Collaborative Writing in L2 Classrooms

NEW PERSPECTIVES ON LANGUAGE AND EDUCATION
Series Editor: Professor Viv Edwards, *University of Reading, Reading, Great Britain*
Series Advisor: Professor Allan Luke, *Queensland University of Technology, Brisbane, Australia*

Two decades of research and development in language and literacy education have yielded a broad, multidisciplinary focus. Yet education systems face constant economic and technological change, with attendant issues of identity and power, community and culture. This series will feature critical and interpretive, disciplinary and multidisciplinary perspectives on teaching and learning, language and literacy in new times.

Full details of all the books in this series and of all our other publications can be found on http://www.multilingual-matters.com, or by writing to Multilingual Matters, St Nicholas House, 31–34 High Street, Bristol BS1 2AW, UK.

Collaborative Writing in L2 Classrooms

Neomy Storch

MULTILINGUAL MATTERS
Bristol • Buffalo • Toronto

Library of Congress Cataloging in Publication Data
A catalog record for this book is available from the Library of Congress.
Storch, Neomy.
Collaborative Writing in L2 Classrooms/Neomy Storch.
New Perspectives on Language and Education: 31
Includes bibliographical references and index.
1. Second language acquisition. 2. Written communication. 3. Language and languages—Study and teaching. I. Title.
P118.2.S85 2013
418.0071–dc23 2013012576

British Library Cataloguing in Publication Data
A catalogue entry for this book is available from the British Library.

ISBN-13: 978-1-84769-994-7 (hbk)
ISBN-13: 978-1-84769-993-0 (pbk)

Multilingual Matters
UK: St Nicholas House, 31–34 High Street, Bristol BS1 2AW, UK.
USA: UTP, 2250 Military Road, Tonawanda, NY 14150, USA.
Canada: UTP, 5201 Dufferin Street, North York, Ontario M3H 5T8, Canada.

Copyright © 2013 Neomy Storch.

All rights reserved. No part of this work may be reproduced in any form or by any means without permission in writing from the publisher.

Typeset by Techset Composition India (P) Ltd., Bangalore and Chennai, India.
Printed and bound in Great Britain by Short Run Press Ltd.

Contents

	Preface	vii
	Acknowledgments	ix
1	Introduction	1
	The Aims of the Book	1
	What Does Collaborative Writing Mean?	2
	Outline of the Book	4
2	Theoretical and Pedagogical Rationale for Collaborative L2 Writing	6
	Introduction	6
	Theories of Language Acquisition and Learning	7
	Pedagogical Support for Collaborative L2 Writing	18
	Conclusion	25
3	Collaborative Writing: L2 Learning and Practice Opportunities	27
	Introduction	27
	Collaborative Writing and the Nature of Languaging	28
	Feedback and Collective Scaffolding	37
	Opportunities for L2 Use	39
	Conclusion	42
4	Factors Affecting Languaging in Collaborative Writing	44
	Introduction	44
	Task Type	45
	Grouping Learners: Composition and Size	57
	Relationships Formed	60
	Conclusion	70
5	Collaborative Writing and Language Learning	71
	Introduction	71

	Comparing Individual and Collaborative Texts	71
	Evidence of Language Learning	76
	Conclusion	91
6	Learners' Perspectives of Collaborative Writing	93
	Introduction	93
	Language Learning Beliefs and Attitudes	94
	Attitudes to Group and Pair Work	98
	The Main Concerns About Group and Pair Work	100
7	Computer Mediated Collaborative Writing	118
	Introduction	118
	First-Generation Web Technology and L2 Collaborative Writing Tasks	119
	Second-Generation Technology (Web 2.0) and Collaborative Writing Tasks	123
	Research on Wikis in Mainstream Education (L1 Context)	125
	Wikis in L2 Classes	136
	Conclusion	154
8	Conclusion: Pedagogical Implications and Research Directions	155
	Introduction	155
	Overview of the Main Themes	155
	Decisions to Make When Implementing Collaborative Writing Tasks	158
	Challenges and Suggested Strategies	164
	Research Directions	168
	Concluding Remarks	171
	References	173
	Author Index	193
	Subject Index	199

Preface

My interest in collaborative writing arose unintentionally when I was collecting data for my PhD dissertation. The original purpose of the PhD project was to investigate how second language (L2) learners, and in my context ESL learners, make decisions regarding grammar, and what knowledge sources they draw on, if any. Instead of using think-aloud protocols, a difficult procedure especially for second language learners, I decided to collect data by having students work in pairs on a range of tasks. Furthermore, rather than just using grammar-focused tasks, such as a passage editing task, I decided to also use a short composition task. Over the semester, as I listened and observed my students working in pairs on these tasks, I became aware that the learners' interactions while writing in pairs, the relationships they formed and the outcomes of their joint activity were more fascinating areas for research than the original quest. The joint composition seemed to elicit engagement with ideas as well as language choice. It also elicited quite robust debates (some quite loud). Clearly, there was a notion of text ownership at play, not present when students complete editing tasks based on texts that they did not compose.

When I consulted published work on collaborative writing activities, I found that most of the work was by composition scholars, writing on the merits of collaborative writing for the development of good writing skills (e.g. Bruffee, 1984; Elbow & Belanoff, 1989) that could also prepare students for the kind of writing they are likely to encounter in the workplace (Ede & Lunsford, 1990). These scholars were writing about learners developing advanced writing skills in their first language (L1). However, as an ESL teacher, my interest was also in whether collaborative writing provides a site for second language learning. That is, I was interested in whether collaborative writing could provide language learners with opportunities not only to learn how to compose well-structured texts in the L2, but also opportunities to learn and consolidate knowledge about L2 grammatical structures and vocabulary. In the literature on L2 learning, there were certainly studies about the nature and benefits of small group and pair work, but most of these studies employed oral tasks (e.g. information gap tasks) rather than writing tasks (e.g. Pica, 1994, 1996; Polio & Gass, 1998).

In my PhD dissertation (published as a monograph in 2009) I reported on the nature of the relationships learners formed when working in pairs on writing and grammar tasks. My study found that although collaboration can result in language learning, not all pairs form collaborative relationships and that some relationships are not conducive to learning. My subsequent research projects in ESL as well as EFL contexts (my own as well as that of PhD students I supervised) aimed to shed further light on the nature of such joint writing activities and on factors that may promote or impede collaboration.

Throughout this journey of investigating collaborative writing activities in L2 classes, I was informed by the writing of a number of L2 scholars. However, it was (and continues to be) the work of Professor Merrill Swain that was particularly informative and that played a major role in shaping my thinking. Her explanation of cognitive processes and affective states enriched my own understanding of the potential benefits of collaborative writing for L2 learning.

Acknowledgments

Thanks...

The first seed to write a book on collaborative writing was planted in my head by my colleague from New Zealand John Bitchener. I owe him and my colleagues at the University of Melbourne, particularly Jo Tapper, Celia Thompson, Janne Morton and Tim McNamara, my heartfelt gratitude for their continuous encouragement and moral support. I want to thank Jo in particular for her careful proofreading of the manuscript. I also owe much to my students: students in the ESL classes that I taught and who agreed to participate in many of my studies on collaborative writing, and graduate students whose research helped to shed further light on collaboration in different L2 contexts. Finally, I would like to thank my family, and particularly my husband Paul, for his love and support, and for never wavering in his belief that this book project was achievable.

The book is dedicated to the next generation of collaborative writers in my family: my sons Amir and Edan Nissen and my nieces Tia and Corenne Storch.

1 Introduction

The Aims of the Book

Writing is generally perceived as a solitary, individual activity. Writing in pairs or small groups is a novel activity and there are reported observations of teachers' reluctance to implement such activities (e.g. McDonough, 2004). Some of this reluctance may stem from the perception of writing as an individual act as well as from assessment practices that tend to measure individual achievement. It may also stem from a lack of awareness of the potential benefits of collaborative writing for language learning or a lack of knowledge of how best to implement such writing activities. However, collaborative writing is likely to increase given developments in Web 2.0 technology, and particularly the use of wikis and Google Docs – new collaborative writing platforms. Ortega (2009a) argues that in our technologically driven world, the inclusion of computer mediated activities in language classes is no longer a choice but an imperative. Research on the use of wikis in second language classes suggests that, as in the case of face-to-face collaborative writing, online collaborative writing activities need to be carefully designed.

Thus this book has two overarching goals. The first goal is to encourage language teachers to consider implementing collaborative writing activities in their classes. The book attempts to provide a theoretical, pedagogical and empirical rationale for the use of collaborative writing activities in second language (L2) classes as well as some guidelines about how to best implement such activities in both face-to-face and online modes. The second goal is to encourage researchers to continue investigating collaborative writing activities. The book critically reviews the available body of research on collaborative writing and identifies future research directions. It should be noted at the outset that throughout the book the term second language (L2) is used as an umbrella term to refer to both second and foreign languages, although I acknowledge that there are important differences between second and foreign language contexts in terms of exposure to the target language and learners' need and motivation to write in the target language (see Manchón, 2011a).

What Does Collaborative Writing Mean?

Let me begin by defining collaboration, the central term in this book. Collaboration means the sharing of labour (co-labour) and thus collaborative writing, in its broadest sense, means the co-authoring of a text by two or more writers. Some writing scholars (e.g. Bruffee, 1984; Harris, 1994) assert that all writing is collaborative to some extent. Individual writers composing with a certain reader in mind or seeking assistance from others at some stage of their writing can be said to engage in collaborative writing. Under such a broad definition, peer editing or peer planning would also qualify as collaborative writing.

An alternative view of collaborative writing is offered by Ede and Lunsford (1990). The authors identify three distinguishing features of collaborative writing: (1) substantive interaction in all stages of the writing process; (2) shared decision-making power over and responsibility for the text produced; and (3) the production of a single written document. From this perspective, collaborative writing is a distinct process and product. The process is one where participants work together and interact throughout the writing process, contributing to the planning, generation of ideas, deliberations about the text structure, editing and revision. This process is not merely an exchange of ideas but negotiations which often arise as a result of a struggle to create a shared understanding and shared expressions (Schrage, 1994). The product of the collaborative writing process is the jointly produced and shared text, a text that cannot easily be reduced to the separate input of individuals (Stahl, 2006). As such the text produced is also jointly owned, with all writers sharing in the ownership of the text produced.

On the basis of this definition, peer planning or peer editing (often referred to as peer response) do not qualify as collaborative writing because the interaction occurs only at one stage of the writing process (planning or editing) and the process of writing remains a private act. More importantly, ownership of the text produced rests with the individual writer rather than being jointly owned. Hirvela (2007) uses the term 'collaborative approaches to writing' to describe peer planning or peer editing, rather than 'collaborative writing'. Collaborative writing also excludes editing tasks where the learners are asked to amend a text that they did not compose, or a text-reconstruction task where learners have to reconstruct a text based on given content words (see Storch, 1998a, 2001a).

Although I have previously referred to such tasks as collaborative writing tasks, on reflection I think that these kinds of grammar-focused tasks, where learners are not involved in constructing a text, should be labelled collaborative editing or reconstruction tasks rather than collaborative writing tasks.

Similarly, group projects, a frequent form of assessment at universities (Leki, 2001; Strauss & U, 2007) which are said to emulate the kind of writing prevalent in the workplace (Ede & Lunsford, 1990; Lay & Karis, 1991; Mirel & Spilka, 2002), do not necessarily qualify as collaborative writing activities. Here Dillenbourg *et al.*'s (1996) distinction between cooperation and collaboration is useful. Whereas cooperation involves the division of labour between individuals in order to complete a task, collaboration involves individuals in a coordinated effort to complete a task together. Research (e.g. Ede & Lunsford, 1990; Lay & Karis, 1991; Leki, 2001) has shown that in group projects, responsibilities are often divided, either by negotiation or by an assigned group leader, with each member of the group having a defined role. These roles may include the drafting of one discrete section or the editing of the entire document once it has been completed. Thus, what such an activity describes is cooperative writing (Dillenbourg *et al.*, 1996), a form of co-authoring which involves the production of 'a singular text by multiple authors' (Ede & Lunsford, 1990). In collaborative writing, roles and contributions to text creation are not split up. Instead, there is mutual engagement and a coordinated effort by all members of the group or pair throughout the composing process.

Thus, in this monograph, collaborative writing describes an activity where there is a shared and negotiated decision making process and a shared responsibility for the production of a single text. In the L2 class, the text produced may be a composition or a report, but can also include more language-focused tasks such as a dictogloss, where students work in small groups or pairs to reconstruct a text based on notes taken from a dictated text (Wajnryb, 1990). However, it excludes grammar exercises such as joint editing, cloze or text reconstruction. In such tasks, students do not compose a text, rather they 'reprocess language previously produced by others' (Manchón, 2011b: 76). Nevertheless, I will refer to studies reporting on learners completing such grammar tasks in pairs as their findings are of relevance to a discussion of collaborative writing as a site for language learning.

It should be noted that the outcome of a collaborative writing activity is not just the jointly produced text. It is also collective cognition, emerging when two or more people reach insights that neither could have reached alone, and that cannot be traced back to one individual's contribution

(Stahl, 2006). In the context of L2 learning, it is cognition related to language learning, including, for example, learning new vocabulary, improved ways of expressing ideas, gaining a greater understanding of certain grammatical conventions or greater control over the use of a particular grammatical structure.

Outline of the Book

Chapter 2 presents the theoretical and pedagogical rationale for the use of collaborative writing tasks in L2 classes. The chapter also includes a brief review of collaborative writing in first language (L1) composition literature, where collaborative writing is relatively well established. However, as noted above, L1 scholars promote collaborative writing as a vehicle for developing good writing skills. In L2 contexts, the rationale for collaborative writing is generally to develop language skills. Manchón (2011b) distinguishes between using writing activities as the means to develop writing skills; that is, learning to write (LW) and activities which use writing to learn language (WLL). Using this distinction, the rationale for collaborative writing in L1 is predominantly couched in terms of learning to write (LW); in L2 it is writing to learn language (WLL).

Chapter 3 reviews empirical research on collaborative L2 writing showing that such tasks provide learners with language learning and language practice opportunities. It presents excerpts from a range of studies on collaborative writing showing what learners focus on when they deliberate about language, and how they use language in their deliberations. The chapter also discusses extensively the unit of analysis used in this research, the language-related episode (LRE).

Chapter 4 discusses the factors that may impact on the number and quality of the LREs found in the talk of learners when they write together. Here I include reference to studies where the learners completed grammar-focused tasks in pairs. The factors discussed include the type of task, the learners' L2 proficiency and the relationships they form. Chapter 5 reviews the relatively small body of research investigating the outcomes of collaborative writing activities. The outcomes considered are in terms of the nature of the co-authored text and evidence of longer term language learning.

As mentioned previously, language teachers may hold some reservations about using collaborative writing tasks for language practice or assessment purposes. Learners have also been observed to be reluctant to participate in collaborative writing activities. Chapter 6 discusses the language learning beliefs and concerns that underpin teachers' and students' attitudes towards group and pair work in general, and by implication to collaborative writing tasks. The chapter then presents the findings of a relatively small number of studies which have elicited learners' evaluations of collaborative writing once they had experienced such activities.

Whereas the previous chapters focused mainly on face-to-face collaborative writing activities, Chapter 7 focuses on collaborative writing that is computer mediated. It discusses briefly research on collaborative writing using text-based online communication, but the main focus of this chapter is on wikis, the new collaborative writing platforms. Wikis have a number of features which facilitate the creation of collaborative texts by multiple authors. The chapter describes these features and then reviews the main strands of research on wiki collaborative writing in both L1 and L2 contexts.

Chapter 8 concludes with a summary of the main themes covered in the book, reiterating the main reasons for implementing collaborative writing activities, both in face-to-face and online modes. It then identifies the decisions that L2 instructors need to make before implementing collaborative writing activities in their classes and the challenges they may face. Some suggestions are put forward for how such writing activities could be implemented in order to maximise the language learning opportunities they offer. Throughout the book, I note the dearth of research on a number of aspects related to collaborative writing. The final section of the chapter thus identifies future research directions.

2 Theoretical and Pedagogical Rationale for Collaborative L2 Writing

Introduction

Collaborative writing involves learners interacting in pairs or small groups on a writing task. Thus the two key components in collaborative writing are verbal interaction and writing. Verbal interaction has been identified as fundamental in both cognitive and sociocognitive theories of second language (L2) learning. The act of writing also has language learning potentials. The cognitive processes that occur in the production of oral language also occur in the production of written language and in fact some research suggests that writing may be superior to speaking as a site for L2 learning.

The first section of this chapter discusses the importance of interaction from both theoretical perspectives. It describes the evolution of Long's (1983, 1985, 1996) interaction hypothesis and Swain's (1985, 1993, 1995) output hypothesis, leading cognitive theories of second language acquisition (SLA). It then presents arguments and some research evidence which suggest that tasks which combine speaking and writing may be better than speaking only tasks in promoting interaction with a focus on language. A discussion of sociocognitive perspectives, and in particular Vygotsky's (1978, 1981) sociocultural theory of mind, follows. Vygotsky's sociocultural theory is, strictly speaking, not a theory of second language learning, but rather a psychological theory that explains the development of complex human cognitive abilities. The ability to acquire a second language is one such cognitive ability.

It is relatively recently that sociocultural theory has gained recognition within Applied Linguistics research and has been used to explain second language learning processes. The work of scholars such as Lantolf (2000), Lantolf and Thorne (2006), Ohta (1995, 2001), and particularly Swain (2000, 2006, 2010), provides a radically different conceptualisation and analysis of interaction. Swain's notions of collaborative dialogue and languaging are pertinent here; they provide a cogent argument in support of tasks that combine speaking and writing.

The second section presents the pedagogical rationale for the use of collaborative writing tasks. The discussion here first focuses on communicative and task-based approaches, considered to be best practice approaches to L2 instruction. These approaches promote interaction on tasks that require learners to reflect on language form while still being oriented to meaning. Collaborative writing tasks combine a focus on language form and meaning. The discussion then turns to the pedagogical rationale for collaborative writing as the means to advance not only language but also writing abilities. Here I draw mainly on the work of composition scholars (e.g. Bruffee, 1984; Dale, 1994a, 1994b) who have long championed the benefits of collaborative writing in general education and first language (L1) writing classes. Their arguments are equally applicable to L2 writing contexts.

Theories of Language Acquisition and Learning

Although a number of theories have attempted to explain how humans acquire or learn a second language, the two perspectives discussed here are cognitive and sociocognitive. Long's (1983, 1996) interaction hypothesis and Swain's (1985, 1993) pushed output are considered cognitive theories of SLA. Such theories view language acquisition as primarily a cognitive process and thus focus on what triggers learner internal cognitive processes. These processes include noticing, hypotheses testing and how the mind stores and retrieves information. In these theories, the learner's existing mental capacity is the source of their own learning.

Vygotsky's (1978, 1981) sociocultural theory, on the other hand, represents a sociocognitive view of learning. From this perspective, language learning has both social and cognitive dimensions. Sociocultural theory views the learner as a social being, and all cognitive development (including language learning) as essentially embedded in social interaction. Swain's notions of collaborative dialogue and languaging (2000, 2006, 2010) are informed by sociocultural theory. They explicate how the use of language in social interaction mediates language learning.

Cognitive theories: Long's interaction hypothesis and Swain's output hypothesis

One of the most influential theories of SLA is Long's (1983, 1985) interaction hypothesis. The genesis of this hypothesis is Krashen's (1981, 1982, 1985) comprehensible input hypothesis, but Long's hypothesis diverged from Krashen's in terms of what makes the input comprehensible. Krashen claimed that the necessary and sufficient condition for SLA is for learners to be exposed to language that they can understand (comprehensible input) and which contains linguistic structures which are just beyond their interlanguage, their current L2 knowledge ($i + 1$). Krashen (1982) explained that what enables a learner to comprehend input beyond their interlanguage is the learner's existing L2 knowledge and extralinguisitic knowledge. Long (1983, 1985) accepted that comprehensible input is key to L2 learning but claimed that a more consistently used and prevalent way of making input comprehensible is via interactional modifications during conversations. It is this claim that first highlighted the importance of verbal interaction for language learning.

Long's (1983) claims were based on his own study which compared the conversations of native-speaker (NS) and non-native speaker (NNS) dyads with those of dyads composed of two native speakers. Long found that what distinguished the conversations between these two types of dyads were certain conversational moves that were used by the interlocutors to keep the conversation going. In NS–NNS dyads, the conversational moves included clarification requests, confirmation and comprehension checks. These moves were grouped under the umbrella term negotiation for meaning. Long found that when linguistic input was not comprehensible, and there was the potential for a communication breakdown, speakers engaged in negotiations to avoid or repair such breakdowns. Such negotiations led to modifications of the input (e.g. rephrasing) making it more comprehensible. Thus Long argued that verbal interactions in the form of negotiations for meaning promote acquisition because the interactions provide learners with the comprehensible input they need for acquisition to take place.

However, as a number of case studies of unsuccessful language learners (e.g. Schmidt, 1983) showed, exposure to comprehensible input is insufficient for successful L2 learning. More convincing evidence for the insufficiency of comprehensible input for L2 learning came from reports on the Canadian immersion programmes (Harley & Swain, 1984; Swain, 1985). Learners in these programmes were found to be able to use the L2 fluently but not necessarily with native-like accuracy, despite many years of exposure to presumably comprehensible second language input in the classroom. These findings led Swain (1985) to propose a comprehensible output hypothesis. Without denying the essential role of input in SLA, Swain argued that producing language (output) also plays an important role in SLA. Swain pointed out that comprehension and production involve different processes. Comprehension can be achieved by processing language input for gist by relying on understanding key content words or on general knowledge. Production requires learners to process language syntactically. Thus for successful L2 learning, learners need to be not only exposed to comprehensible input but also to produce spoken or written language.

In 1993 Swain revised her claim for comprehensible output calling for pushed output. Swain argued that just speaking and writing may provide learners with practice opportunities and hence develop their fluency but it may not develop their accuracy. For accuracy to develop, learners need to be pushed to produce language that is not only understood, but that is also grammatically accurate and which stretches their linguistic resources. Swain's (1993, 1995) arguments in support of pushed output were based on important cognitive processes activated during language production. While attempting to produce in the L2, learners may notice gaps in their knowledge, gaps which arise when they encounter difficulties in expressing their intended meaning. This noticing may prompt learners to look for ways to address their gaps, including exploring their own internal linguistic resources and testing various hypotheses, processing language input more deeply (syntactically rather than semantically), and reflecting on their language use.

The study by Swain and Lapkin (1995), using think-aloud protocols of learners writing in their second language, showed evidence of learners engaging in the kind of cognitive processes identified by Swain's pushed output hypothesis. Studies by Izumi (2002) and his colleagues (Izumi & Bigelow, 2000) further substantiated Swain's claims. The studies, which compared learning gains arising from input and output conditions, showed greater learning gains from the output condition. Learners who were exposed to input immediately after they were required to produce output significantly outperformed the learners who were only required to process the input for comprehension. Izumi (2002) proposed that the need to produce output pushes learners to process language more deeply and thus establish a more durable memory trace. It should be noted that in Izumi's studies, learners were required to produce written output.

Long's (1996) revised interaction hypothesis took account of Swain's arguments for the importance of pushed output for language acquisition, but also drew on the work of Schmidt (1990, 1994) on the importance of noticing (selective attention) for language learning, and on the work of Pienemann (1989) on processing capacity. As Long writes (1996: 451–452):

> I would like to suggest that *negotiation for meaning*, and especially negotiation work that triggers interactional adjustments by the NS or more competent interlocutor, facilitates acquisition because it connects input, internal learner capacities, particularly selective attention, and output in productive ways. (original emphasis)

Long conceded that comprehension alone was insufficient for SLA, particularly for the development of native-like L2 proficiency. Thus in subsequent writing, the importance of negative feedback for SLA was highlighted (e.g. Long, 2007; Long & Robinson, 1989). It is negative feedback which is said to draw learners' attention to gaps in their L2 knowledge, either in their comprehension or their production. Such negative feedback can be provided during negotiations. For example, a clarification request is an implicit form of negative feedback. Another form of negative feedback is a recast which involves the correct reformulation of an incorrect utterance. The recast generates a negotiation of form. In sum, the argument put forward was that negotiations and negative feedback provided during such negotiations will lead to acquisition but only if the learner pays attention to the feedback (Schmidt, 1990, 1994), the learner is developmentally ready to attend to such feedback (Pienemann, 1989), and the learner attempts to incorporate the feedback in their modified or pushed output (Swain, 1985, 1993).

Although the interaction hypothesis focused on the language learning opportunities created in negotiations between a learner and a native-speaker or with a more competent peer, others (e.g. Gass, 1997; Pica, 1994) suggested that the benefits could also accrue to pairs of students of similar L2 proficiency. During such pair interaction, if the lack of comprehension stems from an ill-formed message, the request from the listener acts as negative feedback and encourages the speaker to pay attention to the grammatical accuracy of their utterance, making connections between grammatical form and meaning, and pushing the speaker to modify their output to make it more target-like. These negotiations allow for language hypotheses to be tested and refined in response to feedback. If the negotiation is triggered by a perceived or imminent misunderstanding, comprehension and confirmation checks may require the speaker to repeat, elaborate or rephrase the original message, providing the speaker with additional speaking practice. The listener also gains because presumably the input they are exposed to is now more comprehensible.

Researchers informed by Long's original hypothesis set out to identify how to best pair students and what tasks to use in order to maximise negotiations. The assumption underlying this research was that the more negotiations learners engage in, the better. Thus it was found that if learners share the same L1 or are at a similar level of L2 proficiency, they are likely to engage in fewer negotiations than if they come from a different L1 backgrounds or have different levels of L2 proficiency (e.g. Iwashita, 2001; Polio & Gass, 1998; Takahashi, 1989; Varonis & Gass, 1985). Fotos and Ellis (1991) also found that assigning students to work in pairs rather than in small groups marginally increases the number of negotiations. A great deal of attention was also paid to the tasks used. Long and Crookes (1992) argued for the use of meaning-focused tasks rather than language exercises. In meaning-focused tasks the shift to linguistic code features occurs incidentally, triggered by perceived problems with comprehension or production. Such incidental focus on language is termed Focus on Form (FonF). This is distinct from traditional Focus on Forms (FonFs) approaches to language instruction where the focus on grammatical structures is pre-determined and class time is spent on explaining and practicing the structures in language exercises.

Careful analysis of various task dimensions by researchers (e.g. Pica et al., 1993) produced a theoretical typology of tasks which predicted that meaning-focused problem-solving tasks that require an exchange of information and allow for only one solution (e.g. picture differences) are likely to generate more negotiations than open-ended tasks where the exchange of information is optional (e.g. discussion task). It should be noted that the typology only considered speaking tasks. Furthermore, although Swain's (1985, 1993, 1995) notion of output encompassed both spoken and written language, research informed by the revised interaction hypothesis continues to use primarily oral tasks (see for example reviews of studies in Gass, 2003; Mackey, 2007).

This research, however, also identified some limitations with the oral tasks used and with the analysis of interaction that focused only on identifying and quantifying negotiation moves. For example, Nakahama et al. (2001) compared the talk produced by NS–NNS dyads in an unstructured conversation activity with a structured information gap activity (spot the differences). The researchers reported that although the structured task elicited more negotiations for meaning, the unstructured conversation elicited longer and more complex utterances. Fotos and Ellis (1991) also found that in their structured task (two-way communication exchange) the learners' negotiations often consisted of one or two word utterances. Similar evidence was reported by Pica et al. (1996): the negotiations data consisted of frequent use of simple signals of non-understanding and modifications. Nakahama et al. (2001) also found that in the open conversation task the learners paid attention not only to linguistic features but also to affective aspects of the overall discourse such as textual coherence, the maintenance of face, and the exchange of information. The authors argued that such open-ended tasks therefore offer potentially more language learning opportunities.

Of greater concern were the findings by Foster (1998). Foster reported that the oral information exchange tasks, which are predicted to encourage negotiations, did not elicit much negotiation when implemented in regular L2 classes. The study, implemented in an adult intermediate level ESL class, found few instances of negotiations, with many students choosing not to contribute to the interaction. Foster suggested that learners, when speaking to their peers in a regular classroom environment, might be unwilling to divert attention to errors and negotiate for form, unless a true communicative breakdown occurs. Although Gass et al.'s (2011) study found that students working in regular L2 (Spanish) classes generated, on average, a similar number of negotiations as students working in language laboratories, the range and standard deviations reported in this study suggest that some pairs generated no or very few negotiations in both contexts.

A number of studies have found that learners tend to negotiate primarily over lexis (Pica, 1992, 1994; Pica et al., 1993; Williams, 1999). For example, Pica (1992), in a large-scale study, found that breakdowns and the ensuing negotiations occurred only in response to problems in lexis. No negotiation sequences were found in response to problems in morphosyntax. Pica (1992) explained that errors in morphosyntax do not usually lead to communication breakdowns.

These research findings raise some concerns about whether oral tasks do provide learners with opportunities to negotiate and focus on form as suggested by Long or to produce the kind of pushed language output suggested by Swain. This may be the case particularly with intermediate and advanced L2 learners where grammatical errors may not impede meaning. It may also be that learners perceive oral tasks as meaning focused rather than accuracy focused (Foster, 1998; Williams, 1999). In other words, what we need is tasks which provide learners with incentives to focus on form. Such tasks may be particularly important for intermediate and advanced learners whose interlanguage growth may slow down unless they are encouraged to pay attention to how they are expressing their intended meaning (Kowal & Swain, 1994).

An alternative suggestion put forward by a number of researchers working within this cognitivist theoretical framework (e.g. Adams & Ross-Feldman, 2008; Williams, 2008, 2012), is to use tasks which require written output. The main advantages of writing over speaking are that writing does not require online processing and thus enables learners to focus on form more easily. In speaking tasks, the pressures of conducting a conversation means that the learner may not have sufficient time or memory space to process language for form and for meaning, to notice feedback (Mackey et al., 2002), or indeed have the opportunity to produce modified output (Oliver,

1995). Conversations tend to be naturally more meaning focused, with the aim being to get the message across. When writing, learners have more processing time. This enables them to reflect on their language use drawing on their explicit knowledge of the language (Adams & Ross-Feldman, 2008; Williams, 2008, 2012). Furthermore, as Cumming (1989) and Williams (1999) point out, writing is a task that naturally encourages learners to pay attention to grammatical accuracy because writing, in the absence of immediate signals of non-comprehension, as is the case in speaking, demands more precise expression. The quality of attention to language use may also be different in writing. The focus on accuracy can occur during the process of composing, as the writer deliberates on how to best express their ideas, recursively reading, re-reading and evaluating what has been written, and in response to feedback.

To conclude, Long's (1996) interaction hypothesis suggests that receiving comprehensible input and interactional feedback while negotiating for meaning and form facilitate L2 learning. This hypothesis provides a rationale for the use of small group and pair work in the language classroom. Research informed by this hypothesis showed that small group work (and more commonly pair work), if carefully implemented, encourages negotiations for meaning, some of which include a focus on form. These negotiations are in turn said to trigger cognitive processes important for language learning. Most of this research has focused on interaction arising in work on oral tasks, and particularly on the facilitative role played by recasts for SLA (see review of studies in Gass, 2003; Long, 2007). A number of researchers argue, quite convincingly, that tasks which contain a writing component may be a better alternative to oral tasks in terms of eliciting a focus on form.

Sociocognitive theories: Vygotsky's sociocultural theory and Swain's notion of languaging

Vygotsky's sociocultural theory of mind (SCT) is a sociocognitive theory which also highlights the importance of verbal interaction for learning. Interaction, however, from this perspective is viewed more than just the means to make input comprehensible or as an opportunity to provide negative feedback and for modified output. Rather, from this perspective, interaction and the use of language in interaction play a key role in all cognitive development, including language learning.

The underlying premise in sociocultural theory is that all cognitive development, and in particular the development of higher order cognitive functions, such as voluntary attention, intentional memory and language learning, is socially situated (Vygotsky, 1981). It occurs in interaction between humans, where an expert participant (an adult, or a more knowledgeable peer) provides carefully attuned assistance to the novice (a child, or a less knowledgeable peer). Thus all cognitive functions originate in social activity, in dialogues between individuals (on the interpersonal or interpsychological plane) and are eventually internalised to become the individual's own resources that can be used independently (on the intrapsychological plane). Internalisation is the movement from social ways of knowing to increasingly internal ways of knowing and thus constitutes cognitive development (Lantolf, 2005).

A key element in the interaction on the interpsychological plane is the nature of the assistance provided by the expert. Not all forms of assistance are effective and lead to development. To be effective, the assistance provided by the expert needs to take into consideration the novice's current state of knowledge, and the potential state achievable with assistance (Vygotsky, 1978). The distance between these two states is referred to as the Zone of Proximal Development (ZPD). The ZPD is not a fixed property of an individual but a collaborative activity, involving both the novice and the expert. The novice's actions or utterances cue the expert about their needs. The role of the expert is not only to finely tune the assistance so that it is contingently responsive to the novice's level of performance and perceived needs but also to encourage the novice to participate and take an increasingly greater responsibility for the activity. This fine tuning and encouragement is referred to in the literature as scaffolding (Wood et al., 1976).

Scaffolding is mediated by language. It is language which enables the novice and expert to communicate and coordinate their action (Wells, 1999). Language also reflects development. On the interpsychological plane speech is social: it is vocalised and other-directed. As development progresses, speech assumes a different function and external form. Social speech develops into what Vygotsky (1986) referred to as egocentric or private speech. Novices (e.g. children) use private speech for cognitive purposes, to help structure and organise their own thinking (Lantolf, 2000). Private speech may be observed as children talk to themselves when they perform a task. Private speech like its precursor, social speech, is vocalised. However, what distinguishes private speech is that it is self-directed, and hence often spoken more softly. It is also likely to be short and simplified, often consisting of single word or a few words (Ohta, 2001). Such speech is meaningful for the person who produces it, but may be difficult to decipher for the person overhearing it.

At the final stage of development, as novices assume increasing control over their mental activity, private speech becomes inner speech. Inner speech is self-directed and also functions to organise thinking but, unlike private speech, it is no longer vocalised. Inner speech is language at its deepest level; it loses all its formal properties and is condensed into pure meaning. It is thought without words and without syntax (Swain et al., 2011). Private speech resurfaces when a person (child or adult) faces a complex problem and tries to regain control over the activity, often without being aware of it (Lantolf, 2006; Lantolf & Yañez Prieto, 2003).

Thus Vygotsky's sociocultural theory establishes learning as a fundamentally social experience and provides a rationale for the use of interaction in the classroom, interaction between an expert (e.g. teacher, native speaker) and the novice learner as well as peer interactions. SLA researchers, informed by sociocultural theory, have focused on the nature of the scaffolding and the use of language during such interaction, whether it is between the teacher (expert) and the learner or between learners in group and pair work. It is the latter that is of relevance here.

In L2 classes a number of studies, conducted with young adolescents (e.g. Kowal & Swain, 1994) and adults (e.g. Donato, 1988; Ohta, 1995; Villamil & de Guerrero, 1996), found that peers with a similar level of L2 proficiency, and thus no identifiable or constant expert, were able to provide each other with scaffolding. Some studies (e.g. Kowal & Swain, 1994; Ohta, 2001) reported that the role of the expert was fluid, with learners taking this role in turn. Fluidity in expert/novice roles is perhaps not surprising, particularly among adult learners who bring with them a range of perspectives, experiences, and levels of linguistic expertise (Jacoby & Gonzales, 1991; van Lier, 1996). Jacoby and Gonzales (1991), who investigated the expert-novice relationships in a group of peers (scientists), argue that in any group interaction of adult individuals, to view expert-novice as a preordained bipolar dichotomy may fail to capture what it means 'to know things' (p. 152).

Other researchers, such as Donato (1988, 1994), found evidence of mutual scaffolding in peer interaction, which Donato termed collective scaffolding. Collective scaffolding episodes are instances where the learners pool their partial knowledge of the L2 to reach solutions to decisions concerning vocabulary or linguistic structures. Donato argued that collective scaffolding enabled his learners, who worked in small groups, to perform beyond their existing level of linguistic expertise. However, such scaffolding was found mainly in groups that functioned as a collective (see Chapter 4). Donato also found some evidence that the knowledge co-constructed during these interactions was internalised and used in subsequent independent activity. These findings have led Lantolf (2000: 17) to call for the ZPD to be conceived of more broadly as the 'collaborative construction of opportunities for individuals to develop their mental abilities'.

Language as a tool to mediate cognitive development is a key concept in SCT. However, in the L2 learning context, the use of language in mediating learning is unique. Unlike other learning domains, such as mathematics or science for example, where language mediates the learning process of mathematical or scientific concepts and skills, in the language learning domain, language mediates language learning and the knowledge acquired is language. Swain, perhaps more than any other sociocultural researcher, has succeeded in explaining this important and unique role of language in interaction and in L2 learning.

In 2000, Swain began to question the use of her previously coined metaphor of pushed output and its overtones of information processing. Influenced by SCT, her work began to focus much more on the notion of language as a tool that mediates development. The term output was replaced with words such as verbalisation and collaborative dialogue and finally with the more encompassing term 'languaging' (Swain, 2006, 2010; Swain et al., 2011).

Languaging describes the process of using language in an attempt to make sense of complex information or when confronting a difficult task. It is the articulation of thinking. Such articulation occurs in all domains of learning. In the L2 learning domain it occurs when learners need to solve linguistic problems, such as gaining an understanding of complex grammatical conventions or deciding on how to best express an idea. Languaging has two forms: private speech and collaborative dialogue (Swain, 2006, 2010; Swain et al., 2002, 2009, 2011). Private speech, as discussed previously, is speech directed to the self. Collaborative dialogue is speech directed to others. It is the dialogue that occurs when learners work in groups or pairs and attempt to solve a problem by talking it through together (Swain & Lapkin, 2002; Swain et al., 2002). The importance of languaging is not only that it is the means to solve problems but that in the process new knowledge or new understandings are constructed.

When a learner works alone on a complex task, languaging takes the form of private speech. Although private speech does not guarantee that a problem will be solved (Lantolf, 2005), it may enable the learner to talk him/herself into understanding something that the learner did not understand before. Swain (2000) refers to the work of Chi *et al.* (1989, 1994) in psychology where such private speech is more commonly referred to as self-explanation. When engaging in such dialogue with the self, the learner sounds out and critically evaluates alternative options, draws on their existing knowledge and makes inferences. In other words, verbalising thoughts creates a product, an artefact that can be examined and deliberated about further. More importantly, languaging in the form of private speech is the source of learning. Swain *et al.* (2009), for example, documented instances of learners engaging in self-talk as a means of struggling to understand the difficult grammatical structure of voice in French. The study found that frequent engagement in such talk led to a more accurate and deeper understanding of verb voice, of the form-meaning connections, and an ability to apply that knowledge.

When a learner works with a peer, speech can have private and social functions simultaneously (Wells, 1998) and as such can confer a number of additional language learning advantages. First, overt self-directed verbalisation (private speech) in the social context becomes public. This makes the speaker's thinking accessible to others and therefore able to be examined and evaluated. Second, private speech, for example in the form of vocalised hesitations, can signal appeals for assistance in response to which the hearer may be able to provide timely assistance – whether in the form of a suggestion, an explanation, or confirmation.

In collaborative writing, the need to reach agreement on what and how to express ideas in the jointly produced text makes it imperative to engage in collaborative dialogue (Camps *et al.*, 2000). When encountering a problem, learners writing in pairs or small groups no longer need to rely only on their own linguistic resources to solve the problem. They can also draw on the knowledge of others. Together they can pool their linguistic resources, collectively scaffolding their performance and co-construct new knowledge. In interaction with others, learners are exposed to a range of viewpoints. If disagreements arise, learners may be asked by their partners to provide explanations to justify their suggestions (see Tocalli-Beller, 2003). These requests may force learners to construct a clearer and more coherent representation of their own knowledge and in the process enhance their own understanding (Chang & Wells, 1988; van Lier, 1996).

Thus from a sociocultural perspective, interaction between learners is a site for language learning because it provides opportunities for languaging, for private and for collaborative talk. The collaborative form of languaging is different to Long's negotiations for meaning. Collaborative talk does not necessarily aim to make the message more comprehensible, nor does it arise as a result of non-comprehension as argued by the interactionist theorists. Rather, it occurs while learners, for example, deliberate over the best way of expressing an idea. In the process, learners may pool their knowledge sources and co-construct new language or consolidate existing knowledge. This co-constructed knowledge can then be appropriated and internalised by the learners for their own use.

SLA researchers guided by a sociocultural perspective also promote the use of tasks which engage students in interaction. However, in the main, there is no discussion about what type of task to use or whether oral or written tasks may be preferable. Furthermore, as Ohta (2000) and Coughlan and Duff (1994) show, task design does not necessarily predict the activity that the learners will engage in. In Ohta's study, for example, a sentence translation exercise, a very traditional focus on forms exercise, was transformed by two students into a language learning activity with opportunities for scaffolding mediated by the use of language and which resulted in both participants gaining a better understanding of a difficult grammatical construction.

Nevertheless, I argue that collaborative writing tasks may present more optimal conditions for languaging than speaking tasks. In a writing task, there are two artefacts that can be further explored: verbalised thoughts and the co-authored text. In collaborative writing, the thinking that is involved in producing a co-authored text, such as the linguistic choices involved in phrasing an idea or how to organise ideas into a cohesive text, becomes external and explicit (see discussion Chapter 4). Such thinking is not open for inspection by others in private writing. In addition, the co-authored text is also available for examination and for revision, providing additional reasons to language.

Pedagogical Support for Collaborative L2 Writing

Communicative language teaching and task-based approaches to language instruction, both now generally accepted as best practice approaches to L2 instruction, also promote interaction and the use of meaningful tasks in the language classroom. As such they provide a pedagogical argument for the use of collaborative writing tasks. In this section I briefly describe what these approaches entail to show how collaborative writing tasks accord with germane principles of these approaches. I then discuss approaches to writing instruction and the reasons why L1 composition scholars promote collaborative writing.

Approaches to language teaching

Communicative Language Teaching (CLT) and task-based language teaching (TBLT) are approaches to L2 instruction that have substantially influenced the curricula and teaching of second languages worldwide, and particularly the teaching of English as a second and foreign language (Butler, 2011; Littlewood, 2011; Savignon, 2005). The approaches are broadly based on theories of SLA as well as models of what it means to be competent in a second language. However, as TBLT is considered an offshoot of CLT, I focus most of the discussion on CLT.

Although the exact definition of CLT is somewhat elusive (Littlewood, 2011), according to Savignon (2005: 635), one of the architects of this approach, the essence of CLT is 'the engagement of learners in communication to allow them to develop their communicative competence'. Thus the goal of language teaching is communicative competence. Communicative competence describes the ability of a language learner to interact with other speakers of the L2 competently; that is, to produce language that is not only correct but also meaningful and appropriate for the context in which it is used (Canale & Swain, 1980; Savignon, 1983). The competencies that make up communicative competence include linguistic competence (knowledge of grammar and lexis), an understanding of the social context in which the communication takes place (sociolinguistic competence), discourse competence and strategic competence (Bachman, 1990; Canale, 1983; Canale & Swain, 1980). Thus, although linguistic competence is important, it is one type of competence in what constitutes overall communicative competence in the L2.

The means to achieve communicative competence in the L2 classroom is via activities which engage students in communication, in a sharing of ideas, and in negotiation for meaning and form. The term task has been used to describe such communicative activities (Skehan, 2003). Tasks, unlike language exercises, focus primarily on meaning but also allow for an incidental focus on language form (Long, 1991; Long & Crookes, 1992). The tasks most often associated with CLT are speaking tasks (Butler, 2011; Kumaravadivelu, 2006). The tasks require an exchange of information (e.g. picture differences, jigsaw) or an exchange of opinions (e.g. discussion, debate), with the former type of tasks predicted to be more effective in promoting a focus on form. These tasks reflect the underlying premise of cognitive theories of SLA, discussed earlier in this chapter, that language is acquired via verbal negotiations for meaning and form (Long, 1983, 1996).

One of the core features of CLT is the use of group and pair work (Ellis, 2003; Kumaravadivelu, 2003, 2006; Richards & Rogers, 2001). Group and pair work provide learners with opportunity to practice using the target language. This opportunity is particularly compelling in foreign language (FL) classes because the classroom is often the only opportunity that FL learners have to use the L2. In teacher-fronted classes, researchers have consistently observed that teachers control the floor and do most of the talking (Bejarno, 1987; Gutiérrez, 1994; Harklau, 2002; Long & Porter, 1985). For example, in Bejarno's (1987) study, conducted in 33 seventh grade classes of English as a foreign language (EFL), teacher talk amounted to about 80% of the class time. In such classes, research has shown that not only is student talk brief, but it is also usually in response to teachers' questions and elicitations and thus performs a limited range of functions (see Storch & Aldosari, 2013). Class talk may also be dominated by very proficient learners (Pica & Doughty, 1988).

Research has shown that when learners work in small groups, they have more opportunity to use the L2 and for a wider range of functions. Studies have shown that in small group work, learners produce more extended L2 turns (Bejarno, 1987; Gutiérrez, 1994; Storch & Aldosari, 2013). They use the L2 for a range of functions, such as providing corrections and explanations; functions that are generally the reserve of teacher talk (Hall & Walsh, 2002; Ohta, 1995; Storch & Aldosari, 2013). Moreover, studies (e.g. Pica & Doughty, 1988; Rulon & McCreary, 1986) have found that when working in groups, learners are more willing to admit to a lack of understanding and to seek clarification than in teacher-fronted class discussions. They are also more likely to take risks and test hypotheses (Philp & Mackey, 2010; van Lier, 1996).

A number of proposals have been put forward regarding what can constitute the subject matter or the organising principles of the syllabus in CLT (Wesche & Skehan, 2002). One such proposal is a task-based approach. In task-based language teaching (TBLT) the overall purpose is the same as for CLT – learners attaining high levels of communicative competence. The distinguishing feature of TBLT is that an overall task or a series of tasks or group projects form the central components of the syllabus (Skehan, 2003). That is, rather than organising a syllabus according to the grammatical structures to be presented, as in traditional approaches to L2 instruction, or a series of themes, a task-based syllabus proposes to organise the content of the L2 teaching programme in terms of tasks. Such tasks or group projects often involve a writing component. However, discussions of CLT and TBLT have, by and large, paid no attention to the nature of the writing in such projects or to the contributions of writing to language learning.

A controversial aspect of TBLT and CLT has been the kind of activities to be used in the classroom, and in particular what constitutes a meaningful task as distinguished from a language exercise. Researchers such as Ellis (2003), Samuda and Bygate (2008), among others, have tried to synthesise the essential characteristics of tasks. These characteristics emphasise that the task outcome needs to be non-linguistic but at the same time pose learners with linguistic challenges that promote an incidental focus on form. A number of suggestions have been put forward concerning task implementation conditions (e.g. pre-task planning, task repetition) and task design features (e.g. task complexity) that may help promote a focus on form. Ortega (2007), for example, advocates designing tasks that make the need for a focus on certain grammatical structures essential for task completion. Swain *et al.* (2011), however, argue that of utmost importance is that the tasks should be relevant and engaging for the students. Mechanical tasks, which are designed to merely serve the function of practicing a particular grammatical structure, are unlikely to encourage learner engagement, and such lack of engagement has been shown to be detrimental to noticing (Izumi & Izumi, 2004).

To summarise, the distinguishing features of CLT and TBLT are the use of pair and group work on tasks that engage learners in communication. Such tasks need to focus primarily on meaning but, by careful design, also encourage learners to negotiate for form; that is, to focus on language use and accuracy. Attending to form while focusing on meaning highlight the important links between meaning, form and function. Working in groups or pairs on such tasks also provides learners with opportunities to practice using the target language for a range of functions. As mentioned previously, the tasks most often associated with these approaches to L2 instruction are speaking tasks. This is perhaps not surprising given that the interaction hypothesis is often cited in support of claims regarding the importance of tasks for L2 learning, or as support for task-based language teaching approaches (Bygate et al., 2001; Ellis, 2003). However, as Savignon (2005) points out, CLT does not mean exclusive use of oral group work activities. Similarly, Ortega (2007) notes that the overemphasis in SLA on oral tasks as promoting L2 practice is regrettable. Harklau (2002) takes a stronger stance, criticising scholarship in SLA for privileging oral interaction over learning through writing modalities.

Collaborative writing, where students engage in speaking and writing, fulfils all the requirements of tasks noted above. In collaborative writing tasks meaning is primary. If assessed, assessment criteria generally include a measure of task fulfilment. The need to write is more likely to focus learners' attention to form than speaking only tasks, as reported in the research discussed previously. Collaborative writing tasks may also be designed in a way that requires learners to use certain linguistic structures (see Chapter 4). The tasks present learners with opportunities to practice not only speaking but also writing. Indeed from a pedagogical CLT perspective, collaborative writing tasks may confer more language learning advantages than oral tasks.

Collaborative writing tasks may also develop other competencies. It is interesting to note that most of the research on oral tasks has been on whether the task conditions optimise a focus on form and thus develop learners' linguistic competence. The other competencies that make up communicative competence have been largely ignored. For example, very few studies, with the exception of Nakahama et al. (2001), consider the discourse produced during negotiations for meaning and form to examine whether structured two-way exchange tasks provide the conditions to develop or practice strategic and discourse competence. What Nakahama et al. (2001) found was that a discussion task, a less structured task, encouraged learners to practice using discourse markers and use various strategies appropriate for cross-cultural peer interactions. When the impetus for the interaction is the creation of a cohesive written text, there is also attention to discourse, specifically written discourse. This is evident in the deliberations and negotiations over how best to organise the ideas of the co-authors in a jointly owned text (see Chapter 3). The extended discourse often resulting from such negotiations provides learners with comprehension and production practice opportunities and for the development of other competencies that make up communicative competence.

Approaches to writing instruction

Much has been written on collaborative writing in the L1 composition literature. However, it should be noted that in this literature, the term collaborative writing is often used broadly to include peer response activities (e.g. Bruffee, 1980; DiPardo & Warshauer Freedman, 1988) where learners provide each other with feedback on individually written compositions, and cooperative writing (e.g. Leonard et al., 1994).

Support for collaborative writing from L1 composition scholars is based on two main arguments. The first argument is that collaborative writing develops students' writing skills. This argument draws on research on composing processes, activities associated with the process approach to writing instruction, and the benefits that collaboration has over solitary writing, particularly for novice writers. The second, more recent and more pragmatic argument is that collaborative writing tasks prepare students, particularly university students, for the kind of writing they are likely to experience in the work place. This argument draws on research that has documented the nature of writing in various work places.

The main approach that has influenced the teaching of writing in the USA since the 1980s is the process approach (see Reichelt, 2009). The process approach was developed largely (but see Matsuda, 2003) in response to insights offered by research using think-aloud protocols of learners and expert writers composing (e.g. Emig, 1971; Perl, 1980; Sommers, 1980) and models of composing processes based on this research (e.g. Flower & Hayes, 1981; Hayes, 1996). What the research showed is that writing is a recursive rather than a linear activity, where planning, formulation of ideas and revisions take place throughout the writing process. Researchers also uncovered that novice writers, unlike expert writers, do not spend a sufficient amount of time on planning (e.g. Bereiter & Scardamalia, 1982; Emig, 1971; Flower & Hayes, 1981), and that they edit their writing prematurely, focusing on surface level errors (Perl, 1980; Sommers, 1980). Thus the process approach advocates the use of pre-writing activities such as group brainstorming, use of multiple drafts, revision, and teacher and peer feedback (Ferris & Hedgcock, 2005). The focus is very much on the articulation and development of ideas, with teachers acting as guides and the use of peer response, where learners provide each other with feedback on their drafts. The process approach, or elements of it, is also used in foreign language classes in the USA (Reichelt, 2009) and ESL classes.

The philosophical underpinnings motivating the process approach are social constructivism, which draws on the work of scholars such as Vygotsky (1978), Dewey (1938/1970) and Freire (1970). This philosophy views the classroom not as a site where teachers 'deposit' knowledge into learners, but rather as sites where knowledge is produced through dynamic interaction. Freire (1970), for example, argued that literacy is best taught in social contexts, with students actively involved in creating knowledge.

L1 composition scholars, such as Elbow (1973), Bruffee (1984) and Dale (1994a, 1994b, 1997), among others, advocated the use of collaborative writing as a way of supporting the shift from a product to a process emphasis in writing instruction. Bruffee, who is most often associated with collaborative writing, in his early work (1980) advocated the use of peer response groups. It was only in his later writing (1984) that he argued for collaborative learning including collaborative writing. He noted that when students work together on their writing, 'they converse about and as part of writing' (p. 655); they converse as members of a 'community of knowledgeable peers' (p. 644) who share an understanding of what counts as relevant contributions, what counts as a good argument, and expected writing conventions in the educational context. When engaging in collaborative writing, peers can take on multiple roles. These roles include those of tutors, sounding boards and critical readers. Writing with peers also makes the concept of readership real because in collaborative writing there is an in-built audience and this may be particularly helpful for novice writers. Flower's (1979) study found that less successful writers produce a 'writer-based' text, assuming that the reader will understand their intended meaning. In collaborative writing, such writer assumptions may be questioned.

Collaborative writing also provides a natural environment for peer feedback about writing. During collaborative writing, learners are able not only to receive but also to provide feedback. Such feedback is available immediately and during the entire process of text creation. Feedback is provided on all aspects of writing and explanations are offered in a way that may be perhaps more developmentally appropriate. That is, the feedback may be better aligned with the learners' linguistic and cognitive capacity than teacher feedback (Daiute & Dalton, 1993). In contrast, in solitary writing and peer response activities, feedback is provided once the writing has been completed and only on the product. Furthermore, the level of commitment to editing the text in collaborative writing is likely to be higher than in peer editing because learners share ownership of the text (Tobin, 1991 cited in Dale, 1997).

In collaborative writing, co-authors may hold different opinions and this may compel debates about which ideas to include, how to express such ideas, and how to organise ideas. These debates have been termed 'cognitive conflict', a process of intellectual negotiation and collective decision making (Trimbur, 1989). Johnson and Johnson (1979), writing about cooperative groups, suggest that in a supportive climate, where students feel comfortable in challenging each other's ideas, such a conflict can be a positive force. The conflict can stimulate an exchange of ideas and a critical evaluation of the strengths and weaknesses of alternative suggestions, forcing students to clarify their own ideas. The debate may be a catalyst to a restructuring of ideas to accommodate new perspectives.

Dale's (1994b) research on collaborative writing with groups of high school students attests to the importance of cognitive conflict. Dale found that the most important factor which distinguished the most and least successful groups of collaborative writers in a ninth grade class was the level of cognitive conflict. In the most successful group, 20% of the group talk was spent on resolving cognitive conflict compared to 7% in the least successful group. Dale (1994 a, b) also found that a substantial amount of group writing time was spent on strategic planning and ongoing, recursive revision.

Researchers who have investigated the talk of students writing together found that collaborative writing encourages writers to share ideas about good composing strategies (e.g. Daiute, 1986), and that collaborative writing encourages writers to express and reflect on thinking 'that might otherwise remain unexamined or unelaborated' (Daiute & Dalton, 1993: 293). In interviews held by Louth et al. (1993) with students who were involved in collaborative and cooperative writing activities, the students reported that they had gained from the experience. They felt that they had learned much about the writing process, about how to revise, and developed a better sense of writing for an audience.

Another important reason often given for using collaborative writing activities in the L1 writing literature is that it prepares students for writing in the workplace. Collaborative writing provides learners with the experience needed to work and write together. Ede and Lunsford (1990), who studied writing in a range of professions, reported that the vast majority of professionals write together some of the time. Of the 700 professionals surveyed, 87% of the respondents reported that they worked as members of a team in producing documents. However, the authors also observed that the production of such documents was often a 'hierarchical' co-authoring process, in which the writers involved divided the responsibilities for the text creation, and there was a group leader who was assigned responsibility to ensure that the document was completed. In such teams, the effort is cooperative rather than collaborative. Each team member has limited responsibility, be it for the creation of one section of the document or perhaps one phase (e.g. final editing), depending on how the work is shared.

There have been a number of reports about the merits and pitfalls of such cooperative team writing activities in educational settings, such as group assignments (Leki, 2001; Strauss & U, 2007), but more so in workplace settings (e.g. Colen & Petelin, 2004; Dias *et al.*, 1999; Lay & Karis, 1991; Mirel & Spilka, 2002; Palmeri, 2004). This research suggests not only that team writing is prevalent, but that the abilities to collaboratively or cooperatively create, write and manage group projects are important skills in the professional world. A number of business communication as well as L2 writing scholars now argue that these skills need to be developed in writing and communication classes in higher education (e.g. Bremner, 2010; Dovey, 2006; Ede & Lunsford, 1990; Gollin, 1999; Schneider & Andre, 2005). In this sense, collaborative writing is a potential site for learning how to write, preparing students for future writing tasks.

Conclusion

Second language learning theories from differing perspectives and widely accepted approaches to L2 language instruction seem to concur that: (a) learners should be engaged in interaction; (b) the tasks which promote such interaction should be meaningful; and (c) such tasks should also encourage learners to focus on form. Collaborative writing tasks accord with all three principles. Collaborative writing activities involve students in interactions about their writing. Writing is meaning focused, is more likely to promote a focus on accuracy, and provides learners with the cognitive space to do so. The tool that enables them to deliberate about how to articulate their ideas in writing is language itself. Thus language is learnt in and through such task performance.

The arguments in support of collaborative writing put forward by L1 composition scholars are perhaps even more compelling for L2 writers. Research using think-aloud protocols of L2 writers composing shows that although the composing processes in L2 are the same as in L1 writing, writing in the L2 is more difficult and time consuming as L2 writers have to search their existing knowledge not only for ideas related to the topic but also their existing knowledge of the L2 (Chenoweth & Hayes, 2001; Manchón *et al.*, 2009; Roca de Larios *et al.*, 2006). When writing collaboratively, L2 writers have access to the ideas and to the linguistic resources of other L2 writers. It enables them to draw on this larger pool of knowledge rather than relying only on their own knowledge sources. Collaborative writing can also provide advanced L2 writers more generally with practice opportunities for the kind of writing they are likely to experience outside the L2 writing class (Leki, 2001) and writing in the workplace (Ede & Lunsford, 1990). Thus collaborative writing has potentially a number of advantages over solitary writing, both in terms of language learning and learning to write in the L2. In the next two chapters these potentials are explored further by reference to empirical research findings.

3 Collaborative Writing: L2 Learning and Practice Opportunities

Introduction

As the previous chapter has shown, collaborative writing seems well supported theoretically and pedagogically. Collaborative writing may provide learners with opportunities to shift their attention to deliberation over linguistic elements while completing meaning-focused language production tasks. Swain (2006, 2010) has used the term languaging to describe these deliberations when attempting to solve linguistic problems. Long (1991, 2000) and researchers informed by the interaction hypothesis use the term focus on form. Regardless of the terms used, SLA researchers agree that attention to language form is important for L2 learning. This chapter presents research findings on the nature of the talk that occurs during collaborative writing activity.

The chapter is divided into three sections. The first section considers the nature of languaging during collaborative writing. Excerpts from a range of studies are given to illustrate what learners focus on and how during collaborative writing activities. The second section discusses the attributes of the feedback that learners provide each other during these instances of languaging. The third section considers the language practice opportunities that collaborative writing provides L2 learners. Here the focus is not only on the amount of talk but also on the range of rhetorical functions that learners practice when writing collaboratively.

Collaborative Writing and the Nature of Languaging

When learners compose a text in an L2 and become aware of gaps in their knowledge or are uncertain about how to best express an idea, their attention turns to language choice and form. Research conducted with individual writers using think-aloud protocols (e.g. Cumming, 1990; Roca de Larios *et al.*, 2006) or with pairs (Storch & Wigglesworth, 2007) using pair dialogues has shown that L2 writers devote much attention and time to such deliberations. For example, using think-aloud protocols, Cumming's (1990) study found that about 30% of the decision-making episodes in L2 writers' protocols focused on their gist and language use concurrently, particularly on searching for appropriate words to express their ideas. In our study (Storch & Wigglesworth, 2007) we analysed transcripts of collaborative writing activities to assess the amount of time learners spent on the different phases of composing a text (planning, generating ideas, revising etc.), and found that over 30% of the talk concerned specifically deliberations about language choice. However, although the portion of time devoted to such deliberations may be similar, whether writing individually or in pairs, the major difference between collaborative writing and individual writing is the opportunity to interact with a peer during these deliberations about language in collaborative writing activities.

Before illustrating and discussing the nature of these interactions about language evident in research on collaborative writing tasks, it is important to note the unit of analysis used in this research. In research on focus on form, informed by Long's interaction hypothesis, the unit of analysis is generally the turn (e.g. Foster & Ohta, 2005; Mackey *et al.*, 2003; Pica & Doughty, 1986). Turns are coded for the kind of negotiation moves identified by Long's (1983, 1996) taxonomy of negotiations: confirmation checks, clarification requests, comprehension checks, and recasts. In research on collaborative writing, the unit of analysis tends to be a language-related episode (LRE).

An LRE is a segment in the learners' talk where learners deliberate about language while trying to complete the task (Swain, 1998; Swain & Lapkin, 1995, 2001). That is, in these episodes learners focus their attention explicitly on language use. They deliberate about the language they are producing, self and other-correct. Deliberations can be about grammatical form (morphology and syntax), lexical choices and meaning of words and phrases, mechanics (punctuation, spelling), as well as cohesion at sentence and discourse level. The following are examples of the different types of LREs taken from studies conducted in a range of L2 learning settings. What these examples also show is evidence of several cognitive processes taking place during these deliberations.

The first two examples are of LREs which focus on grammatical form. Example 1 comes from a study that I conducted, as part of my PhD research (see 2009 monograph: 145), in an ESL class with adult learners of high intermediate ESL proficiency. Here the two female students (Olivia and Shirley) are composing a data commentary text based on a graphic prompt which shows the English language proficiency of different migrant groups in Australia. Olivia suggests the simple present form of the verb *participate* and Shirley corrects her, suggesting the form *participating* (turn 17). Although Olivia accepts the correction by repeating the suggested verb form (turn 18), Shirley seems surprised that her correction has been accepted (turn 19). This note of surprise perhaps signals that what appears as a recast in turn 17 may in fact have been an instance of hypothesis testing. It is interesting to note that it is Olivia who then reassures Shirley (turn 20) that it is the appropriate verb form in this sentence. She provides a justification by noting the verb phrase that they are using in their text. Although not using grammatical terminology, she is clearly referring to a grammatical rule in her justification. Such reassurances and explanations are not available during individual writing.

Example 1: Form-based LRE

16	Olivia:	Figure 3 shows that there were Vietnamese and Laotians participate
17	Shirley:	Participating
18	Olivia:	Participating
19	Shirley:	Is correct? (sounds incredulous)
20	Olivia:	(laugh)…Because there were. We are using there were

Example 2 comes from Swain (2000: 110–111), from a study conducted with young learners, Grade 8 French immersion students (the study was also reported in Swain & Lapkin, 1998). The task involved the learners composing a text based on a set of pictures. In the example reproduced below (English translations of the French words are given in brackets), Kathy and Doug are co-constructing a sentence and become aware of their errors in verb choice and form. Kathy becomes aware of her error in verb choice (turn 3), but not in verb form. Doug then becomes aware of the wrong verb form. He points out (through emphasis) that *brosse* is a reflexive verb: *elle SE brosse* (turn 4). Kathy accepts Doug's correction and incorporates this information in her subsequent utterances (turns 5, 7, 11). Doug confirms that the revised idea is now acceptable (turns 6, 8).

Turn 7 is an interesting one to examine more closely. Here we have Kathy hesitating, self-correcting and also admonishing herself. Ewald (2005) suggests that some of the characteristics of private speech during interaction are low volume and self-corrections. Turn 7 in this excerpt may very well be an instance of Kathy's private speech used in an attempt to organise her thoughts and direct her attention. However, because this private speech is externalised, it makes her thinking public and invites a confirmation from Doug (turn 8). Thus what we see in this lengthy episode, which deals with verb choice and form simultaneously, is evidence of both forms of languaging, of private speech and of collaborative dialogue.

In this excerpt we also see evidence of learners pooling their linguistic resources: Kathy self-corrects for verb choice, Doug other-corrects for the reflexive form and ultimately the jointly constructed sentence is improved. The writing activity thus offers the learners opportunities to deliberate about their language use, to self- and other-correct, to pool their linguistic knowledge, and to provide and receive confirmation. The pooling of resources represents collective scaffolding (Donato, 1994). The knowledge co-constructed in this episode may not be new knowledge but consolidation of existing knowledge, which can lead to more accurate subsequent language use.

Example 2: Form-based LRE

1	Kathy:	Et brosse les cheveux.
		(*and brushes her hair*)
2	Doug:	Et les dents.
		(*and her teeth*)
3	Kathy:	Non, non, pendant qu'elle brosse les dents et...
		(*No, no, while she brushes her teeth and...*)
4	Doug:	Elle se brosse... elle SE brosse.
		(*She brushes... she brushes [emphasises the reflexive pronoun]*)
5	Kathy:	Pendant qu'elle se brosse les dents et peigne les cheveux
		(*while she brushes her teeth and combs her hair*).
6	Doug:	Ya!
7	Kathy:	Pendant qu'elle... se brosse... les cheveux, I mean, no, pendant qu'elle se PEIGNE les cheveux.
		(*while she... brushes... her hair, I mean, no, no, while she COMBS her hair*)
8	Doug:	Ya.
9	Kathy:	Et se brosse...
		(*and brushes*)
10	Doug:	Les dents.
		(*her teeth*)

11 Kathy: Pendant qu'elle SE peigne lex cheveux et SE brosse les dents.
               (While she combs her hair and brushes her teeth [emphasises the reflexive pronoun].

Example 3 is of a lexical LRE. It comes from the data of Aldosari's (2008) PhD study (see also Storch & Aldosari, 2010: 369). The study was conducted with adult (male) learners in an EFL class in Saudi Arabia. The learners were paired according to their L2 proficiency. The data come from the pair Nabeel and Naif, two relatively low-proficiency learners, writing a short composition about how to maintain good health. Translations of the Arabic words are provided in brackets.

In this LRE, the learners are deliberating about word meaning. Naif is not familiar with the word exercise in English and asks for an explanation (turn 62). In this EFL setting, where learners have a shared first language (L1), this L1 can be used as an effective tool. As seen in this example, Nabeel is able to provide an explanation of the word using the L1 (turn 63). The help offered is immediate: it is given when it is needed during the composing process. Naif seeks confirmation, repeating the word in Arabic and in English, and Nabeel confirms (turns 64–65). Thus the LRE shows that the collaborative writing activity provided Naif with an opportunity to gain new knowledge (new word), knowledge that can be appropriated and internalised by him and used in subsequent individual performance. Such an opportunity would not have been available had Naif been writing on his own.

Example 3: Lexis-based LRE (word meaning)

61 Nabeel: Any exercising... exercising...
62 Naif: Leesh *(what do you mean)* exercising?
63 Nabeel: Tamareen
              (exercise)
64 Naif: Exercise *tamareen?*
65 Nabeel: Yeah

Example 4 contains two consecutive LREs. The first LRE (turns 276–280) is a lexical LRE, the second (turns 281-282) is a short, form-based LRE. The example is taken from the data of an experimental study we (Wigglesworth & Storch, 2009: 459) conducted with adult ESL learners writing and processing feedback in pairs. These were advanced L2 learners, completing graduate degrees at our university. One of the tasks the participants had to complete was an argumentative essay. The example is drawn from the pair talk data of Mat and Emily. Here the lexical LRE is not triggered by an error or by uncertainties. Instead, Emily, the more proficient learner, suggests a number of what may be considered more sophisticated expressions (turns 277, 279). Thus the advantage for Mat in this collaborative writing activity is the exposure to a greater range of expressions. Matt readily accepts the suggestions, he repeats the suggestion (turn 278) and praises Emily (turn 280). It should be noted, however, that Emily also gains from this interaction. Her deliberations, self-repairs, and self-directed questions (in turn 281) may be self-directed speech. However, in this context, this audibly signalled need for assistance receives an immediate response. Mat, although the less proficient of the two learners, provides the needed assistance (turn 282), confirming that the gerund is the better alternative. Thus the contributions of both learners in this episode, regardless of proficiency differences, were valuable (see also Ohta, 2000).

Example 4: Two consecutive LRES

276	Mat:	By forcing the students to revising
277	Emily:	Encouraging would be a nicer word
278	Mat;	Ha ha ha. In the encouraging the students…
279	Emily:	To take the initiative
280	Mat:	Yeah, great.
281	Emily:	To take initiatives to start revising… to start a revision. Oh no, to start revising, no¿
282	Matt	mmm… to start revising.

Example 5 is of a mechanical LRE. It comes from the study by Tan *et al.* (2006) who compared the nature of learners' interactions when completing a range of collaborative writing tasks in a face-to-face and a computer mediated mode (see also Tan *et al.*, 2010). The learners were adult beginner learners of Chinese as a foreign language (FL) in Australia. In this example we see two learners, Ivan and Lisa, deliberating about the form of a Chinese character. As in the case of Aldosari's (2008) study, these FL learners use their shared L1 (English) to deliberate about this fairly difficult aspect of Chinese orthography. However, unlike the LREs in all the previous examples, here the LRE remains unresolved.

Example 5: Mechanical LRE

64	Ivan:	Is that how you write 真¿ Or does it have leg with them¿ Got long thing at the bottom¿
65	Lisa:	No
66	Ivan:	Got long ones at the bottom…真

67	Lisa:	And it's got cross on the top, yeah¿
68	Ivan:	Cross¿ It's not dot¿ Are you sure¿
69	Lisa:	No
70	Ivan:	On the top…

Example 6 is one where the focus of the LRE is on cohesive links between sentences. The example comes from a study conducted by Niu (2009: 391) with upper intermediate EFL learners in China. The task used was a text reconstruction. One group of learners was asked to reproduce in written form a text that they had first read but which had been removed after they had read it. In this example the two learners, Yu and Liu, deliberate about the need to link two sentences and the appropriate linking word or phrase. Yu (turn 1) knows that they need a link between the two ideas, but is uncertain about the use of *but* reflected in her hesitations. These hesitations signal a need for assistance. However Liu is unable to assist (turn 2), and Yu resolves the problem on her own. Perhaps verbalising her uncertainty helped her in deciding that it is the appropriate linking word here. Liu agrees with the resolution (turn 6). For Yu, this may be an occasion for consolidation; for Liu an occasion for learning.

Example 6: Discourse focused LRE

1	Yu:	Ok, but … er…we must make the first sentence and the second sentence er… make some linking.
2	Liu:	It's pretty difficult for me.
3	Yu:	The… er… predicting the future is always perilous, but it…
4	Liu:	Perilous.
5	Yu:	But it is safe… it is safe to say that … er….
6	Liu:	Yeah, I agree with you.

It is important to note that when learners work collaboratively, not all LREs are resolved (see Example 5) and some are not resolved correctly. The following example is of an LRE where, despite the deliberations and explanation, the resolution the learners reached was grammatically incorrect. The data come from a study (Storch, 2001b: 44) that was conducted in an ESL class with adult learners of high intermediate ESL proficiency, using a data commentary task. Here the two male students (Howard and Sam) re-read the text they jointly composed which describes the writing proficiency of two migrant groups before and after coming to Australia. As he re-reads what they had collaboratively composed, Howard expresses his uncertainly about the verb tense chosen, and suggests that the verb *have* should be changed to the past tense form. In a sense he is testing a hypothesis about the use of the past tense in this context (turn117). Sam seems a bit confused by this suggestion (turn 118), perhaps he is not sure which of the two instances of *have* should be replaced with the past tense form *had* that Howard is referring to. Howard attempts to provide a clarification by repeating and spelling out the past verb form (turn 119). Although Sam agrees with the suggested amendment (turn 120), Howard feels the need to justify his suggested amendment and thus offers an explanation for his verb tense choice (turn 121). Here we see some use of simple metalanguage ('it's past') and implied reference to a grammatical rule about past tense forms. Sam accepts and repeats the justification, but it is not clear whether he's agreeing with the use of the past tense form in this instance or that *had* is the past tense of *have*. The resolution is incorrect in this instance. In their jointly produced text the learners wrote: 'The majority of Vietnamese have learn English before and had English language fluency above or equal to low'.

Example 7: An incorrectly resolved LRE

117	Howard:	The majority of Vietnamese Vietnamese…have learnt English before and have English language is fluency… above or equal to low. And had is it¿ We should put had¿
118	Sam;	Had¿
119	Howard:	Had, H-A-D¿
120	Sam:	Yeah
121	Howard:	Because it's past
122	Sam:	Yeah past

Studies on collaborative writing conducted with different cohorts of L2 learners, such as adult ESL learners (e.g. Storch, 2001a, 2001b; Wigglesworth & Storch, 2009), adult FL learners (e.g. Aldosari, 2008; Alegría de la Colina & García Mayo, 2007; Niu, 2009; Tan *et al.*, 2006), and adolescents in L2 immersion programmes (e.g. Swain & Lapkin, 1998, 2001) have shown that when engaging in collaborative writing activities learners focus on both lexical choices and grammatical forms, and on structures beyond those necessarily targeted by the teacher or researcher. The proportion of each type of LRE may depend on the task type. Tasks which are more grammar focused (e.g. passage editing) seem to elicit more LREs, particularly form-based LREs, than meaning-based tasks such as picture description and compositions (see discussion in the next chapter). Regardless of task type, however, research shows that mechanics (spelling, punctuation) receive the least attention, although this may be a function of the relatively high L2 proficiency of learners in research to date on collaborative writing.

Research on collaborative writing tasks has also shown that the length of the LREs and the nature of their resolutions may vary. LREs can vary in length and depth of engagement, ranging from one turn (e.g. a self-repair) to extended negotiations consisting of a sequence of turns and involving both learners (see Example 2 above). However, it should be noted that length of LREs does not necessarily equate with level of engagement. Long LREs may consist of a monologue by one learner and merely expressions of agreement by the other (see the example provided in Chapter 4). Thus in one of my studies (Storch, 2008), I distinguished between LREs showing substantial and elaborate levels of engagement by both members of the dyad, those showing elaborate engagement by one member only, and those showing limited engagement by both. Fortune (2005) suggests that what he labelled discontinuous LREs reflect sustained engagement. In discontinuous LREs learners re-engage with an issue because an earlier LRE dealing with the issue was left unresolved or because the learners determine that their original resolution is incorrect (see also Storch, 2009).

Although LREs may not always be resolved, nor necessarily resolved correctly (as in Example 7 above), there is now sufficient empirical evidence (e.g. Adams & Ross-Feldman, 2008; Alegría de la Colina & García Mayo, 2007; Niu, 2009; Storch, 2001b; Storch & Aldosari, 2013) to suggest that the majority of LREs are resolved, and resolved correctly (see also Chapter 6). In resolving lexical LREs, particularly in the FL setting, the shared L1 helps learners to explain word meanings. In resolving grammar-based LREs, particularly in the case of more advanced L2 learners, resolutions are sometimes reached by recourse to previously learnt grammatical rules and conventions as well as intuitions of what sounds correct, with a higher rate of successful resolutions generally occurring when learners draw on considerations of form and meaning (Fortune, 2005; García Mayo, 2002a, 2002b; Storch, 1997, 1998b). However, learners do not always verbalise the reasons for their decisions, nor do they use metalinguistic terminology when offering explanations or justifications for their suggestions (see Example 1). This is particularly the case with simple morphosyntactic structures (e.g. subject-verb agreement), and even more so in cases which require more complex form-meaning mapping (Fortune, 2005; Storch, 2008). Furthermore, the use of metalinguistic terminology does not necessarily lead to a correct LRE resolution (see Example 7).

Fortune and Thorp (2001) and Fortune (2005) provide extensive discussions of some of the difficulties involved in identifying, classifying and quantifying LREs, including how to code instances of overlapping and embedded LREs which deal with more than one item of language simultaneously. Although the definition of LREs is largely similar across the studies, slight differences exist. For example, Fortune (2005) excludes episodes containing only self-repairs, arguing that such episodes do not reflect collaborative activity. Swain and Lapkin's (1995) definition of LREs includes such episodes, not surprising given that LREs were used in the researchers' analysis of individual think-aloud protocols. There are also some variations in categorising LREs, particularly episodes where learners focus on prepositions and on mechanics (e.g. spelling). For example, talk about choice of prepositions was coded by Leeser (1994) as form-based LREs, arguing that in such LREs his learners were basing their decisions on grammatical conventions rather than meaning considerations. Others (e.g. Williams, 1999) codes LREs dealing with prepositions as lexical. This is a practice I tend to adopt (e.g. Storch, 2008; Storch & Wigglesworth, 2010a, b) because in my analysis of pair talk about prepositions, the deliberations seem to be about a choice between alternative prepositions, and the semantic meaning of prepositions. Mechanical or orthographic LREs, given their infrequency in pair talk data, are often collapsed and included as lexical LREs (e.g. Niu, 2009) or form-based LREs (e.g. Swain & Lapkin, 1998). Despite these differences in coding, the LRE does seem to provide a useful unit of analysis for learners' deliberations about language. It is interesting to note that it is now also used in research informed by the interaction hypothesis, to complement analysis of negotiation moves (e.g. see Gass et al., 2011).

As noted in the previous chapter, a number of researchers (e.g. Cumming, 1989; Williams, 1999, 2008, 2012) claim that writing, being less ephemeral than speaking, encourages and enables learners to pay more attention to language. Studies that have compared the frequency and nature of LREs in collaborative writing tasks with LREs generated by oral tasks confirm these claims. For example, in a series of studies Adams (2003, 2006) compared learners' interaction in two phases of a task. The first phase was an oral information gap task involving learners in an exchange of information about their pictures in order to compose a joint story (orally). The second phase required the learners to write up their story. Adams found that the writing phase of the task elicited more LREs than the speaking only phase. In the speaking phase, there were often missed opportunities for negotiations about language. The students did not always signal a lack of understanding, nor did they always correct their partner's incorrect utterances. In contrast, in the writing phase the students seemed more willing to engage in lengthy discussions about language and to pool their linguistic resources.

These findings about the superiority of writing over speaking tasks in encouraging learners to focus on language were replicated in subsequent studies (Adams & Ross-Feldman, 2008; Niu, 2009) using slightly different writing tasks. Niu's (2009) study, mentioned earlier, had one group of EFL learners work in pairs reconstructing a text orally, the other group reconstructing a text in written form. Niu found that the written reconstruction task drew more attention to language than the oral reconstruction task. The writing task generated more LREs, and these LREs dealt with a wider range of grammatical and discourse structures than the oral task. Furthermore, deliberations about language was more extensive (quantified in terms of number of turns) in the collaborative writing task. In these deliberations, the learners were willing to offer explanations and justifications for their choices. This was not the case in the oral task.

Feedback and Collective Scaffolding

Cumming's study (1990), mentioned earlier, which analysed think-aloud protocols of learners composing in their L2, showed that students often put a great deal of effort into their deliberations about language choice. In the process of composing a text, learners generate and evaluate alternative expressions before reaching a choice that is deemed to be satisfactory. The following excerpt from Cumming's study (1990: 491) illustrates this struggle to find an appropriate word:

> I'm looking for a word. 'Not even are they...' Are they...' I was going to say 'enable.' Able? Ah. I don't want to say 'able'. I don't want to say 'efficient'. Ah, I'm looking for words 'Are they ...' 'Not even are they able'? Ah. How do you say someone who has the qualification of doing something? Are they qualified? 'Qualified' would be too much. No, no, that's not what I want to say. 'Capable', yah, 'capable'. Well is it the same than 'able'? Yah, okay, Okay.

What stands out in this protocol is that the learner in the solitary writing mode can only rely on her own linguistic resources to resolve her deliberations. Manchón et al.'s (2009) study, using think-aloud protocols with EFL learners composing individually, reported similar findings. The L2 writers drew predominantly on their first and second languages. However, the researchers also noted that these L2 writers drew on their existing knowledge rather than generating new or novel language creations. In contrast, when writing collaboratively, as illustrated in the LREs discussed earlier, learners no longer need to rely only on their own knowledge sources when grappling with how to express an idea. They have a larger pool of knowledge to draw on. Their deliberations about language are vocalised and may thus elicit assistance from their peers. This assistance can be in the form of suggesting alternative forms of expressions, negative feedback (e.g. explicit corrections, recasts) as well as positive feedback (confirmation). Furthermore, the availability of assistance and the opportunity to pool resources means that in collaborative writing, unlike in solitary writing, learners can co-construct new language knowledge.

The feedback provided by peers in collaborative writing activities has a number of attributes which make it particularly valuable for second language learning. First and foremost it is timely. As the LREs in the previous section demonstrate, such feedback is provided in response to cues signalling a need for assistance (e.g. deliberations, self-repairs) as well as overt requests for assistance. The feedback provided is immediate and available throughout the composing process, unlike teacher and peer feedback (in peer response activities) which is usually given when the writing has been completed.

Research conducted by Brooks and Swain (2009) also suggests that peer feedback given during a collaborative writing activity may be more developmentally appropriate than teacher feedback and hence more useful. In their multi-staged study, Brooks and Swain examined not only whether learning occurred as a result of collaborative writing, but also the most effective source of learning. In Stage 1, two pairs of adult ESL learners co-authored a text. The text was then reformulated by one of the researchers (native speaker) and in Stage 2, the participants were asked to compare their text to the reformulated version of their text. In Stage 3, they were given an opportunity to ask the researcher further questions about the reformulations. The students were then asked to revise their jointly produced text individually. This revised version was used as a post-test, to assess the learning that took place as well as the source of the learning given that the learners had three different sources of expertise: peers, the reformulations, and interactions with the researcher in the third session. The study found that the most effective source of expertise was in fact the peers. A very high proportion of the solutions to language problems that the learners discussed and resolved during the co-authoring session (Stage 1) were maintained in the post-tests. In contrast, some of the language problems on which the students received reformulations and discussed with the researcher, reappeared in the final version. One possible explanation offered by the researchers for these findings is that the reformulations and assistance provided by the native speaker researcher dealt with structures that were perhaps beyond the learners' developmental stage. Peers, on the other hand, provided each other with assistance that was more attuned to the learners' needs and developmental stage.

Feedback during collaborative writing activities is generally readily given, negotiated, and often accepted and incorporated in the text co-authored. This is unlike feedback provided in peer response activities, where research (e.g. Carson & Nelson, 1994; Connor & Asenavage, 1994; Nelson & Carson, 1998;

Nelson & Murphy, 1993; Yang *et al.*, 2006) has shown that learners may be reluctant to provide corrective feedback, reluctant to question the feedback given, and indeed to take up the feedback given. A number of reasons have been suggested which may explain this reluctance, including cultural differences, perceived roles and L2 proficiency. However, another important reason for this reluctance may be related to text ownership. In peer response activities, the text reviewed is owned by the writer. The learner providing the corrective feedback may be concerned that the corrective feedback may be perceived as offensive by the writer, leading to a loss of face. Furthermore, as McCarthy and McMahon (1992) point out, the peer providing the feedback has no ownership of the text and thus little power to affect change. When composing collaboratively, ownership of the text is shared and thus corrective feedback is not directed at any one learner's text but at the jointly created and owned text. This in a sense may mitigate any individual loss of face. The joint responsibility over the creation of the text also means that the students may be more accepting of peer suggestions and corrective feedback. Furthermore, such feedback may be more readily acceptable because it is bi-directional. In teacher feedback, there are generally few opportunities to discuss and negotiate the feedback once it is given on the written text. During collaborative writing, feedback is provided in the context of the writing activity and may therefore trigger a chain of suggestions and counter suggestions (see Example 5 above).

Thus the feedback provided during collaborative writing is a form of scaffolded assistance (Ohta, 2000); it is timely and developmentally appropriate, responding to the learners' expressed need for assistance. It can also be a collectively constructed scaffold (Donato, 1994). In such instances, novices guide and support each other, pooling their linguistic knowledge to reach an outcome that they may not have been able to achieve had they been composing on their own. This is evident in Examples 2 and 4 in the previous section. In Example 2, we noted that Kathy's deliberations about verb choice led to the correct verb choice, and Doug's correction then led to the correct form of the verb. Similarly, in Example 4, it was Emily's and Matt's joint effort which resulted in a sentence which was more linguistically sophisticated and grammatically accurate. Together these learners' performance outstripped their individual L2 competence.

Opportunities for L2 Use

Collaborative writing tasks provide learners opportunities not only to focus on language use but also to use the target language and use it for a range of functions that are normally the purview of the language teacher. As the

LREs in the earlier section demonstrate, these functions include providing negative feedback (e.g. recasts, corrective feedback) as well as positive feedback (e.g. confirmation, praise), seeking confirmation, explaining grammatical choices and word meanings. In addition, research on talk generated by collaborative writing has shown that in such tasks, learners provide suggestions and counter suggestions and extend on each other's suggestions to compose complex ideas. The following examples illustrate these latter functions of L2 use.

Example 8 is taken from the data of a study conducted with advanced ESL learners (Storch & Wigglesworth, 2007: 171) writing in pairs. The task used was a data commentary report based on a graph showing levels of rainfall in different cities in the world. As the example shows, in their attempt to co-construct a sentence the learners offer suggestions and counter suggestions about choice of expression (turns 195–196), provide an explanation for their preferred expression (turn 197), correct for grammatical form (turn 198), seek and receive confirmation (turns 199–200), incorporate and extend on each other's ideas (turns 201–202).

Example 8: Co-constructing a sentence

193	Eik:	Both city have the same trend throughout the year
194	Lily:	Yep yep yeah
195	Eik:	During the four seasons... during the four seasons, can I say that? Seasons... both city have
196	Lily:	During the year maybe, yeah?
197	Eik:	But I don't want to repeat throughout the year
198	Lily:	Ok... both cities
199	Eik:	Both cities you know we should... we should use past tense always.... Lagos... had or has?
200	Lily:	Had
201	Eik:	Had... had throughout the year except in winter which average rainfall
202	Lily:	Much less than

Such opportunities to use the L2 for a range of functions is particularly important in FL contexts, where the classroom is often the only opportunity learners have to use the target language. The following two examples, from a study conducted in EFL classes in Saudi Arabia (Storch & Aldosari, 2013), show quite starkly the difference in opportunities for learners to use the L2 in teacher-fronted and pair interaction when writing collaboratively. The first excerpt is fairly typical of the class talk recorded and observed in a number of EFL classes in the college (Arabic words are in italics followed by their English translation in brackets, T stands for teacher, S for a student).

Example 9: Teacher led class talk

37	T:	For present simple ... simple present ... did for ... simple past ... So if we ... if we are to negate drank ... how do we do that? How to negate drank? I ... I
38	S:	Did
39	T:	Did (writing on the board) ... *aywah* (*ok*) not
40	S:	Drink
41	T:	Drank?
42	S:	Drink...
43	T:	Drink ... *mumtaz* (*excellent*) I did not drink ... negation ... With negation you have to use the simple form ... I did not drink water. I did not drink water. Aaaa if I say for example ... I aa ummm I write on the board ... Can can some one negate it? I want some one to negate *el* (*the*) sentence.

The teacher talk clearly dominated class talk, forming almost 90% of all talk. The typical pattern of the teacher's turns in this class involved explanations of grammatical structures followed by elicitations (e.g. turn 37, 43) or a repetition of a student's response to confirm that the response was correct. The students' responses in the L2 were fairly short, often consisting of one word. These utterances served basically one function: a response to an elicitation. Thus students' use of the L2 was limited not only in terms of the length of their L2 utterances but also in terms of the functions their utterances fulfilled. The limited quantity and function of learner talk in teacher-led classes has been reported previously in studies which compared teacher talk and oral group interactions (e.g. Bejarno, 1987; Pica & Doughty, 1986).

When we implemented our study in this EFL class and had the learners work in pairs on a range of writing tasks, the talk that the tasks elicited showed evidence not only of longer L2 turns (averaging six words), but also that the turns served a wider range of rhetorical functions. The extract in Example 10 illustrates the nature of the learners' talk when the learners were asked to collaboratively compose an essay about factors that contribute to good health. The learners, Ali and Naser, were considered of relatively low proficiency. In this dialogue we see evidence of the learners elaborating on each other's ideas (turns 58-60), offering counter suggestions (turns 65), and providing corrective feedback (turn 63). Thus the task provided the learners with opportunities to practice genuine and extended communication in the L2.

Example 10: Pair talk during CW

58	Ali:	Do the do the sport
59	Naser:	Yes … and swimming and aaa and swimming
60	Ali:	Walk
61	Naser:	Swimming and
62	Ali:	Walked
63	Naser:	Walkeding the aaa
64	Ali:	Or do any anything do anything do any sport
65	Naser:	Do something to help to help us

Other studies, conducted in a range of settings, also show the opportunities that collaborative tasks offer learners in terms of L2 use. Abadikhah's (2012) study, which compared the nature of learner talk generated by so-called mechanical tasks (i.e. grammatical drills) with that generated by meaning-focused writing tasks, also found that meaning-focused writing tasks generated longer discussions.

One reason that may explain why collaborative writing tasks provide learners with greater opportunities to use the L2 and for a range of functions is that such activities engage the learners in a multitude of roles. As noted by Bruffee (1984), writing about collaborative writing in L1 contexts, and Weissberg (2006), writing about collaborative writing in L2 contexts, these roles include co-authors, sounding boards, critical peers and tutors. As co-authors, learners engage in co-constructing ideas, suggesting and counter-suggesting alternative ways of expressing ideas, and extending on each other's suggestion or completing an idea that their partner may have difficulties with. As sounding boards, they confirm or disconfirm any expressed uncertainties or question the language used to express an idea. When proposing alternative suggestions or agreeing with proposed changes, they are in fact acting as critical peers, who are responding after evaluating the ideas put forward (Camps *et al.*, 2000). When providing negative and positive feedback, and explanations to justify corrective feedback, they take on the role of tutors.

Conclusion

Research using think-aloud protocols has shown that when composing a text, L2 learners spent substantial time and effort deliberating about language; that is, on how best to express their ideas. That is, they language. They engage in private speech using language as a tool to direct their thoughts in order to solve problems about language. They search their existing knowledge sources, testing and evaluating alternative forms of expression. However, in resolving these problems they can rely only on their existing knowledge sources.

Research on collaborative writing shows that when learners co-author with peers, they deliberate about similar types of issues as when writing alone: grammatical forms, word choice and meaning, orthography, and cohesion. These deliberations have been operationalised in this literature as LREs. In essence, these LREs show learners engaging in problem solving. However, what distinguishes the deliberations that occur during collaborative writing activities from solitary writing is the forms that languaging can take and the pool of available knowledge.

In collaborative writing, as indeed in any problem-solving group work, languaging has two forms: vocalised and hence audible private speech and collaborative dialogue. These forms of languaging direct learners' attention to a particular linguistic problem and may elicit a response from the others in the group or pair; responses such as suggestions, counter suggestions, negative feedback (e.g. recasts, explicit correction) as well as positive feedback (e.g. confirmation, praise). Thus the writer no longer needs to rely solely on their own knowledge sources to resolve deliberations about language when writing. Furthermore, learners can build on each other's suggestions, collectively scaffolding their performance to a level unattainable had they worked on their own. Thus collaborative writing tasks may be more conducive to language learning than solitary writing. Writing collaboratively provides learners with occasions to consolidate existing linguistic knowledge as well as to co-construct new knowledge that can then be internalised and used subsequently in individual writing production.

Furthermore, studies investigating the nature of the dialogue that takes place during collaborative L2 writing activities have shown that these activities provide learners with opportunities for extended L2 use. Deliberating about composing a text provides leaners with a meaningful and genuine need to communicate, and to use the L2 for a range of functions, including functions that learners rarely practice (e.g. explaining, providing feedback, inviting opinions, expressing disagreement) in teacher-fronted classes.

The importance of the incidence of LREs in the students' dialogues as they engage in collaborative writing is not only that they represent a focus on language, but that they are occasions for language learning. However, a number of factors may affect the quantity and quality of these LREs. These factors include the type of tasks used, the L2 proficiency of the learners, and the nature of the relationships the learners form when composing together. The next chapter discusses these factors in greater depth.

4 Factors Affecting Languaging in Collaborative Writing

Introduction

The empirical studies discussed in the previous chapter show that collaborative writing provides learners with opportunities to language and to practice using the target language. However, a number of factors may affect the volume and quality of languaging, operationalised in terms of the quantity and nature of LREs. These factors include the type of writing task, the L2 proficiency of the learners and the size of the small group, and the relationships learners form when writing together. Each of these factors is discussed in turn.

Table 4.1 presents a summary of the published studies that I refer to in this chapter. It should be noted that the table does not present a comprehensive summary of all studies which have investigated collaborative writing. I have included only studies which analysed the learners' dialogues for instances of languaging, and which have tended to use LREs as units of analysis. Thus, for example, the table excludes the study by DiCamilla and Anton (1997) which analysed pair talk during collaborative writing for the use and functions served by repetitions. The table, however, does include studies which investigated learners' dialogue on a range of grammar tasks (e.g. editing), tasks which, as I noted in Chapter 1, do not constitute collaborative writing. These studies have been included because their findings are informative in this discussion on LREs. The table provides brief details about the context in which the studies were implemented, the task used, and how the task was implemented. Information about implementation, where available, includes whether the students worked in pairs or small groups; how the pairs/groups were formed (self-selected or assigned by the researcher/teacher);

whether there were any pre-task activities such as a brief (usually grammar) instruction session, modelling of interaction and/or practice sessions; and the time allocated to complete the task. Where the author/s draws on the same data set in a number of published studies, these studies are collapsed under the one entry. It should be noted that one of the studies in this table used computer mediated communication (Tan *et al.*, 2010). This is one among the very few studies where this mode of communication was used to complete collaborative writing tasks (see discussion in Chapter 7).

As the table shows, although these studies have been implemented in a range of L2 contexts, the predominant cohort is adult ESL and EFL learners (university), of intermediate to advanced proficiency. However, how the proficiency level was determined is not always stated by the researchers, and where it is, it is often based on local language tests or the classroom teacher's assessment. This makes the concept of proficiency somewhat elusive. What intermediate means in one context could be vastly different to what it means in another context. Thus comparisons between studies and generalisations about the impact of L2 proficiency on languaging are problematic. The studies range in size and research design. Some are experimental studies, conducted in language laboratories; others are quasi-experimental classroom-based studies. As the table shows, the most commonly used task in research to date has been the dictogloss (elucidated below). In many studies, students were given some practice sessions before data collection. The time given to complete the set tasks varied, with many researchers not setting time restrictions. Where a time limit was set, it tended to average 30 minutes. In the majority of studies, students worked in pairs rather than small groups, and these pairs were self-selected rather than assigned by the teacher/researcher. This is perhaps not surprising given that many of these studies were conducted in regular and intact language classes where students are familiar with each other.

Task Type

A range of writing tasks have been employed in studies investigating collaborative writing. These tasks can be distinguished in terms of whether they are meaning-focused or language-focused. A meaning-focused writing task requires the writers to compose a text based on a written or pictorial prompt. Attention to language form (Focus on Form) in such tasks is incidental; it occurs while the co-authors focus on creating a meaningful text and encounter a difficulty. As such it is difficult to predict which language forms the learners will focus on. In contrast, language-focused tasks attempt to draw learners' attention to a set of pre-determined language forms while completing the task.

Table 4.1 Studies reporting on L2 learners writing in pairs/small groups

Study	Learners and context	Tasks	Implementation
Abadikhah (2012)	N = 36 EFL low intermediate Iran, university Experimental study	Mechanical exercises e.g. substitution + Meaning and language-focused tasks e.g. description, dictogloss	Some practice Pairs (self-selected) 15 minutes on mechanical exercises
Alegría de la Colina & García Mayo (2007)	N = 24 EFL elementary Spain, university Experimental (lab)	3 tasks: jigsaw, dictogloss, text reconstruction	Prior practice Pairs (self-selected) No time restrictions (within 50 minutes)
Aldosari (2008) Storch & Aldosari (2010, 2013)	N = 36 (18 pairs) EFL Mixed proficiency Saudi Arabia, university	Jigsaw, composition, text editing	Pairs assigned. 6 pairs each of: High–High High–Low Low–Low 20–25 minutes
Eckerth (2008)	N = 31 L2 = German Lower (n = 14) and upper intermediate (n = 17) USA, university Regular classroom	Consciousness raising tasks: Text reconstruction (adapted dictogloss) + Text repair (similar to a text reconstruction)	Pairs

Fernández Dobao (2012) See also Fernández Dobao (forthcoming)	$N = 111$ L2 = Spanish Intermediate USA, university 6 intact classes	Story based on a set of pictures	Grammar lesson Pairs ($n = 15$) and small groups ($n = 15$) of 4 students, all self-selected. 21 individual writers Approx 30 minutes
Fortune (2005)	$N = 8$ ESL Advanced UK, university	Dictogloss	Pairs
Fortune & Thorp (2001)	$N = 28$ ESL Intermediate UK, university Intact classes	Dictogloss	5 triads and few dyads Students assigned to ensure approx. same L2 proficiency and different L1
García Mayo (2002a, 2002b)	$N = 14$ EFL High intermediate Spain, university Experimental (lab)	Range of grammar exercises/tasks: multiple choice, cloze, text reconstruction, editing, dictogloss	Pre-task training Pairs (self-selected) 10–15 minutes
Kim (2008)	$N = 32$ L2 = Korean as second language (KSL) Intermediate Korea, university	Dictogloss (text read 3 times)	Modelling + Practice sessions 8 pairs (+ 16 individuals) 30 minutes

(continued)

Table 4.1 (continued)

Study	Learners and context	Tasks	Implementation
Kim & McDonough (2008)	N = 24 L2 = KSL Intermediate and Advanced Korea, pre-university intensive programme	Dictogloss	Modelling and Practice session 8 intermediate learners paired first with same proficiency, then with higher proficiency learners 30 minutes
Kim & McDonough (2011)	N = 44 EFL Korea, middle school students (13–14 yr) Regular classes	Dictogloss	Pre-task modelling Pairs Maximum 45 minutes
Kowal & Swain (1994)	N = 19 L2 = French Mixed proficiency Canada, Grade 8 (immersion) Intact class	Dictogloss	2 practice sessions 9 pairs + 1 triad Pairs mostly self-selected 20 minutes
Kuiken & Vedder (2002)	N = 34 EFL Netherlands, high school	Dictogloss	Experimental group (n = 20): groups (3–4). Control group (n = 14): worked individually 45 minutes on each of 2 dictogloss tasks

Study	Participants	Task	Procedure
Leeser (2004)	N = 42 L2 = Spanish Mixed proficiency USA, university Regular classes	Dictogloss	Short grammar + practice session + modelling Paired according to L2 proficiency High–High ($n = 8$) High–Low ($n = 9$) Low–Low ($n = 4$) 10 minutes
Malmqvist (2005)	N = 12 L2 = German Mixed proficiency Sweden, university preparation course	Dictogloss (not focusing on particular structures)	Practice session Implemented 3 times: 1st and 3rd individual work 2nd session: Small groups (3–4 per group) Teacher assigned to ensure heterogeneity 25–30 minutes
Nassaji & Tian (2010)	N = 26 ESL Low intermediate Canada, university intensive programme Two regular classes	2 grammar exercises: cloze and editing	Mini lesson Pairs Random assignment by researcher All completed 2 versions of each exercise, once individually and once in pairs 8 minutes

(continued)

Table 4.1 (continued)

Study	Learners and context	Tasks	Implementation
Niu (2009)	N = 16 EFL Upper intermediate China university	Oral vs. Writing text reconstruction based on prior reading of a text	Practice session Pairs (assigned to ensure homogeneity and familiarity with each other) 4 pairs in each modality Oral task: 15 minutes Writing task: 25 minutes
Storch (1997)	N = 14 ESL Intermediate Australia, university	Editing task	4 pairs (and 2 triads) - Self-selected
Storch (1998b, 1999)	N = 9 ESL Interm – advanced Australia, university	3 grammar exercises (multiple choice, cloze, text reconstruction) and composition task	3 pairs and 1 triad – self-selected No time restrictions
Storch (2005)	N = 19 ESL Intermediate/ advanced Australia, university Regular class	Data commentary	Students given choice to work in pairs or individually. 7 pairs – self-selected No time restrictions
Storch (2007)	N = 66 ESL Intermediate	Editing	In 2 classes, students given a choice to work in pairs (self-selected) or individually:

	Australia, university Regular classes		Pairs ($n = 9$), triad ($n = 1$), individuals ($n = 25$). Within 30 minutes
Storch (2008)	$N = 22$ ESL Intermediate Australia, university Regular classes	Text reconstruction	Pairs – self-selected Within 30 minutes
Storch (2009) Storch (2001a)	$N = 20$ ESL Intermediate Australia, university Regular class	3 tasks/exercises: Data commentary, text reconstruction, editing	Pairs – self-selected No time restrictions
Storch & Wigglesworth (2007) (Wigglesworth & Storch, 2009)	$N = 72$ ESL Advanced Australia, university	Data commentary and argumentative composition	Pairs ($n = 24$) – self-selected Individuals ($n = 24$) Pairs: 40–60 minutes Individuals: 20–30 minutes
Swain (1998)	$N = 48$ L2 = French Canada, Grade 8 (immersion) 2 intact classes	Dictogloss	Pre-task modelling (± metalanguage), practice sessions Pairs

(continued)

Table 4.1 (continued)

Study	Learners and context	Tasks	Implementation
Swain & Lapkin (1998)	N = 24 (focus on 1 case study pair) L2 = French Canada, Grade 8 (immersion)	Jigsaw	Mini lesson + modelling practice Pairs No time restrictions
Swain & Lapkin (2001)	N = 65 L2 = French Canada, Grade 8 (immersion) 2 classes	Dictogloss and jigsaw (each class completed one of the tasks)	Mini lesson + modelling, practice Pairs No time restrictions
Tan et al. (2010)	N = 12 L2 = Chinese Beginners Australia, university Intact class	7 tasks: 5 compositions, editing, translation	7 pairs (self-selected) Completed 2 versions of each task, in face-to-face and computer-mediated mode
Watanabe & Swain (2007, 2008)	N = 12 ESL Mixed proficiency Canada, university	Essay	4 core participants worked with 4 higher and then with 4 lower proficiency learners No time restrictions

Meaning-focused tasks that have been used in research on collaborative writing include descriptive and argumentative compositions, data commentary reports and jigsaw. A data commentary report requires students to summarise information presented in a graph or table. A jigsaw is an information gap task (see Pica *et al.*, 1993) where each member of the pair (or small group) receives part of the necessary information and must exchange that information in order to complete the task. The information given to the participants is usually visual (e.g. pictures). The task requires each participant to describe the pictures that he/she holds and together with other members of the group or pair compose a coherent story or narrative based on the entire set of pictures. The jigsaw has been used in oral tasks as a way of promoting negotiations of meaning (e.g. Gass & Mackey, 2007). When used as a collaborative writing activity, the participants also write a story or narrative based on the entire set of pictures.

As noted above, the most commonly used language-focused task in research on collaborative writing has been the dictogloss. The dictogloss, developed by Wajnryb (1990), is a procedure that requires students to listen twice to a short passage (about a paragraph in length) which is read at normal speed. The first time the students simply listen to the passage, the second time they take notes (not in complete sentences). They then use the notes to reconstruct the passage. Reconstruction is generally done in small groups or pairs, with students pooling their individual notes to reconstruct the text. The reconstructed text does not necessarily have to be identical to the original text, it simply needs to be grammatically accurate, meaningful, and resemble in gist the original text (e.g. see Fortune & Thorp, 2001). The dictogloss is generally seeded with a set of pre-determined grammatical forms and aims to encourage learners to use these forms in their reconstructed text. However, researchers (e.g. Eckerth, 2008; Kuiken & Vedder, 2002) frequently report that in reconstructing the text based on their notes, learners focus on language items not targeted by the task.

Some researchers have varied the dictogloss procedure slightly. For example, Niu (2009) had the students read the passage rather than listening to it being dictated. The passage was then removed and the learners reconstructed the text (orally or in written form) using their notes and a handout with key words that had to be incorporated in their reconstructed texts. Eckerth (2008) also provided learners with a set of key words to help them in listening to the dictated task and in the reconstruction process (note also the somewhat confusing terms used to describe the tasks in Eckerth's study). Malmqvist (2005) did not seed the task with a set of pre-determined language structures.

Other more explicitly grammar-focused language tasks that have been used in this body of research include passage editing, cloze and text reconstruction. These are, strictly speaking, grammar exercises rather than tasks, as they focus primarily on grammatical accuracy (see discussion in Chapter 2). However, researchers commonly use the term tasks to describe these activities. In such grammar tasks, unlike meaning-focused tasks and the dictogloss, the learners are not required to compose a text. In an editing task, students are given a passage that they need to edit for accuracy. The passage may be one written by other students in the class, or one created by the instructor/researcher and which contains the kind of errors commonly found in the writing of this group of students (see Storch, 2009). In a text reconstruction, students need to insert appropriate words and inflect word stems in a given text containing key content words (see Storch, 1998a). These grammar tasks are thus more controlled, attempting to direct the learners' attention to a pre-determined set of language items.

In an attempt to identify which type of task is most effective in drawing learners' attention to language, researchers have compared the number and type of LREs that different types of tasks generate. This research (e.g. Alegría de la Colina & García Mayo, 2007; García Mayo, 2002a, 2002b; Storch, 1998b, 2001a) has shown that the more controlled grammar tasks (e.g. text reconstruction, editing) tend to generate more LREs than meaning-based tasks (e.g. composition, jigsaw). Furthermore, and perhaps not surprisingly, meaning-based tasks tend to generate more lexical LREs, dealing with word meanings and word choice, whereas grammar tasks tend to generate more form-based LREs, dealing with a range of morphosyntactic forms.

However, as Fortune and Thorp (2001) correctly point out, researchers need to look beyond quantification of LREs. For instance, Alegría de la Colina and García Mayo (2007) found that although the text reconstruction elicited more LREs than the jigsaw, a large proportion of these LREs were not resolved correctly. The researchers suggested that the text reconstruction may be useful in raising learners' attention to form, but these pre-determined forms may be beyond the learners' linguistic knowledge. On the other hand, meaning-focused tasks, such as the jigsaw, are more likely to focus learners' attention to those forms that are driven by the learners' own needs and which are therefore more likely to be within their linguistic knowledge range. Furthermore, Nassaji and Tian (2010) found that although structured grammar tasks (e.g. editing, cloze) elicited a large number of LREs, deliberations about the targeted language forms (English phrasal verbs) were often quite brief and superficial. In my own research (Storch, 1998b, 1999), the text reconstruction, a grammar-focused task, elicited more LREs than the composition, and a large proportion of these LREs showed extensive engagement. In resolving these LREs, the learners drew on their knowledge of grammatical conventions, word meanings, as well as form-meaning mapping.

However, the learners in my studies were of high intermediate L2 proficiency; in Nassaji and Tian's study they were of low intermediate proficiency. Thus task type may determine the number and focus of LREs, but the learners' level of engagement in LRE resolution may also be affected by a number of other factors, including L2 proficiency.

The dictogloss has been used in research on collaborative writing with both adult (e.g. Abadikhah, 2012; Eckerth, 2008; Fortune & Thorp, 2001) and adolescent L2 learners (e.g. Kim & McDonough, 2011; Kuiken & Vedder, 2002). However, several studies have shown that the dictogloss may not generate many LREs, particularly when used with low-proficiency L2 learners (e.g. Alegría de la Colina & García Mayo, 2007; García Mayo, 2002a, 2002b; Leeser, 2004). For example, García Mayo (2002a), who compared attention to language generated by a range of grammar tasks (e.g. editing, cloze) and a dictogloss, found that the grammar tasks elicited the highest number of LREs, the dictogloss the smallest number. Researchers who compared the quantity of LREs and their resolution generated by a dictogloss task when employed with intermediate and with advanced learners have shown quite clearly that the dictogloss is more successful when employed with more advanced learners (Fortune, 2005; Leeser, 2004). Leeser (2004) points out that low-proficiency learners may struggle to understand the dictogloss passage, and therefore may not be able to contribute to the reconstruction of the passage and to discussion of grammatical forms that the task is designed to generate.

Studies on the relative efficacy of different meaning-based tasks in drawing learners' attention to language are scarce. Our study (Storch & Wigglesworth, 2007), one of the few studies to compare the attention to language generated by two meaning-based tasks, used an argumentative essay and a data commentary report. The study, conducted with high-proficiency ESL learners, found that both tasks generated a similar number of LREs and that a higher proportion of the LREs were lexical rather than grammatical. The findings were attributed not only to the nature of the tasks, but also to the relatively high L2 proficiency of the learners. These advanced learners perhaps had little need to deliberate about grammatical accuracy.

What the above studies highlight is that it is not only task type but also the L2 proficiency of the learners that may determine the number and type of LREs that the different task types generate, and thus the suitability of certain tasks for different cohorts of L2 learners. Whereas the jigsaw task, with its pictorial stimulus and the built-in need to exchange information, may be suitable for relatively low and intermediate L2 learners (see Storch & Aldosari, 2013); language-focused tasks, and particularly the dictogloss, may be more suitable for advanced L2 learners.

Task implementation conditions may also impact on the type and number of LREs generated. Pre-task mini grammar lessons and/or modelling of desired metalinguistic interactions (using video clips or role plays) may encourage a focus on language form. In Swain's (1998) study, in one class the teacher and researcher modelled negotiations on language form using metalanguage (e.g. explanations using grammatical terms). In the other class, the modelling drew attention to grammatical forms but did not invoke any grammatical metalanguage. Swain reported that the group exposed to the metalinguistic modelling produced a substantially greater number of LREs than the other group. Swain and Lapkin's (2001) study, conducted in the same context (Grade 8, French immersion), had one class completing a jigsaw task and the other a dictogloss task. Both classes received a mini grammar lesson as well as pre-task modelling of interactions. The mini lesson covered the grammatical forms seeded in the dictogloss and thought likely to be used in the jigsaw. The study found that both tasks generated a similar number of form-based LREs, and that form-based LREs exceeded lexical LREs even in the meaning-based jigsaw task. The researchers suggested that it was the mini lesson and modelling that preceded the tasks which encouraged the learners to focus on grammatical accuracy in both tasks.

Kim and McDonough's (2011) study provided additional evidence for the impact of pre-task teaching and modelling on languaging. The study was implemented in two intact EFL classes in a middle school in Korea. Three communicative tasks were used: two oral tasks and one writing task (the dictogloss). In one class (the experimental group) students were given pre-task modelling of the interaction the researchers hoped to encourage; the other class did not receive such modelling and acted as the control group. The study found that learners who were exposed to pre-task modelling produced more LREs, and that more of these LREs were resolved correctly, compared to the control group. However, it should be noted that in Leeser's (2004) study, despite the practice and modelling sessions, pairs composed of low-proficiency learners generated few LREs when completing the dictogloss, and most of these LREs were lexical rather than grammatical.

Finally task familiarity may also need to be taken into consideration when explaining the impact of task type on languaging. The dictogloss task is unfamiliar and thus getting acquainted with the procedure poses additional challenges. For example, Dunn (1993) reported that the passages her students reconstructed often resembled a string of phrases that made little sense because the dictogloss encouraged the learners to adhere to their notes. On the other hand, the composition task is a familiar task to all students; however, implementing such a task as a collaborative activity is unfamiliar. It requires students to overcome years of institutional practice and assessment based on individually produced compositions. Such experiences may explain students' observed reluctance to write compositions collaboratively (Storch, 2005).

Thus in choosing a task for collaborative writing activities, it is important to consider not only the type of task but also its suitability for a particular group of L2 learners. The learners' L2 proficiency and their familiarity with the task are important considerations when selecting and implementing tasks to be used for collaborative writing. Task choice may also depend on the instructor's pedagogical aims, although learners' interpretation of what a task requires them to do may differ to that intended by the instructor (or researcher).

Grouping Learners: Composition and Size

In any one L2 class, students may vary in terms of their L2 proficiency. Thus an important decision that a teacher needs to make in implementing group and pair work, whether on oral or written tasks, is how to best group learners in such activities. Is it best to have students of similar or different levels of L2 proficiency work together? Which proficiency grouping will optimise the language learning opportunities for all students, the lower as well as the higher proficiency learner? Such decisions can be informed by research on the impact that proficiency differences within the pair or group have on the quantity and quality of languaging.

Studies investigating the impact of proficiency pairing on interaction, and particularly on attention to language, are relatively rare. Leeser's (2004) study is one of the few such studies. In the study, 42 adult learners of L2 Spanish were assigned to pairs on the basis of their L2 proficiency (determined by the instructor). There were eight pairs of similar high L2 proficiency (high–high), four pairs of similar low L2 proficiency (low–low) and nine pairs of mixed proficiency (high–low). It should be noted that these proficiency levels were relative: a learner was rated as of higher or lower proficiency in comparison to other students in the class. All learners completed a dictogloss task after a practice session and exposure to a short video clip modelling how the learners should talk through their linguistic problems. The recorded pair talk data were analysed for the number, type of LREs (whether lexical or form focused), and LRE resolution (resolved correctly, incorrectly or unresolved).

The study found that L2 proficiency pairing affected how much the dyads focused on form, which linguistic forms, and the nature of LRE resolution. The number of LREs, the proportion of form-focused LREs, and whether they were resolved decreased in line with the proficiency of the pairs. The high–high pairs produced the largest number of LREs, most of which were grammatical, and most LREs were resolved correctly. The low–low pairs produced the smallest number of LREs, most of them were lexical, and about a third of all the LREs were left unresolved. The high–low proficiency dyads produced more grammatical LREs than low–low pairs, but the difference was not statistically significant. Thus although the dictogloss task seemed successful in terms of eliciting attention to form for high-proficiency learners when paired with fellow high-proficiency learners, it seemed less successful for low-proficiency learners.

The findings led Leeser to question the benefits of pair work (particularly using dictogloss) for low-proficiency learners, whether teamed with fellow low-proficiency learners or high-proficiency learners. Low-proficiency learners, working in low–low pairs, generated few LREs; that is, there was little focus on form in such pairs. Furthermore, because of their limited L2 knowledge, the learners had difficulties in resolving LREs and thus a relatively high proportion of their LREs were unresolved. Although high–low pairs produced more LREs than low–low pairs, in these high–low pairs the contributions of the low-proficiency learners to the LRE deliberations were minimal. The majority of the LREs generated by mixed-proficiency pairs were resolved by the higher-proficiency learners. Leeser also questioned whether exposure to correct resolutions of grammatical LREs that low-proficiency learners experienced when working with high-proficiency learners is beneficial. He suggested that low-proficiency learners may not be developmentally ready to learn grammatical information arising from LREs initiated and resolved by higher proficiency members of the dyads.

Aldosari's PhD study (2008) built on Leeser's study. The study investigated the impact of proficiency pairing and task type on learners' interactions. Rather than employing a dictogloss task, shown in previous research to be difficult for low-proficiency learners, in Aldosari's study the students completed two meaning-focused tasks (jigsaw and a composition) and an editing exercise. In one published paper (Storch & Aldosari, 2013) we focused on a subset of Aldosari's data. We looked at the interaction of 15 pairs (five from each proficiency grouping) on the composition task. We analysed the pair talk not only for the number of LREs but also for the amount of L2 used by the learners in their interaction.

The findings concerning the quantity of LREs in relation to the proficiency grouping of the dyads were similar to those reported by Leeser. The highest number of LREs was generated by the high–high pairs, the lowest by the low–low pairs. The low–low pairs seemed more intent on task completion (generating ideas for the composition) than on deliberations about language, and thus most of their LREs were lexical. LRE resolution was also impacted by the proficiency of the dyads. The proportion of incorrectly resolved LREs was higher in the low–low pairs than in high–high and high–low pairs.

Our findings concerning the mixed-proficiency pairs differed to those presented by Leeser. Whereas Leeser (2004) reported that high–low pairs generated more LREs than low–low pairs, in our study, this was not always so. In the case of two mixed-proficiency pairs, the number of LREs generated was very low, lower than the number generated by low–low pairs. In these high–low pairs, the low-proficiency learner adopted a very passive role, whereas the high-proficiency learner dominated the interaction, producing long L2 turns, but initiating very few LREs.

Similar dominant–passive roles were also observed by Kowal and Swain (1994), in their study conducted in a Grade 8 French immersion context, but only in pairs composed of learners of different L2 proficiency. Kowal and Swain (1994) observed that in such heterogeneous pairs, the weaker students seemed intimidated, allowing the more proficient students to dominate the interaction. These dominant–passive roles were not observed in pairs composed of similar proficiency learners.

However, not all high–low-proficiency pairs necessarily develop a dominant–passive relationship. In our study (Storch & Aldosari, 2013) we found that of the five high–low pairs, only two exhibited a dominant–passive relationship. Another high–low pair worked collaboratively, and generated a large number of LREs, with both learners initiating and contributing to the resolutions of these LREs. In this pair there was also evidence of collective scaffolding, with both learners contributing to the resolutions of the LREs. Ohta's study (1995, 2000), which examined the talk of a pair of tertiary learners of Japanese, also found evidence of collective scaffolding in the talk of this pair that was clearly heterogeneous in terms of language proficiency. The two learners drew on their varying levels of linguistic expertise to contribute to the interaction. These findings suggest that the number of LREs generated in mixed-proficiency pairs may be affected not only by the proficiency of the learners but also by other affective factors.

Yule and Macdonald's (1990) study used an interesting research design to investigate the role of L2 proficiency and role assignment in an oral task. In the study, high-and low-proficiency learners were paired together. However, one member of the dyad was assigned a more dominant role and was given information that the other member of the dyad needed. The study found that when the dominant role was assigned to the high-proficiency learner, little negotiations took place. When the dominant role was assigned to the lower proficiency learner, the dyads interacted successfully and engaged in negotiations of meaning. In the next section I discuss relationships learners form when working in pairs in greater detail.

One other decision that classroom teachers need to make is whether it is best to use pairs or small groups when deploying collaborative writing tasks in their classrooms. In the research reviewed, and as shown in Table 4.1, pairs are more commonly used than small groups. Pair work offers more opportunities for individual learner contribution. In small groups, the task can be completed with some members contributing very little to the activity. However, a recent study by Fernández Dobao (2012) suggests that small groups may provide more opportunities for language learning than pairs. The study compared, among other issues, the LREs produced by learners working in small groups (of four students) and pairs on a collaborative writing task (a modified jigsaw task). The researcher found that groups produced more LREs than pairs and were able to solve a higher proportion of LREs correctly compared to pairs. These findings were attributed to the greater linguistic resources at the disposal of the groups compared to the pairs. In small groups, four different learners could draw on their knowledge sources and solve the problems encountered. Thus, Fernández Dobao suggests that small groups may be preferable to pairs in collaborative writing tasks. Nevertheless, she notes that in group interactions, the LREs did not always involve the active participation of all four group members; and as in the case of pair work, some group members adopted a more passive role, and contributed very little to the interaction. In a study which compared small groups and pairs but which only considered LREs dealing with vocabulary, Fernández Dobao (forthcoming) found that whereas in pairs 89% of all the lexical LREs were interactively resolved by both members of the dyad, in small group interactions only 25% of lexical LREs involved all four members of the small groups. In the group data, the bulk of these lexical LREs (75%) were resolved by three or two members of the group.

Taken together, the findings suggest that it is not just proficiency levels or the group size but the relationships that learners form and the roles that they adopt (or are assigned) which affect the interaction between learners. These relationships affect both the quantity and quality of languaging, and thus have implications for language learning. These relationships are discussed in the next section.

Relationships Formed

Much of the research on learner interaction, particularly in the 1980s and 1990, and informed by psycholinguistic perspectives, tended to focus heavily on quantitative accounts of linguistic behavior (e.g. counting negotiations of meaning). Little attention was paid to the socially constructed nature of interaction. In my PhD dissertation (see Storch, 2009) I attempted to address this research gap. The classroom-based study set out to investigate the relationships that the learners formed when working on a range of collaborative writing tasks. The students worked in the same self-selected pairs over the semester on three tasks: a meaning-focused task (data commentary report) and two grammar-focused tasks (text reconstruction and passage editing). All the pair talk was audio recorded. The students were also interviewed individually on four occasions: after the completion of each task type and at the end of the study. Of the students who agreed to participate, the data of 20 students (i.e. 10 pairs) were analysed.

Over the semester, I observed that these ten pairs formed distinct relationships and that these relationships, once established, tended to persist, regardless of task type or passage of time. Based on the analysis of learner talk and informed by the work of Damon and Phelps (1989), Donato (1988) and Lockhart and Ng (1995), I proposed a model of dyadic interaction with two intersecting continua: equality and mutuality.

In the model, equality, the horizontal continuum, reflects the learners' level of contribution and control over the task. Thus high equality describes not merely equal contributions to the task but also equality in the decision making or perceived authority over the task. Mutuality, the vertical continuum, reflects the learners' level of engagement with each other's contribution. High mutuality describes interactions which show evidence of co-construction and that are rich in reciprocal feedback. As shown in Figure 4.1, the two intersecting continua form four quadrants, representing four distinct patterns of dyadic interaction.

In Quadrant 1, both equality and mutuality are relatively high and the relationship is labelled collaborative. In pairs working collaboratively, both members of the pair contribute to all aspects of the task and engage with each other's suggestions, often pooling their linguistic resources (collective scaffolding) in resolving deliberations about language (LREs). They both share responsibility for the task.

In Quadrant 2, equality is high, but mutuality is low. The pattern is labelled dominant/dominant or cooperative (see Storch, 2001b). What distinguishes this pattern from a collaborative pattern is that although both members of the pair contribute to the task, they do not engage or are unwilling to engage with each other's contributions. In the dominant/dominant pattern, the talk shows high levels of conflict, but not the type of cognitive conflict referred to in the literature on L1 collaborative writing (see Dale, 1994b, discussed in Chapter 2). In the pair displaying this pattern of interaction in

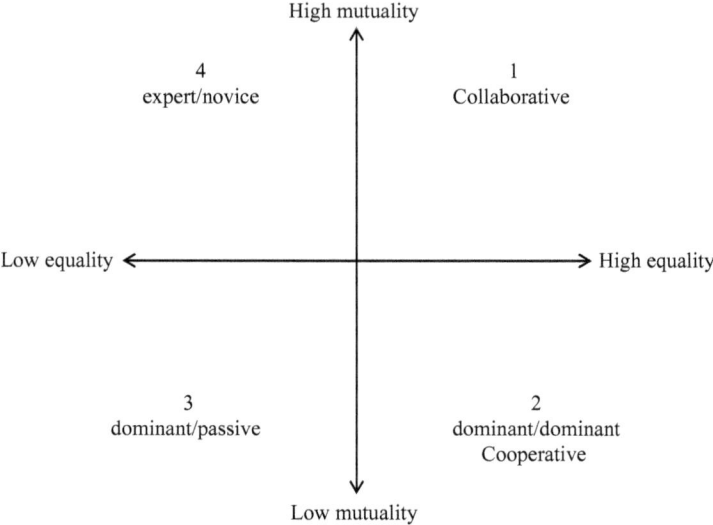

Figure 4.1 A model of dyadic interaction (Storch, 2001b, 2002, 2009)

my study, the conflict did not seem to be a positive force where alternative suggestions were evaluated critically. Rather, the learners seemed unwilling to consider each other's suggestion. The text produced by this pair often had two alternative sentences side by side, forming parallel texts rather than a joint single text. In the cooperative pattern, both members contribute to the task and create one text, but do not engage with each other's contribution, behaving as if they have responsibility only over their own contributions.

In Quadrant 3, both equality and mutuality are low. One member of the pair takes or is afforded control of the task; the other member contributes very little to the task. Hence the pattern is labelled dominant/passive. The dominant participant in such dyads takes on an authoritarian stance and seems to appropriate control over the task. The passive participant's contributions to the task are not only minimal in quantity but also in quality (e.g. rewriting the text to make it 'neater').

In Quadrant 4, equality is low but mutuality is high and the pattern is labelled expert/novice. There is an unequal level of contributions and control over the task. However, what distinguishes this pattern from the dominant/passive pattern is that in this pattern the dominant participant acts as an expert or tutor and actively encourages the other participant (the novice) to contribute to the task.

It is important to note at the outset that coding for patterns of interaction is by its very nature imprecise. In any one activity, learners may display instances of different relationships. Thus in coding for relationships, a global analysis needs to be undertaken, describing the predominant pattern observed in the pair talk in one activity. The following excerpts, taken from different studies, illustrate the kind of pair talk that typifies each pattern.

The excerpt in Example 1 (Storch, 2001b: 38–39) is representative of the type of interaction found in collaborative pairs. The two students, Mai (a Vietnamese female) and Charley (a Thai male), worked collaboratively throughout the semester on all the tasks. As the example shows, their pair talk is highly cohesive. Cohesion is created by the learners repeating and elaborating on each other's utterances (e.g. turns 2–3, 7–8) or by completing each other's ideas (e.g. turns 3–4, 6–7). Mai and Charley contribute jointly to all aspects of the text: generating ideas (e.g. turns 2–9), suggesting how to organise the ideas (e.g. turns 11–12), and deciding on how to best express their ideas (e.g. turns 5–6, 14–15). They provide each other with assistance in response to requests about vocabulary (e.g. turns 1–2), corrective feedback such as explicit other repairs (e.g. turn 15) and recasts (e.g. turns 3, 6), as well as positive feedback in the form of confirmations (e.g. turns 9, 10). There is also evidence of collective scaffolding (e.g. turns 16–20), where the learners pool their linguistic resources. In turn 16, the pauses suggest that Mai may be searching for an appropriate verb. Charley suggests a verb (show) but then Mai notes a problem with subject verb agreement and Charley provides the appropriate correction.

Example 1: Collaborative pattern of dyadic interaction

1	Charley:	This (reads instructions)... What is this?
2	Mai:	From the chart
3	Charley:	This chart about
4	Mai:	The data
5	Charley:	With percentage and ah...
6	Mai:	Describe describe the percentage of
7	Charley:	English language fluency
8	Mai:	English language fluency between two countries yeah? Vietnam and Laos
9	Charley:	Yes and compare before they came here and now
10	Mai:	Yes
11	Charley:	You can separate it here
12	Mai:	Yeah... first we... mm the
13	Charley:	Perhaps you should write

14	Mai:	Yeah I write yeah from the information of the chart yeah... (writing) information of the chart
15	Charley:	No from figure 3
16	Mai:	Ah figure ... figure 3? From figure 3 ... figure 3 ah
17	Charley:	Show the information
18	Mai:	Show the information ... it it's
19	Charley:	Yeah it's ok it shows... the data or the percentage?

Example 2 illustrates the kind of interaction found in a pair who formed a dominant/dominant relationship. It comes from a study (Tan *et al.*, 2010: 27.11) conducted with beginner L2 learners of Chinese in a university class. The learners worked in pairs on a range of tasks in two modes: face-to-face and computer mediated (the study is discussed in greater detail in Chapter 7). One of the tasks required the learners to write up a plan. In this example, the two learners, Ivan and Lisa, negotiate about what to write and how to write it using the correct Chinese characters (translations of Chinese words are given in brackets immediately after each turn). The excerpt in this example was typical of the pair talk throughout the task. As the excerpt shows, although both participants contribute to the task (e.g. turns 50, 59, 62, 77, 78), there is a high level of disagreement (e.g. turns 51-54, 64-74, 78-79). The two learners frequently reject each other's suggestions (e.g. turns 54, 69–72, 79). There was no evidence of collective scaffolding in the pair talk.

Example 2: Dominant/dominant pattern of dyadic interaction

50	Ivan:	zhong-wen-ke *(Chinese class)*
51	Lisa:	Most people use Hanyu
52	Ivan:	I can't write Hanyu
53	Lisa:	Yes, you can. It's on your book, hurry.
54	Ivan:	I'll stick to zhongwen, shi zhongwe ke de jiaqi...danshi *(Chinese...is Chinese class's holiday...but)*
55	Lisa:	Danshi *(But)*
56	Ivan:	Is this dan?
57	Lisa:	You need .... Yeah
58	Ivan:	Danshi *(But)*
59	Lisa:	Women haiyao *(We still need)*

60	Ivan:	Xuyao... women... is it hai?
		(Need... we... is it still?)
61	Lisa:	Yeah
62	Ivan:	Xuyao...Women xuyao... are you sure?
		(Need...we need)
63	Lisa:	Hm ... something like that
64	Ivan:	I know what it look like
65	Lisa:	it doesn't look like
66	Ivan:	Hm ... maybe a bit, but not really
67	Lisa:	I know, that's what I saw
68	Ivan:	I didn't find
69	Lisa:	Yes, it is
70	Ivan:	No it is not
71	Lisa:	Yes, it is
72	Ivan:	No it's not
73	Lisa:	look, it is exactly... hm
74	Ivan:	What ... come on, I mean things have legs
75	Lisa:	I mean this too, in the middle it's like that
76	Ivan:	Yeah
77	Lisa:	so you got that, you just need a horizontal line
78	Ivan:	danshi women hai xuyao xiaban...zuoyi women meiyou jihua (laugh)
		(But we still need work...therefore we don't have plan)
79	Lisa:	(laugh) no, you can't write it

Example 3 comes from the same study as Example 2 (Tan *et al.*, 2006) and illustrates a cooperative pattern. Here both participants, Ben and Jan, construct a text but their interaction is computer mediated (using MSN messenger). Both learners contribute to the task by taking turns to compose a sentence. As such equality is high. However there is not much evidence of engagement with each other's contributions. Unlike Example 1, here the learners behave as if composing the text on their own. Each learner simply contributes one sentence at a time (see turns 9, 10, 11) and the discourse seems disjointed (e.g. turns 9–11). There is not much evidence of deliberations about language, of seeking or providing feedback.

Example 3: Cooperative pattern of dyadic interaction

7	Jan:	Do you want to start?
		Is our student studying at Moerben daxue?
		(Is our student studying at Melbourne University?)

8	Ben:	Dui ta jiudian chi zaofan
		(*Yes, he eats breakfast at 9 o'clock*)
9	Jan:	Shierdian shangke xuexi yingyu
		(*At 12 start class to study English*)
10	Ben:	Jiudianban ta zu moerben daxue
		(*at 9.30 he goes to Melbourne University*)
11	Jan:	Hao
		(*Good*)
12	Ben:	Hao
		(*Good*)
		yidian zai fandian chi wufan
		(*At 1 o'clock at restaurant eat lunch*)

Example 4 is typical of the talk found in dominant/passive pairs. The data come from Aldosari's (2008) study with EFL learners in Saudi Arabia. The excerpt in this example comes from the pair talk of Talal and Saber (see Storch & Aldosari, 2013), a mixed-proficiency pair (high–low), composing a short essay about health. As shown in the example, Talal, the higher proficiency learner, produces long monologues. He first generates ideas and then dictates them to Saber. Saber's contributions are often limited to single word turns, simply expressing agreement. Indeed in the entire interaction of this pair, the average length of Talal's turns was about 17 words, and that of Saber three words. Evidence of languaging was scarce. There were only two LREs found in the data of this pair on the composition task.

Example 4: Dominant/passive pattern of dyadic interaction

1	Talal:	I think we had to choose the second subject … we can talk about it. Aaa it's about health. Health is very important or people must be concern about health because they had to keep his health good. So, I think there are three things that we have to follow to keep our health … our health good. The first thing. The first thing is kinds of food. Food must be good must be rich of aaa good elements.
2	Saber:	Yes
3	Talal:	Aaa the other thing the second is sport … We have to do sports every day we have to do the exercise every day … Third is to keep ourself away from the pollution sources
4	Saber:	Yes
5	Talal:	We we'll talk about all of these things … First food we have to to take food or to make our food I mean we have

		to take more than one kind of food every day, specially fruits and aaa we must we must eat foods every day and drink milk in the morning and I think those are very important for us. Aaa the other thing is the aaa sport we have do the sport every day ... aaa walking and playing football and and do any do any kind of sports ... aaa.
6	Saber:	Write?
7	Talal:	Yes you can write now.

Example 5 shows the nature of the talk found in pairs who formed an expert/novice relationship. The excerpt also comes from Storch and Aldosari (2013). Gamal and Sahafi, another mixed-proficiency pair, formed a very different relationship to that formed by Saber and Talal. Here, Gamal, the higher proficiency learner, seems to take a greater responsibility for task completion, including the role of the scribe. However, unlike Talal in Example 4 above, Gamal encourages Sahafi, the lower proficiency learner, to participate by asking him overtly to provide or confirm ideas (e.g. turns 65, 75). He also provides corrective feedback (e.g. turns 75, 77) and checks on Sahafi's knowledge of vocabulary (turn 77).

Example 5: Expert/Novice pattern of dyadic interactions

65	Gamal:	(writing) All kinds of food ... right?
66	Sahafi:	Yeah
67	Gamal:	Of food ... We say meat ... rice
68	Sahafi:	Juice rice...
69	Gamal:	Something like this
70	Sahafi:	Yeah
71	Gamal:	What else? Umm ... following some kind of books, they are forbiddening a lot kind of food. Like meat, like milk ... ok? Let see what else what about the food what else. Health also about the food ... also sport or food. (writing) also sport are important
72	Sahafi:	Important
73	Gamal	To keep
74	Sahafi:	To keep health
75	Gamal:	To keep your health. Health good. What kind of sport for example?
76	Sahafi:	Walked
77	Gamal:	Walking what else ... biking ... you know biking ... bicycles
78	Sahafi:	Yeah

My model of dyadic interaction has since been applied to code interactions of L2 learners in different contexts. For example, Ives (2004) found evidence of collaborative, expert/novice, and expert/passive patterns of interaction in a primary class (Grade 6) where ESL learners were paired with native English speaking children. Watanabe and Swain (2007), who investigated the patterns of interaction formed by four core learners who worked alternatively with a participant of a lower proficiency and with a higher proficiency learner, reported that they found collaborative, expert/novice, and dominant/passive patterns of interaction. No pairs formed a dominant/dominant or cooperative pattern, and one pair formed a pattern they labelled expert/passive. In the expert/passive pair, despite the expert's attempts to encourage the less proficient learner to contribute to the task, the less proficient learner was reticent and reluctant to contribute.

What these studies show quite clearly is that simply assigning students to work in pairs does not guarantee collaboration. More importantly, as a number of studies (e.g. Kim & McDonough, 2008; Storch, 2002, 2009; Storch & Aldosari, 2013; Tan, *et al.*, 2010; Watanabe & Swain, 2007) have shown, there is more evidence of languaging in the data of pairs who adopt a collaborative orientation (collaborative and expert/novice patterns), than is the case in pairs who adopt a non-collaborative orientation (dominant/dominant and dominant/passive patterns). These findings have implications for language learning (see discussion in Chapter 5).

Similarly, simply assigning students to work in small groups does not mean that they will work 'as a group' rather than merely 'in groups' (see Donato, 1988; Fernández Dobao, 2012; Leki, 2001). Donato (1988) argued that in order to investigate the potential of group work for language learning, we need to consider the dynamics of the group. Drawing on the work of Petrovsky (1983a, 1983b), Donato distinguished between diffuse or loosely knit groups and groups which formed a collective, a socially cohesive unit. He analysed two sets of data of L2 learners of French working in groups. One set of data was from groups working on a writing task; the other was from groups working on an oral classroom presentation. In both sets, evidence of collective scaffolding was only found in the talk of groups forming a collective. In loosely knit groups, instances of collective scaffolding were rare, and requests for help were often ignored. Clearly, more consideration needs to be given to group dynamics. Not all group activities provide opportunities to learn.

A number of individual learner factors have been proposed to explain why learners form different relationships when working in small groups or pairs, whether on collaborative writing tasks or in peer response activities. These factors include: personality (e.g. Alvarado, 1992; Malmqvist, 2005), cultural differences (e.g. Lockhart & Ng, 1995; Nelson & Carson, 1998), differences in L2 proficiency (e.g. Kim & McDonough, 2008; Storch & Aldosari, 2013; Watanabe & Swain, 2007), as well as the classroom environment, including the teacher's teaching style (see DiNitto, 2000). Most of this research has been conducted with pairs rather than small groups.

No doubt differences in proficiency may affect the relationships learners form. As shown by several studies conducted with adult learners (e.g. Kim & McDonough, 2008; Leeser, 2004; Storch & Aldosari, 2013; Watanabe & Swain, 2007) as well as adolescent L2 learners (Kowal & Swain, 1994), in mixed-proficiency pairing, we are more likely to see dominant/passive patterns, with the lower-proficiency learner adopting a passive role and the higher proficiency learner adopting a dominant role.

In pairs formed of similar proficiency learners, there is more evidence of a collaborative orientation, with pairs working collaboratively or forming expert/novice relationships. For example, in Kim and McDonough's (2008) study, eight intermediate Korean L2 learners were paired first with fellow intermediate learners and subsequently with eight advanced learners to complete dictogloss tasks. The study found that the intermediate learners tended to collaborate when working with the same proficiency learners but tended to become more passive when working with advanced learners.

However, it is important to note that it is not necessarily measured proficiency but perceived proficiency which may affect how learners interact (Storch, 2004; Watanabe & Swain, 2008). For example, Watanabe and Swain (2008), in a closer analysis of one case study learner, Mai, drawn from the researchers' larger data set (Watanabe & Swain, 2007), found that when Mai interacted with a lower proficiency learner who acted confidently, Mai judged her as of equal proficiency and thus the relationship formed was collaborative. In my own study (Storch, 2004), in the case of one pair, Tanako (a Japanese female) and Victor (a Vietnamese male), Tanako's assessed writing proficiency was higher than that of Victor. Yet, in the interviews it became clear that Tanako perceived Victor to be of a much higher proficiency. This affected her self-confidence and, together with her dislike of pair work, led to her adopting a fairly passive role.

Thus perhaps a more important factor, which may explain the kind of relationships learners form and in turn the nature of their engagement and contribution to the collaborative writing activity, is how the learners orient to the activity. This notion of orientation encompasses the learners' attitude to the tasks given and to being asked to work in groups/pairs, as well as the goals that drive their action. In the case of group and pair work, another consideration is whether these goals overlap or compete.

Thus in my investigations of why learners formed distinct patterns of interaction (Storch, 2001b, 2004, 2009), using in-depth interview data supplemented by discourse analysis of pair talk, I found that pairs who formed collaborative and expert/novice relationships had positive views about collaborative writing and valued each other's contributions. Stone (1993), among others, noted the importance of respect for each other's opinions in collaborative situations. The participants in my studies who formed collaborative relationships viewed the collaborative text as a shared responsibility. A discourse analysis of the talk of such pairs showed frequent use of first person plural pronouns (we, our), reflecting the sense of a joint ownership of the text produced. The learners who formed an expert/novice relationship had complimentary goals. The expert wanted to provide assistance; the novice sought to learn from the activity and from the expertise of his co-participant. In contrast, the learners who formed dominant/dominant and dominant/passive relationships saw little value in collaborative writing, preferring individual writing. In their pair talk, the use of first person pronouns predominated, suggesting that the task was viewed as an individual responsibility. In the interviews, learners who adopted a dominant role expressed desires to display their knowledge. Such learners were often also driven by expediency (a desire to complete the task quickly) rather than by a desire to learn from each other. In the case of the passive participant, passivity marked disengagement from a dispreferred activity (see further discussion in Chapter 6).

Conclusion

The above discussion has shown that a number of interrelated factors affect the language learning opportunities that collaborative writing affords L2 learners. These factors affect the quantity of the languaging episodes (LREs), their focus (lexis or form), the quality of engagement in resolving the LREs, and the outcomes of these LREs (resolved correctly, incorrectly or left unresolved). These factors have implications for how to best implement collaborative writing tasks in L2 classes in order to maximise the occasions for language learning afforded by collaborative writing tasks. I discuss these pedagogical implications in the final chapter. In the next chapter, however, I review the available evidence about the language learning outcomes of collaborative writing activities.

5 Collaborative Writing and Language Learning

Introduction

The previous chapters (3 and 4), on pair (and small group) collaborative writing tasks, have shown that if carefully implemented, collaborative writing tasks seem to provide learners with ample opportunities to language: to deliberate about language choices, to test hypotheses about language, to draw on their linguistic knowledge and pool that knowledge to resolve problems that the learners may not have been able to resolve had they been working on their own. However, the question that needs to be addressed is whether engagement in collaborative writing tasks contributes to L2 learning.

In this chapter I review the relatively small number of studies that investigated the outcomes of collaborative writing activities, discussing their research methodology and their findings. Some of these studies have been discussed in the previous two chapters. The first section discusses the outcomes of collaboration on the product; that is, the text produced. The second section focuses on evidence for L2 learning, including what constitutes such evidence. I conclude by calling not only for more research on the impact of collaborative writing on L2 learning, but also for research which considers more broadly the potential advantages of collaborative writing for L2 learners.

Comparing Individual and Collaborative Texts

Several studies have investigated the benefits of collaborative writing by comparing the texts produced by learners composing collaboratively with those produced by learners working individually. These studies have been conducted with L1 and, more recently, with L2 learners. However, whereas in the case of L1 writers, the comparisons are based on the quality of the texts produced, in the case of L2 writers, the comparisons tend to focus on the grammatical accuracy of the texts.

Studies conducted with L1 college students (e.g. Hillebrand, 1994; O'Donnell *et al.*, 1985) found that the texts produced collaboratively were of better quality than those produced individually. For example, O'Donnell *et al.* (1985) compared the quality of writing of 36 Psychology undergraduates, half of whom were assigned randomly to a collaborative (nine pairs) and the other half to an individual writing condition ($n = 18$). The time allocated to both pairs and individuals was the same (50 minutes). The task (writing instructions) was assessed for its communicative quality and completeness. The study found that dyads outperformed individuals on the measure of communicative quality but showed a similar performance on the measure of task completeness.

In L2 contexts, most of the studies comparing collaborative and solitary writing have focused on whether the collaborative effort results in more accurate performance. These studies have employed a range of tasks including grammar type tasks such as editing, cloze, text reconstruction (e.g. Nassaji & Tian, 2010; Storch, 1999), language-focused tasks such as the dictogloss (e.g. Malmqvist, 2005; Reinders, 2009), and meaning-focused writing tasks including data commentary reports, descriptive and argumentative compositions (e.g. Fernández Dobao, 2012; Storch, 2005; Storch & Wigglesworth, 2007; Wigglesworth & Storch, 2009). Measures of accuracy also vary depending very much on the kind of exercise or task used. Most of these studies suggest that collaboration results in more accurate task completion.

In one of the earliest such comparison studies (Storch, 1999), I investigated the impact of collaboration on writing, focusing in particular on grammatical accuracy. The study was small scale ($N = 11$), the students were high intermediate ESL, and the tasks used were: cloze, text reconstruction and a short descriptive composition. All three tasks had two very similar versions. One version was completed by the learners in pairs (and one triad) in one session; the other was completed individually in the following session. This design eliminated the potential effects of individual differences because all the learners completed all tasks both collaboratively and individually. The data included the completed tasks, transcribed pair talk and observation notes.

As the focus was on the impact of collaboration on grammatical accuracy, all completed work was analysed using task-relevant measures of grammatical accuracy. Thus in the cloze and text reconstruction tasks, the measures took into account whether the amendments made were appropriate (e.g. the insertion of appropriate words in the cloze task, changing the form of words in the text reconstruction). In the composition task, the measure used was the percentage of error free clauses of all clauses (EFC/C). The study found a positive effect of collaboration on grammatical accuracy. The grammar and the composition tasks completed collaboratively were more accurate than those completed alone.

Greater accuracy in the performance of learners working collaboratively over learners working alone was also reported by two other studies, using grammar-focused tasks. Nassaji and Tian's (2010) study compared individual and collaborative work by low intermediate ESL learners on a cloze and an editing task and focused on the use of phrasal verbs. All the students in this study completed the tasks in both conditions, collaboratively and individually. In the study conducted by Reinders (2009) with upper intermediate ESL students, one group ($n = 11$) completed a dictogloss task in pairs, the other group ($n = 8$) individually. Reinders compared the correct use of negative adverbs in the reconstructed texts of the two groups. In both studies, the use of the targeted structures was more accurate in the pair than in the individual condition.

In my 1999 study I observed that pairs took much longer to complete all the tasks, almost double the amount of time it took them to complete the tasks when working individually. Thus one explanation for the improved accuracy could be the longer time spent by the pairs. However, the recordings of the pair talk and observation notes suggested that it was the learners' motivation and focus on accuracy that led to the greater accuracy. Whereas learners who worked individually submitted their tasks directly after completing the tasks, those that worked in pairs spent time revising their work a number of times. I observed a similar tendency in a later study (Storch, 2007), where one group of ESL learners completed an editing task in pairs and another group individually. Students who worked in pairs spent more time on the editing task and also made more amendments to the text given than the students who completed the task individually. Thus the additional time students take to complete tasks when working in pairs seems to be spent on revising and improving their texts. Peers seem to exert pressure on each other to complete a more accurate text and this may explain why collaborative tasks are more accurate than individually completed tasks.

I also observed in both studies (Storch, 1999, 2007) that accuracy scores for individuals and pairs varied for the use of certain grammatical structures. For example, no differences were apparent in the use of articles, in the work of pairs and of individuals. The use of articles in English is renowned as difficult for ESL learners. However, less complex, rule bound structures (e.g. word forms) were produced more accurately by pairs than by individuals. Thus the impact of repeated revisions and deliberations that occur in pair work may sometimes depend on the language structures that they deliberate about.

Malmqvist's (2005) study also showed a positive impact of collaboration on accuracy. The study, conducted with L2 learners of German, used a series of dictogloss tasks. The first and third tasks were completed by the students individually, the second in small groups of three. No specific measures of accuracy were employed in this study. However, the author observed that whereas several of the individually produced texts contained incomplete sentences, all group texts consisted of full sentences. Furthermore, the reconstructed dictogloss texts produced by the small groups tended to be longer (in terms of words) and showed greater linguistic complexity. They contained more subordinate clauses and a greater variety of such clauses than the individually reconstructed dictogloss texts. Malmqvist observed that the groups and individuals spent approximately the same time on completing the task. Thus the results cannot be attributed to time on task.

In another of my studies I considered the impact of collaboration not only on accuracy but also on text quality. The study (Storch, 2005) compared the performance of intermediate ESL students on collaborative and individually completed data commentary tasks. The study was classroom based, and the task formed part of the regular class work. The study design had two distinguishing features. First, in this study, the students were given a choice: they could complete the task individually or in pairs. The majority (18 out of 23) chose to work in pairs. Second, both quantitative and qualitative measures were used to analyse the texts produced. Quantitative measures included measures of fluency (total number of words), accuracy (percentage of error free clauses, errors per words), and syntactic complexity (e.g. proportion of dependent clauses to clauses). In terms of quality, the texts were assessed globally using a five-point scale which took into consideration content, structure, and task fulfilment. The amount of time the learners took to complete the task was also noted.

The study found that pairs took a longer time to complete the task but produced more accurate and linguistically complex writing. Furthermore, as in the case of O'Donnell *et al.*'s study (1985) with L1 writers, texts produced collaboratively were shorter but of better quality. They had a clearer structure and focus. However, the differences in the global scores awarded to individually composed texts and those composed collaboratively were not statistically significant, not surprising given the relatively small-scale nature of this study.

In a series of subsequent studies (Storch & Wigglesworth, 2007; Wigglesworth & Storch, 2009), part of a large-scale experimental research project, we compared collaboratively and individually produced compositions of advanced ESL students. For example, the Storch and Wigglesworth (2007) study compared the writing of 24 pairs and 24 individuals on two writing tasks (data commentary and argumentative essay) and found that although there were no differences in the texts in terms of fluency and complexity, there was a statistically significant difference in terms of grammatical accuracy. In the Wigglesworth and Storch (2009) study, we compared argumentative essays produced by 48 pairs with essays produced by 48 learners working individually, and reported similar results to those of Storch and Wigglesworth (2007). Thus the results of these larger scale empirical studies confirm the positive impact of collaboration on accuracy.

Fernández Dobao (2012) extended the analysis of pairs versus individuals by also including small groups. The study thus compared the texts produced by individuals, pairs, and small groups. Over 100 intermediate learners of Spanish participated in this classroom-based study, with classes assigned randomly to one of the three conditions. There were 21 students working individually, 15 pairs and 15 small groups (of four students). The task used was a narrative based on a series of pictures that the learners had to sequence and then describe the events (a modified jigsaw task). All learners were allowed the same time (30 minutes) to complete the task. The texts were analysed for fluency (length), accuracy, linguistic and lexical complexity. Transcribed data of group and pair talk were analysed for LREs.

The study found that texts produced by the small groups were the most accurate. Although the texts produced by pairs were more accurate than those produced by individual writers, the difference was not statistically significant. Texts produced by individual writers were the least accurate, but the longest. There were no differences between group, pair and individually produced texts on measures of complexity. Fernández Dobao attributes her findings concerning accuracy to the availability of resources. As noted in the previous chapter, Fernández Dobao's analysis of pair and group talk for LREs showed that groups produced a larger number of LREs compared to pairs, and a higher proportion of LREs found in the group data were correctly resolved compared to those in the pair data. Thus groups produced more accurate texts than pairs because in the groups learners had more resources to draw on compared to pairs when encountering language problems. Learners' individual performance was the least accurate because when writing alone, the learners had recourse only to their own linguistic resources.

These findings suggest that collaborative writing results in qualitatively better and more accurate but perhaps somewhat shorter texts. This greater accuracy does not seem to be related to time, as even when the time given to complete the tasks is the same (e.g. Fernández Dobao, 2012;

Malmqvist, 2005), pairs outperform solitary writers. The analysis of the interactions (see Chapter 3) suggests rather strongly that the greater accuracy of collaboratively produced texts is attributable to the greater availability of linguistic resources and an opportunity to pool these resources in collaborative writing.

However, whether the production of more accurate texts means that the learners have acquired new knowledge or are able to apply their newly co-constructed knowledge when working individually is controversial. Ellis (1994: 283), writing about research on verbal interactions, claims that 'evidence that learners improve the grammaticality of their utterances when pushed does not of course constitute evidence that acquisition takes place.' However, Loewen's (2005) study showed that modified output following recasts was a good indicator of noticing and, of all variables considered, proved to be the best predictor of acquisition. Extending this to the domain of writing, does that mean that linguistic knowledge co-constructed during a collaborative writing activity, and which is manifested in a more accurate text, endures? Studies which attempted to address this question are discussed in the next section.

Evidence of Language Learning

A relatively small number of studies have attempted to investigate the short and long term impact of collaborative writing on L2 learning. Three different approaches have been used in these investigations. One approach is to compare pre-post tests results of learners who complete a task individually with those who complete the same task collaboratively. The pre- and post-tests generally test explicit knowledge of a pre-determined set of linguistic items. The other two approaches look quite specifically at the language learning outcomes of collaborative dialogues, and thus require researchers to first identify the linguistic items that the learners discuss during their collaborative writing activity (i.e. in the LREs). Researchers then either proceed to test the learners' explicit knowledge of these items using tailor made tests or they test the learners' implicit knowledge by tracing the learners' ability to use these items in their subsequent writing. (For an extended discussion of the difference between tests of explicit and implicit knowledge, see Purpura, 2004; Storch, 2010.)

Pre-post tests research design

A handful of studies (Kim, 2008; Kuiken & Vedder, 2002; Nassaji & Tian, 2010; Reinders, 2009) have investigated the impact of individual and collaborative tasks on language learning using a pre-post test research design.

These studies tend to use language-focused tasks, such as the dictogloss, seeded with a set of targeted language structures, and the tests measure gains in explicit knowledge of these structures. The results of these studies are mixed. Whereas Kim's (2008) study shows an advantage for collaboration, the other three studies show no such evidence.

Kim's study (2008) used a dictogloss task and focused on the learning of targeted vocabulary items (15 items). The pre- and post-tests (immediate and delayed) used a Vocabulary Knowledge Scale (VKS) – a test which measures learners' self-reported vocabulary knowledge on a five point scale, developed by Paribakht and Wesche (1997). On the test, a score of 1 is awarded if the learner claims no knowledge of the word; a score of 2 if the learner claims familiarity with the word but cannot supply the word meaning; a score of 3 if the learner can provide a correct synonym or translation; a score of 4 if the learner can use the word appropriately in a sentence and 5 if the word is used appropriately and correctly.

The participants ($N = 32$) were intermediate learners of Korean as an L2. Half of the participants completed the dictogloss in pairs and the other half alone. Individuals and pairs were given the same time to complete the task (30 minutes). The interesting design feature of this study was that the individual learners were asked to produce think-aloud protocols when completing the task. This enabled the researcher to compare, to some extent, the nature of languaging that occurs when learners write individually and languaging that occurs in pair talk and the impact of these two forms of languaging on vocabulary learning. It should be noted, however, that a think-aloud protocol is not equivalent to self-directed talk. Self-directed talk arises spontaneously when the learner encounters a difficulty. In think-aloud protocols, learners are verbalising their thoughts because they are complying with the researcher's instructions. Nevertheless, think-aloud protocols do provide researchers with an insight into the individual writer's thinking processes.

Kim identified lexical LREs in the transcribed pair talk and in the individual think-aloud protocols and coded these LREs for whether they were resolved correctly, incorrectly, or left unresolved. Learners' performance on the post-tests was analysed for all 15 targeted items, with a closer examination undertaken of post-test performance on those vocabulary items that the learners focused on in their LRES (in pairs or individually in the think-aloud data). The study found that overall learners who worked in pairs had significantly higher gain scores on both the immediate and delayed vocabulary post-tests than those who worked alone. In terms of performance on vocabulary items that were discussed in the LREs, pairs again outperformed individuals. The study found that 70% of the words discussed by learners when working collaboratively received test scores indicating that they knew the meaning of the words (i.e. a score of 3 on the five point scale), compared to 35% of words in the case of individuals. Delayed post-tests results showed that pairs retained their knowledge of vocabulary. Pairs received scores of 3 or higher for 74% of their words and the individuals received such scores for only 13% of their words.

Analysis of the transcripts of the pair talk and think-aloud protocols provided a possible explanation for these results. The study found that although the total number of LREs in the pair talk and individual think alouds was almost identical, what distinguished the LREs in the two data sets was their resolution. Most of the LREs in the pair work data were resolved correctly (53%) because the learners could pool their linguistic knowledge. In the case of individuals, who could only draw on their own linguistic resources, many of the LREs (39%) were left unresolved. Thus the findings show that collaboration impacts positively on vocabulary learning, but it is the quality of LRE resolutions and not merely the quantity that is an important variable. The link between the quality of LREs and performance on post-tests corroborates the findings of Swain's (1998) study discussed in the subsequent section of this chapter.

The other three studies that investigated the impact of collaboration on language learning gains reported no effect for collaboration. Nassaji and Tian (2010), who also used the VKS test used by Kim (2008), found no advantage for the collaborative condition. In this study (mentioned in the previous section), the 26 low intermediate ESL learners completed a cloze and an editing exercise, each seeded with phrasal verbs. The study was conducted over two weeks, each week beginning with a pre-test, mini lesson on the targeted phrasal verbs, treatment (i.e. completion of the exercises either in pairs or individually), and then four days later, a post-test. Students were given eight minutes to complete each of the tasks, whether they worked in pairs or alone, and all pair work was audio recorded. Although the study found that learners working in pairs produced more accurate instances of the phrasal verbs than learners working alone, particularly in the editing task, a comparison of the pre- and post-test performance showed that all learners improved in their knowledge of the targeted phrasal verbs, with no effect for condition (collaborative vs. individual). These findings suggest that superior performance on the tasks by pairs did not necessarily lead to superior learning gains. Analysis of the pair talk for LREs dealing with the targeted phrasal verbs showed that these LREs were brief and limited in scope, often consisting of one or two turns. The authors admit that such LREs were not rich in opportunities for language learning. They attribute the limited nature of the LREs to the difficulty of phrasal verbs for low intermediate L2 proficiency students.

The study by Reinders (2009) also found that improved performance on a given task does not necessarily mean that learning has taken place. Informed by a cognitive perspective of SLA, in this study the pre- and post-tests used were grammaticality judgement tests (timed and untimed) which are purported to tap into implicit linguistic knowledge. The learners (two groups of intermediate ESL) completed three dictogloss tasks over a three-week period. One group worked in pairs, the other individually. The study found that although those who completed the tasks in pairs used the targeted structure more accurately on each iteration of the task than those who worked individually, a comparison of pre- and post-test performance showed that neither group showed evidence of learning. However, a note of caution is needed when interpreting these results given the type of tests used. There has been extensive debate in the literature about grammaticality judgement tests and particularly about their suitability for L2 learners (see Birdsong, 1989). Although the learners who worked individually completed think-aloud protocols, neither the think-aloud data nor the pair talk were analysed.

Kuiken and Vedder (2002) also reported no language learning advantage for group over individual task completion. In a study conducted with 34 Dutch high school learners of English, the experimental group ($n = 20$), completed two dictogloss tasks in small groups of three or four learners; the control group ($n = 14$) completed the same tasks individually. The dictogloss tasks targeted the use of passive verb structures of different levels of complexity, depending on the number of auxiliaries needed to form the structures. The pre-, immediate and delayed post- tests were recognition tests, asking students to simply underline the targeted structures in a set of sentences.

The study found that all learners performed slightly better on both the immediate and delayed post-tests than on the pre-test. However, there was no difference in the performance of the experimental and the control groups. Analysis of the texts reconstructed showed that the learners tended to avoid using passive sentences, particularly sentences with more complex passive structures. Analysis of the group interaction data for LREs showed that the learners noticed the passive structures as well as other structures not targeted by the researchers. The researchers concluded that collaboration and the interaction it engenders leads to noticing but not necessarily to acquisition. However, the analysis of the group talk also found that some groups engaged in lengthy deliberations about the use of passives, which the authors coded as elaborate noticing, whereas other groups simply mentioned the passive structures with emphasis, coded as simple noticing. The authors did not investigate whether the groups that engaged in more elaborate noticing performed better on the post-tests than the groups that engaged in simple noticing.

A number of factors may explain the mixed results of these studies including differences in the tests used and the complexity of the language items targeted by the researchers. Other, and perhaps more important, factors are whether learners focus on these targeted structures and the quality and outcome of these deliberations. As a number of studies have shown, learners do not always focus extensively on items targeted by the task, even in language-focused tasks such as the dictogloss (e.g. Abadikhah, 2012; Swain & Lapkin, 1998, 2001). This means that the use of a pre-post test research design is problematic and unless we consider data of pair talk and individual think-aloud protocols, we have no way of determining whether in fact the post-test items correspond to what learners focused on in their deliberations when completing collaborative or individual tasks respectively.

Even if learners do deliberate about the targeted structures, they do not always reach correct resolutions. Of the studies discussed, only Kim's (2008) study considered the nature of LRE resolution. Her findings suggest direct links between LRE resolutions and performance on post-tests. Pairs outperformed individuals because most of the pairs' LREs dealing with the targeted vocabulary item were resolved correctly. In contrast, in the case of individuals, over 50% of LREs were left unresolved or were resolved incorrectly (see also Swain, 1998 discussed below). In Nassaji and Tian's (2010) study, the authors mentioned that the targeted structures appeared difficult for the learners and thus it is likely that they may not have succeeded in resolving the relevant LREs, or resolving them correctly.

The quality of learners' engagement is also an important consideration. Nassaji and Tian (2010) noted that their low-proficiency learners showed limited engagement with the targeted structures. Kuiken and Vedder (2002) noted differences in levels of noticing and deliberations with the targeted structures in the case of some groups as well as learners' tendency to avoid using the targeted structures in their reconstructed texts. There are now a number of empirical studies (e.g. Leow, 1997; Qi & Lapkin, 2001; Storch, 2008; Swain *et al.*, 2009) which suggest that the quality of noticing and deliberation about language can have an impact on language learning.

One frequently cited study on the impact of the quality of noticing on language learning is that by Leow (1997). Leow analysed think-aloud protocols of learners working alone on a crossword puzzle in an L2 class (beginner Spanish), distinguishing between two levels of noticing: simple noticing and elaborate noticing. Simple noticing were instances where learners simply repeated the noticed linguistic feature. Elaborate noticing was noticing accompanied by meta awareness, where learners verbalised their noticing processes, with or without verbalising the relevant morphological rules. Leow argued that noticing plus meta awareness is a more elaborate form of noticing because it contains conceptually driven processes such as hypothesis testing and rule formation. Using two immediate post-tests (a recognition test and a fill in the blank production text) the researcher found that elaborate noticers outperformed simple noticers particularly on the recognition test and to a lesser extent on the production test.

Swain *et al.* (2009) also reported links between the quality of languaging episodes and performance on immediate and delayed post-tests. The study involved nine adult L2 learners of French explaining aloud (i.e. languaging) the uses of the French concept of verb voice. Languaging episodes identified in the data were counted and coded for quality of cognitive processes, distinguishing between more and less cognitively complex processing (e.g. drawing inferences versus restatements). Based on this analysis, the learners could be distinguished as high, low and middle languagers. The study found that high languagers performed best on the immediate and delayed post-tests. The researchers suggested that the more able their learners were to externalise their thoughts, the deeper the conceptual understanding they gained of the grammatical structures, and this explains post-test performance. A greater level of engagement represents a higher level of reflection about language and thus a greater depth of understanding. This greater understanding provides a more solid basis for using this knowledge. What this means is that in order to understand why collaborative activity may or may not result in language learning we need a research design which does not just focus on the outcomes but one which also takes into account the nature of learners' deliberations about language.

Tailor made tests: Linking LREs and subsequent performance

An alternative approach to investigate the effect of collaboration on language learning, adopted by a number of researchers, is one which links LREs found in collaborative talk and post-test outcomes but on tailor made tests. The justifications given for the use of such a test design is that no matter how carefully researchers design their tests and manipulate the tasks and task implementation, they cannot predict in advance what learners will focus on during their collaborative activity. For example, Swain and Lapkin (2001) found that regardless of their carefully piloted test, a relatively small number of the LREs in their data of pair talk related to the test items. This meant that any language learning that may have occurred could not be captured by the tests used.

Swain (1998, 2001) thus argues that in order to measure language learning gains arising during collaboration, we need to develop post-tests *a posteriori*; that is, after the collaborative talk has been analysed for LREs. Furthermore, given the observed variations between pairs in what they focus on (Swain & Lapkin, 1998), such tests need to be tailor made so that test items match the linguistic items that the learners considered in their LREs. In a sense, the LREs serve as a type of pre-test. The deliberations captured in the LREs indicate the learners' lack of knowledge of a particular structure or lack of complete mastery. At the same time, these LREs are occasions for language learning. The tailor made tests elicit the learners' explicit knowledge of the specific linguistic item that was deliberated about during the LRE.

A *posteriori* tailor made tests were first used by LaPierre (1994 cited by Swain 1998) and have since been employed by a number of researchers in different contexts. They have been used to assess learning following spontaneous attention to form in various classroom activities (Loewen, 2005; Williams, 2001), learner–learner interactions on oral tasks (e.g. Adams, 2007), interactions on writing tasks via online chats (Shekary & Tahririan, 2006; Zeng & Takatsuka, 2009), as well as interactions which occur when learners engage in face-to-face collaborative writing and feedback activities (e.g. Brooks & Swain, 2009; Swain & Lapkin, 2002).

Studies investigating the impact of collaborative writing on L2 learning employing tailor made tests have shown that collaboration leads to the learning of the lexical and grammatical forms focused on in the LREs. In a series of studies conducted with Grade 8 French immersion students, Swain (1998) and Swain and Lapkin (1998) investigated whether the learners remembered the linguistic targets of their LREs. In Swain's (1998) study, the students completed a dictogloss task collaboratively, and then one week later they completed dyad specific post-tests. Swain reported that learners' retention of the LREs varied according to how they had resolved the LREs. Most (79%) of the LREs that had been correctly resolved in the learners' collaborative dialogue were retained, whereas only 40% of the unresolved LREs and 29% of the incorrectly resolved LREs were correct on the post-test. Similar results were reported in Swain and Lapkin's (1998) study, which focused on the data of one case study pair on a jigsaw task, and by studies investigating chatting to complete collaborative writing tasks online (Shekary & Tahririan, 2006; Zeng & Takatsuka, 2009 - see discussion in Chapter 7).

Eckerth (2008) used a complex study design to investigate language learning gains for targeted and non-targeted language items. The study was conducted with 31 intermediate learners of German who worked in pairs to complete a set of dictogloss and editing tasks targeting the use of complex verb structures (e.g. reflexive prepositional verbs). The study used a pre-, immediate and delayed post-test design. The immediate post-tests, conducted after each task or exercise was completed, were identical to the pre-tests. They consisted of a sentence assembling exercise, testing the learners' knowledge of the pre-determined structures that were targeted by the dictogloss. The delayed post-test had two subtests. One subtest was identical to that of the pre-and immediate post-test; the other subtest was developed retrospectively after analysing transcripts of pair talk. This subtest covered aspects of language that were not targeted by the task and where the learners expressed divergent opinions, reflecting different linguistic hypotheses. These instances were labelled 'controversial language-related episodes'. The test questions on this subtest tested semantic, morphological and syntactic knowledge of these non-targeted linguistic features.

Gains on the targeted items were measured by comparing performance on the pre-test, the immediate post-test, and the recurring subtest of the delayed post-test. To investigate gains on the non-targeted structures, the analysis was more complex. The analysis considered whether the learners maintained or revised their original divergent hypotheses by comparing interaction data with post-test performance, and where revisions of original hypotheses were found, whether these revisions conformed to L2 norms. Gains were thus operationlised as revising incorrect hypotheses by one or both members of the pair. Such gains were also analysed for whether or not the revisions could be directly attributable to the interaction.

Eckerth found statistically significant language learning gains on the grammatical structures targeted by the tasks on both post-tests. For the non-targeted features, results showed that a large proportion of the revisions (38%) accorded with L2 norms, and that most of these revisions (78%) could be directly attributable to the interaction. Thus the findings suggest that collaborative tasks result in learning of structures beyond those targeted explicitly by the task design. Eckerth in fact wonders whether the language learning gains on these non-targeted L2 structures are more durable because they reflect more closely the learners' needs and hence learners may be more receptive to feedback about these structures. The findings of several studies, including those by Brooks and Swain (2009) discussed in a previous chapter (Chapter 3), suggest that this indeed may be the case.

However, although tailor made *a posteriori* tests capture what learners choose to focus on during collaborative activity, they have a number of shortcomings. Loewen and Philp (2006), for example, point out that with the absence of pre-test data, performance on such *a posteriori* post-tests may simply indicate consolidation of existing knowledge rather than evidence of new knowledge. However, some scholars suggest that consolidation of existing knowledge also represents language learning, particularly in the case of more advanced learners. For such learners, L2 learning is not so much the learning of new grammatical structures or rules but more often increased control over forms that have already been acquired (Nobuyoshi & Ellis,

1993), consolidation of existing knowledge, or extension of existing knowledge to new contexts (Swain & Lapkin, 1995, 1998). On a more practical level, as Swain and Lapkin (1998) admit, such tests are difficult to design, not the least because of the considerable time pressure they place on researchers to develop relevant test items within the time span of a study. This is particularly difficult in large-scale studies.

Process-product research design

Another way to gauge the effects of collaborative writing on language learning is to adopt a process-product research approach. This approach involves identifying opportunities for learning that pairs or small groups create in their interaction, often operationalised as LREs, and then examining over time whether the item that is the focus of the interaction is used in a target-like manner in subsequent individual performance. This approach, informed by Vygotsky's sociocultural theory (see Lantolf, 2005; Lantolf & Thorne, 2006), is referred to as microgenetic: documenting development of mental functions and processes over a short period of time. In L2 research, microgenetic analysis has been used to document how knowledge co-constructed during an activity, between a teacher and a student (e.g. Aljaafreh & Lantolf, 1994; Nassaji & Swain, 2000) or by peers working in small groups or pairs (e.g. de Guerrero & Villamil, 2000; Donato, 1994), is appropriated and is utilised by the learners in subsequent cognitive activity. Rather than measuring explicit knowledge about language (e.g. ability to recall a language item), as is the case with the studies employing a tailor made post-test, discussed above, this process-product approach tests implicit language knowledge; that is, ability to use the language item.

One of the earliest studies to use this process-product approach to investigate language learning gains following group work was by Donato (1994). Donato investigated the interaction of one group of L2 learners of French preparing for an oral presentation. The data consisted of the recordings of one session in which three learners prepared for an oral presentation and the subsequent presentations of the three learners (one week later). The learners were told that they could not use notes in their presentations, nor were they to memorise their lines, but they could make notes during the preparation session. The recorded group talk was analysed for instances of collective scaffolding; that is, instances where the learners resolved deliberations about language (e.g. lexical choices, grammatical constructions) by pooling their linguistic resources. Donato found 32 episodes of collective scaffolding in the group planning session. The analysis of the learners' subsequent individual oral presentations found that of the 32 language structures involved in the scaffolding episodes, 24 were used correctly by the learners in their subsequent individual presentations. Donato claims that this is evidence of the appropriation of socially constructed knowledge. That is, the items found subsequently in individual performances represent 'tracers' of socially co-constructed knowledge which has been internalised by the individual learners.

Building on Donato's work, in my own research on pair writing activities (Storch, 2002, 2009), I considered whether the pattern of pair interaction had an impact on subsequent learning. Using the data of four case study pairs, with each pair representing a distinct pattern of interaction, I investigated whether the structures topicalised in the pairs' LREs were evident in the learners' subsequent individual work. The learners completed one version of the three tasks used in this study (data commentary, text reconstruction and editing) in pairs and another very similar version individually. The study found the highest number of instances suggesting evidence of learning in the data of the collaborative pair and, to a lesser extent, in the data of the pair displaying an expert/novice pattern of interaction. Very little such evidence of learning was found in the case of the dominant/dominant and dominant/passive pairs.

Watanabe and Swain's (2007) study provides further evidence concerning the importance of the relationships learners form when engaged in collaborative writing and language learning. As described previously (Chapter 4), in this study four core learners worked alternatively with a lower and with a higher L2 proficiency peer. The researchers treated the first writing task the learners produced as a pre-test and a later writing task (after feedback was provided) as a post-test. The study found a link between the pattern of interaction and post-test scores. When the participants formed collaborative patterns of interaction or assumed the role of the expert in expert/novice patterns, they achieved higher post-test scores than those who acted as novices, dominant in dominant/passive patterns or experts but in expert/passive patterns. Pairs with a collaborative orientation (collaborative and expert/novice) produced more LREs than pairs who displayed a non-collaborative orientation (dominant/passive and expert/passive).

However, it is not just the quantity of LREs that may explain the greater gains achieved by learners forming these patterns of interaction. What became quite apparent when analysing the LREs in my study (2002, 2009) was the importance of the level of engagement in LRE resolution. In the collaborative and expert/novice pairs, both learners engaged extensively in the LRE resolutions; this was often not the case in the dominant/dominant and dominant/passive dyads. In my 2008 study, I examined more closely a subset of the data collected in the larger study (Storch, 2002, 2009). I focused on the nature of LRE resolutions and whether it related to subsequent individual performance. The task used was a text reconstruction, completed one week in pairs (11 pairs of high intermediate ESL learners) and a week later individually. The two versions of the task were similar. Recorded pair talk was analysed for LREs and coded for the language items the pairs focused on; whether they were resolved correctly (√), incorrectly (X) or left unresolved (¿); and, most importantly, for the quality of engagement in resolving the LREs. The latter analysis was based on the work of Leow (1997) and Kuiken and Vedder (2002), and distinguished between LREs displaying an elaborate and those displaying a limited level of engagement. LREs where the participants deliberated over the language items, sought and provided confirmation, explanations, and alternatives, were coded as showing evidence of elaborate engagement. LREs where participants simply stated the linguistic item without further deliberation were coded as showing limited engagement. Taking into consideration each participant's contributions to LRE resolutions yielded three possible engagement categories: both members of the dyad displaying elaborate engagement, coded (E); only one member displaying elaborate engagement whereas the other showing limited engagement, coded (L); both learners displaying limited engagement, coded (L + L).

In order to investigate whether the quality of engagement in deliberations about language had an effect on language learning and/or consolidation, I compared the learners' performance on the individually reconstructed tasks to that completed in pairs, but focused only on language items that were found in both versions of the tasks. Approximately 14 such items were found (e.g. definite articles used with plural country names; adjectival suffixes ('an') denoting nationality).

Adopting a process-product approach, evidence of learning was an instance where a structure that was the topic of discussion in the LRE was then used in the way it was resolved (either target-like or otherwise) in subsequent individual performance. Instances showing evidence of language learning were further coded for who benefitted from the LRE interaction: both learners in the pair, only one learner, neither of the two learners. In instances where only one learner benefited, I also noted whether it was the learner who was more active in the LRE resolution or not.

The following example illustrates the process-product analysis undertaken. Both versions of the text reconstruction task included plural names of countries that necessitated the insertion of a definite article. In the version completed in pairs, the relevant country was *Soviet Union*; in the version completed individually a week later it was *United States*. The example shows the relevant LRE from the data of two learners, Yong and Ed (Storch, 2008: 100–101), deliberating about the use of the definite article with plural names of countries. The LRE was coded as resolved correctly (√) and showing elaborate engagement (E).

Example 1: Process-product analysis

Text reconstruction sentence given: Immigrants East Europe country Soviet Union usual stay Australia

LRE (def + pl. name, √, E)

189	Yong:	Like Soviet Union…
190	Ed:	Like Soviet Union
191	Yong:	Wait a moment … do we have to put the article in the Soviet Union? The Soviet, Soviet Union… the Soviet Union, Soviet Union. Yeah the Soviet
192	Ed:	Are you sure?
193	Yong:	The United States
194	Ed:	Ah yeah…
195	Yong:	The United Nations
196	Ed:	Yeah, yeah…
197	Yong:	The Soviet Union
198	ED:	You're right

As the example shows, Yong initially omits the definite article, but then he realises, after sounding out the noun phrase with and without the definite article that the definite article is needed in this instance (turn 191). Ed, however, is only convinced once Yong presents other examples of plural names of countries and institutions that take the definite article (turns 193, 195). In the following week, both learners inserted the definite article with the plural name *United States*. Thus this instance was taken as evidence of language learning for both learners. Ed learnt that plural names need the use of definite articles and was able to apply this knowledge. The deliberations evident in the LRE suggest that Yong did not have complete control over this use of definite articles. The need to convince Ed, drawing on similar uses of the definite article, helped to consolidate his knowledge.

The analysis found that when the learners engaged with linguistic choices, whether at an elaborate or limited level, this led to learning/consolidation of the structures focused on. However, it was elaborate engagement that was more beneficial to both members of the pair than limited engagement. In well over half the cases showing evidence of elaborate engagement (53.58%), the effect was learning/consolidation for both learners, compared to about a third of cases for limited engagement. That is, elaborate engagement, where learners deliberated over alternatives, questioned and explained their suggestions, and pooled their linguistic knowledge, led to consolidation/learning more so than limited engagement. In instances of uneven engagement (i.e. those coded as L), language learning/consolidation was evident only for the learner actively engaged.

However, it is important to note that lack of engagement does not always mean that learners are not attending to the deliberations. This is particularly relevant in small group work, where not all learners contribute to the resolution of LREs. Fernández Dobao's (2012) study, mentioned earlier, found that small groups generated more LREs than pairs, but that whereas in pairs the majority of LREs were resolved interactively, in many of the LREs resolved by groups, only two or three members of the group contributed to the interaction. However, when Fernández Dobao (forthcoming) analysed the learners' performance on pre- and post- vocabulary tests, she found some instances where a learner in the group did not contribute to a particular LRE resolution, yet showed evidence of learning of the language item deliberated about in that LRE. This is certainly an area that requires further investigation.

A number of studies have examined the nature of peer interaction that occurs during collaborative writing and collaborative processing of feedback given on the jointly written text and then linked these interactions to performance on subsequent writing (e.g. Brooks & Swain, 2009; Storch & Wigglesworth, 2010a, 2010b; Swain & Lapkin, 2001). These studies have focused mainly on how processing of feedback affects the uptake of that feedback. In Brooks and Swain's (2009) study, discussed earlier (in Chapter 3), it was peer feedback given while the learners engaged in co-authoring that was found more effective and enduring than the feedback provided by the researcher on the completed text perhaps because the peer feedback was provided in immediate response to an identified need. Other studies, including those investigating focus on form in class activities (Ellis et al., 2001) and noticing of reformulations (Hanaoka, 2007), have also shown that feedback is most likely to be noticed and retained when it is related to the learner's perceived need. For example, Hanaoka (2007) found that L2 writers were more likely to scan reformulated models for solutions to problems that they had identified when writing, make revisions in accordance with these suggestions and retain this information for longer than was the case for revisions on problems that did not correspond to the learners' perceived needs. Such findings address the query raised by Eckerth (2008) noted earlier. They show that it is those aspects of language that learners identify as problematic, about which they deliberate (language), they receive peer feedback or co-construct a solution, that are most likely to be learnt.

Thus research on language gains adopting a process-product approach suggests that collaborative activity does lead to language learning. Given the detailed analysis that this approach to investigating language learning gains necessitates, the studies tend to be small-scale case studies. These case studies provide insights into the complex relation between interaction and language learning and why studies that compare collaborative and individual performance on pre- and post-test performance, using decontextualised group means, may yield mixed findings.

However, one of the major shortcomings of this body of research on language learning gains following collaborative activities, regardless of the research design employed to gauge gains, is the underlying assumption that we can observe gains after a few or even a single collaborative activity, often of a fairly limited duration. For example, in the Nassaji and Tian's (2010) study, learners were given eight minutes to complete each language exercise in the collaborative and individual mode. Swain and Lapkin (2001) reported that their immersion students spent on average 10 minutes on the collaborative writing tasks used in the study (dictogloss and jigsaw), noting that this is a very brief period to lead to quantitative differences on a test. Kuiken and Vedder (2002), whose students completed two dictogloss tasks within a 90 minute period, admit that learners may need several opportunities to interact before the impact of interaction can be expected to appear in their language production. In order to gauge the impact of collaborative writing on L2 learning we need research which is longitudinal; that is, where learners have opportunities to engage in a number of collaborative writing activities.

Longitudinal research on language learning gains

Shehadeh's (2011) study is the only longitudinal study to date that has investigated the impact of collaborative writing on language learning as well as L2 writing more broadly. The study was classroom based, conducted in two intact classes over a 16-week semester. The students were low intermediate EFL learners. In one class, the experimental group ($n = 18$), the learners wrote in pairs; in the other class ($n = 20$), the control group, learners wrote on the same topics but individually. In each class, learners produced a total of 12 pieces of writing (each of one paragraph in length), one new piece every week. Thus, unlike other studies, in this study, the learners in the experimental group experienced sustained exposure to collaborative writing.

The study compared the performance of pairs and of individual writers using a pre–post test research design. However, rather than using discrete item grammar exercises, the pre- and post-tests used writing tasks which were assessed not only for grammatical accuracy but also for the quality of the writing produced. Using a multiple trait scale, writing performance on the pre- and post-tests was assessed for content, organisation, vocabulary, grammar and mechanics.

One other notable feature of this study was that the students in the experimental groups were encouraged to change partners every two to three weeks. This strategy was adopted in order to avoid the situation of learners working throughout the semester with peers with whom they may form dominant/dominant or dominant/passive relationships, relationships not conducive to language learning. As shown by my research (Storch, 2002, 2009), the type of relationship learners form when working in pairs in a classroom tends to persist over time if learners stay with the same partner.

Shehadeh's comparison of the pre- and post-tests found that students who worked throughout the semester in pairs showed greater improvements in content, organisation, and vocabulary, than those who worked individually. The study found, however, that collaboration did not lead to improvement in grammar and mechanics. Shehadeh suggests that the lack of improvement in accuracy could be attributable to the low proficiency of the learners in the study; that at a low level of proficiency learners may not have sufficient language knowledge to help each other in deliberations about grammar. The learners' L2 proficiency was considered low intermediate in this context, based on the university entrance test scores. These scores are said to be equivalent to writing scores of 3.5–4 on the International English Language Testing System (IELTS). The writing samples Shehadeh enclosed confirm that these learners had a very low level of English language proficiency. In surveys conducted with the students, a number stated that they found deliberating about grammar the most challenging aspect of the collaborative writing. As noted earlier, studies which analysed the dialogues of pairs composed of low-proficiency learners (e.g. Leeser, 2004; Storch & Aldosari, 2013) confirm that such learners encounter difficulties in resolving grammatical LREs.

Nevertheless, it is important to keep in mind that Shehadeh's study found that learners who wrote collaboratively, despite their low L2 proficiency, did show greater improvement on important aspects of writing such as structure, content, and vocabulary, more so than learners who wrote individually. These results accord with the findings of studies investigating collaborative writing with L1 learners, such as the longitudinal study conducted by Yarrow and Topping (2001) with novice writers.

Yarrow and Topping's (2001) classroom study, conducted with young children (10 and 11 year olds), involved the students in producing five pieces of writing over six weeks. A comparison of the pre- and post-test results showed that all the children showed significant improvements in their writing. However, those who wrote interactively showed gains that were significantly greater than those children who wrote individually. The authors attributed these greater gains to the observed behaviour of the learners writing in pairs. Observation notes showed that, with the exception of two pairs, the children who worked in pairs kept each other on task, sought and provided each other with help, shared and explored ideas, and generally seemed to enjoy the co-authoring activity. Furthermore, data elicited via questionnaires, semi structured interviews and informal discussions suggested that the paired writers also gained more confidence in their own writing skills as a result of the collaborative writing activity.

Shehadeh reported similar findings based on his interviews with the learners from the experimental class. These L2 learners felt that their self-confidence as writers improved over time and attributed this improvement to participating in collaborative writing activities (see discussion in Chapter 6). Although Shehadeh did not collect pair interaction data that could be used to explain the gains in writing found in his study, other studies which have collected such data (see excerpts in Chapter 3) provide us with ample evidence that when composing texts collaboratively, L2 learners engage in important cognitive processes such as proposing and evaluating alternative ideas (Gutiérrez, 2008) as well as alternative ways of expressing and organising these ideas (e.g. Alegría de la Colina & García Mayo, 2007; Niu, 2009; Storch & Aldosari, 2013). These processes can lead to gains in language and to writing development.

Conclusion

The body of research reviewed in the preceding sections highlights the dearth of empirical research on the outcomes of collaborative L2 writing and the limitations of the existing small body of research. Most of the research to date, including my own research, has focused on short-term gains. This research has for the most part tended to focus only on one dimension of L2 learning: improvement in L2 accuracy. Clearly much more research needs to be undertaken, particularly longitudinal, carefully designed studies which adopt a broader perspective of L2 learning gains, a perspective that goes beyond grammatical accuracy. If we pay too much attention to learners' progress in accuracy following collaborative writing activities, we may overlook evidence showing developments in other, equally important, aspects of L2 writing.

I would like to conclude this chapter with some final observations about the outcomes of collaborative work, observations that segue to the issues discussed in the next chapter. Roskams (1999: 82) points out that whether a learning activity is beneficial or not 'depends not only on its "intrinsic" educational worth, but on whether students accept that it is a valid and valuable learning methodology.' In the next chapter I discuss students' views about group and pair work in L2 classes per se, and students' perceptions about collaborative writing activities once they had participated in such activities.

6 Learners' Perspectives of Collaborative Writing

Introduction

As a language (ESL) teacher, I have observed over the years that when I ask students to work in pairs (or small groups), particularly on tasks that require written output, some students seem reluctant to write with their peers, preferring to work on such tasks individually. Indeed in a number of my classroom-based studies (e.g. Storch, 2005, 2007), I gave the students the choice of completing the tasks in pairs or individually. Between about a quarter and a third of the students in these classes chose to work individually.

Learners' preferences are important. Language educators have long recognised that their learners bring to the classroom a complex cluster of attitudes, expectations and preferences all of which form significant contributory factors in the language learning process (Breen, 2001). Researchers too have long recognised the importance of learners' attitudes in the ultimate success of L2 learning. There is a large body of research on learners' attitudes towards various teaching approaches and practices. This research shows that learners' engagement with an activity and the outcomes of the activity may be affected by whether the learners believe that the activity is likely to facilitate their language learning. For example, in a study conducted by Dörnyei and Kormos (2000) in British and Hungarian L2 classes, the researchers found that the students' contributions to classroom oral activities (measured by the number of words and turns) correlated significantly with their attitudes towards the language tasks they were asked to perform. In our own research on learners' uptake of written corrective feedback (Storch & Wigglesworth, 2010a, 2010b), we found that the learners' attitudes to the type of feedback given impacted on how much of the feedback they heeded. This research further highlights the importance of taking learners' perspectives into consideration when attempting to understand learners' actions and to explain language learning outcomes.

In this chapter, I focus on L2 learners' perspectives about collaborative writing; that is, their attitudes towards and reflections on collaborative writing. However, given the dearth of research on L2 learners' attitudes towards collaborative writing, such attitudes can only be gleaned indirectly from research on learners' attitude to group and pair work per se. Attitudes towards a particular practice are based on an underlying set of beliefs (Pajares, 1992). In the context of language learning, attitudes towards a particular teaching approach or activity are shaped by beliefs about language learning. The first section of this chapter defines these beliefs and discusses why they are important. I then briefly review research on language learning beliefs, highlighting recent trends in this research. This section forms the foundation for the sections that follow. The second section presents research findings on learners' attitudes towards group and pair work, activities often associated with communicative and task-based approaches to L2 instruction. Although these studies refer predominantly to group and pair work on oral tasks, these attitudes and the concerns students have about group and pair work are likely to influence how they feel about writing collaboratively. The third section focuses on two of the main concerns that learners (and teachers) have about group and pair work, namely learners' excessive use of L1 and learning from each others' errors. The fourth section is devoted to learners' evaluations of collaborative writing activities. In this section I discuss in greater detail the limited number of studies on language learners' reflections and judgements of collaborative writing tasks that these learners had experienced, and conclude by outlining the kind of research that will better inform us about learners' beliefs and attitudes towards collaborative writing.

Language Learning Beliefs and Attitudes

Language learning beliefs can be broadly defined as a set of opinions that learners have about the nature of language learning (Kalaja & Barcelos, 2003), about what constitutes L2 knowledge (Benson & Lor, 1999) and about themselves as learners (Graham, 2006). These beliefs, held consciously or unconsciously, shape learners' attitudes and preferences and may incline them to act and react in certain ways. For example, if learners believe that the best way to learn a language is to memorise grammar rules, viewing language knowledge as mastery of these rules, it is likely that they will hold positive attitudes towards the type of exercises associated with traditional grammar-based approaches to language instruction, such as memorisation and drilling. They may therefore have difficulties accepting and participating in the type of activities associated with communicative approaches to language teaching, such as small group and pair work. If, on the other hand, learners believe that language knowledge includes an ability to use the L2, and that the best way to learn a language is by practicing using the L2, they are likely to be positively predisposed towards participating in communicative tasks. It should be noted that teachers' language learning beliefs are also important in determining the success of a classroom activity or an approach to instruction (see review in Borg, 2003). For example, Yu (2001) attributed some of the difficulties in implementing a communicative approach in EFL classes in China to resistance from teachers who were sceptical about whether this approach is superior to the traditional grammar approach.

Language learning beliefs may also influence how an activity is judged. For example, Green's (1993) large-scale survey ($N = 263$) asked EFL students to rank a list of classroom activities and practices for frequency of exposure, level of enjoyment, and perceived helpfulness for language learning. The study found a weak correlation between levels of enjoyment and helpfulness and previous experience with these activities. That is, the students were willing to rank an activity highly even if they had very little experience with the activity. These findings suggest that students' preconceived beliefs affect their judgement of the enjoyment and the effectiveness of classroom activities (see also discussion of McDonough's 2004 findings in the next section).

A number of factors are said to influence the formation of language learning beliefs. There is generally widespread agreement that one of the most influential factors is prior language learning experience, and in particular formal schooling (see Kern, 1995; Little & Singleton, 1990; Peacock, 2001; Wendon, 1986a). Indeed teachers' own prior language learning experience has been found to be an important factor in shaping their beliefs about effective approaches to instruction (Borg, 2003). Another, more contentious, factor shaping beliefs is the opinions of valued others. Wenden (1999) suggested that beliefs can be acquired consciously from advice given by teachers, parents or peers. However, it is teachers that are generally attributed with the most influence on learners' belief formation. Teachers, who are viewed as experts in language learning matters, and who convey their own beliefs overtly or covertly through their practices, are thought by some scholars (e.g. Horwitz, 1988; Pajares, 1992) to play a key role in learners' belief formation and development. However, Kern's (1995) large-scale survey study showed that teachers' beliefs bore little if any impact on their learners' beliefs.

Research on second language learning beliefs began in the 1980s, following the seminal work by Horwitz (1985, 1987, 1988) and Wenden (1986a,

1986b, 1987), and has flourished since. We now have a substantial body of research on language learning beliefs conducted in a range of L2 settings. However, a review of these studies shows that the definition of beliefs, the research methodology, and focus of research have changed substantially over time, as new theories began to inform SLA researchers.

Early studies (e.g. Horwitz, 1985, 1988; Wenden, 1986b, 1987) tended to view beliefs as stable cognitive entities, almost independent of context. Wenden (1999) refers to these beliefs under the umbrella term 'metacognitive knowledge', which includes knowledge about the learning process and about the learners themselves. The commonly used instruments to collect data were surveys and interviews, often carried out with large groups of students to obtain results that could be tested statistically, but which were notably collected at one specific point of time. The overarching aims of these studies were to describe and catalogue these beliefs in order to explain or predict learner behaviour (e.g. choice of learning strategies), as well as to enhance language teaching and learning. For example, Horwitz (1985) encouraged teachers to use the Beliefs about Language Learning Inventory (BALLI) she designed in the very first class in order to uncover and thus deal with the possible averse repercussions of a mismatch between teachers' and learners' beliefs. This recommendation assumes a direct causal relationship between beliefs, actions and learning outcomes.

This research showed that although learners' beliefs can change over time, some beliefs are deeply entrenched and are resistant to change despite instruction or exposure to new environments. For example, Peacock's (2001) survey with 146 TESL trainee teachers, at the beginning and end of their three year training course, found that these teacher trainees' views differed from those of experienced teachers, particularly regarding the benefits of communicative activities, and stayed the same despite the three-year programme which promoted communicative approaches to L2 instruction. Riley's study (2009), using surveys and focus group interviews administered twice over a nine-month period with EFL students in Japan (and their instructors), showed stability in beliefs on the majority of the questions asked (75% of the survey items). On the other 25% of questions, some student beliefs became more in line with the teachers' beliefs (e.g. usefulness of guessing word meanings). Interestingly, other beliefs such as about the usefulness of communicating in the L2 with peers changed and became less consonant with the views held by teachers.

More recent research, within a sociocultural theoretical paradigm, views language learning beliefs as categories of meaning which are socially constructed and context dependent (Negueruela-Azarola, 2011) rather than stable cognitive entities. As categories of meaning, beliefs are used to interpret and understand the language learning context and oneself. The studies within this paradigm tend to be small scale but longitudinal, often consisting of one in-depth case study (see for example studies in the special issue of *System*, 2011). They are conducted in situ and elicit qualitative data via a range of tools such as open-ended interviews, reflective journals, stimulated recall tasks and narratives. This research has focused on the nature of language learning beliefs, belief change, as well as the relationship between beliefs and actions.

What this research shows is that language learning beliefs are multifaceted and the by-products of internal as well as external factors. Internal factors include emotions (e.g. shyness, fears) and self-concept, a complex set of interrelated self-beliefs (Mercer, 2011). External factors include factors related to the immediate language learning environment, such as the influence of teachers, as well as to the broader socio-political context (for a review see Barcelos, 2003; Barcelos & Kalaja, 2011; Bernat & Gvozdenko, 2005).

Belief change has been shown by a number of studies to be complex and nuanced, influenced by factors such as significant others and self-beliefs. These studies have also shown that change is closely linked to reflection and to action. For example, Navarro and Thornton's (2011) study traced over four months the belief trajectories of two learners. It investigated the influence of factors such as learners' interaction with influential interlocutors (e.g. study advisors, teachers) as well as learners' own reflections on their actions on their beliefs. Thus, in the case of one learner, the study showed that beliefs about how best to improve speaking were influenced by advice given by a teacher. These beliefs led the student to seek speaking opportunities. Her own reflections and positive evaluation of these experiences reinforced and further refined emerging beliefs about L2 speaking, and particularly speaking about a chosen topic, as being beneficial for language learning. This belief became the impetus for her subsequent actions. Thus although the catalyst for the belief formation was advice given by teachers, the student's own reflection and evaluation of the actions undertaken played an important part in belief change.

In-depth longitudinal case studies also show that language learning beliefs are dynamic and embedded in students' language learning contexts. Peng's (2011) longitudinal case study of Weitao, an EFL learner in China, is particularly illuminating. It reveals that changes in beliefs are context-responsive; that is, responding to the nature of the classroom activities, the teachers' communicated beliefs, assessment practices, level of enjoyment, and perceptions of progress. The findings also show that the trajectory in the learner's beliefs is not unidirectional. The study documented how Weitao's positive attitudes to oral communicative activities (group work), as more authentic, enjoyable, and conducive to language learning, became less positive with looming exams and new classes where teachers communicated very different expectations. Towards the end of the study period (seven months), positive attitudes to group work resurfaced in reaction to the dull non-communicative classes Weitao experienced. However, group work activities were no longer perceived as effective means to learn a language but as the means to maintain student interest and motivation. The findings suggest that beliefs can orient the significance of an activity, and that the changes in beliefs can be nuanced.

Thus this body of research suggests that the relationship between beliefs and action is complex and unpredictable. There is no doubt that some beliefs can affect action. For example, in Peng's study (2011), observational data suggest that when the activity (group work) was perceived by Weitao, the case study participant, as meaningful and enjoyable it encouraged him to participate actively in the group discussion. Actions can also reinforce beliefs. Aragão's (2011) study of three EFL teacher trainees showed that because these trainees felt that their own oral skills were inferior to those of their peers, they did not contribute much to class activity. Thus beliefs about their own L2 abilities affected their behaviour but at the same time their behaviour (lack of participation) perhaps further perpetuated these beliefs.

In the next section I discuss what empirical research has revealed about learners' attitudes and underlying beliefs about participating in group and pair work in L2 classes.

Attitudes to Group and Pair Work

There have been a number of studies investigating L2 learners' attitudes to a range of teaching issues, and these issues often include attitudes towards group and pair work. Although not always specified, the reference is to group and pair work on oral tasks. These studies have produced mixed results. Although some studies, both large-scale surveys (e.g. Brown, 2009; Reid, 1987; Riley, 2009) and small-scale studies (e.g. Hyde, 1993; McDonough, 2004), show that learners do not perceive group and pair work favourably; others (e.g. Green, 1993; Littlewood, 2010; Mishra & Oliver, 1998; Trinder, 2013) report on more favourable attitudes among L2 learners towards communicative activities, activities which include small group and pair work.

One reason for the mixed results may be attributed to how the students surveyed conceptualise the activities named in the survey, and as Littlewood (2010) points out, whether students were asked what kind of activities they 'enjoy' versus what kind of classroom activities they think are 'effective' for language learning. Garret and Shortall (2002) found that notions of enjoyment and language learning may also be confounded by L2 proficiency. In their study, 103 EFL learners (beginners and intermediate) were asked to evaluate a range of teacher-fronted and pair work on grammar and fluency activities immediately after the activities were implemented as part of the regular classwork. The students commented on the activities experienced on two dimensions: value for learning and enjoyment. The study found that the beginner learners judged teacher-fronted teaching activities as most conducive to learning, and saw no difference between teacher and student centred activities in terms of enjoyment. The intermediate EFL learners thought that the student-centred activities were more enjoyable but did not necessarily link greater enjoyment to more learning.

Students' attitudes towards group and pair work seem to be more favourable if such activities focus on fluency rather than grammatical accuracy. In a study of ESL high school students' preferences, conducted in Australia, Mishra and Oliver (1998) surveyed 70 ESL high school students and found that although 70% of the students had positive attitudes toward group and pair work, very few of the students, especially from South East Asia, liked group and pair work on grammar exercises. The students preferred to work on such exercises individually because they felt that this could provide them with more opportunities to practice their grammar. These preferences seem to suggest underlying beliefs about language learning, and particularly about learning grammar as well as concerns about learning 'not good English' (Riley, 2009).

McDonough's (2004) study showed that learners' beliefs that pair and group work is not conducive to improving grammar persisted despite evidence to the contrary. The study, conducted with 16 Thai EFL learners, investigated learners' language learning gains (using pre- and post-tests) as well as attitudes to pair work. The study found that although the learners' performance in the use of the targeted structure improved following the pair work activity on two oral communicative tasks, most of the students (12 out of 16) felt that the pair and small group activities were not useful for language learning. The learners seemed concerned about learning the wrong grammar from their peers yet analysis of the pair talk in fact showed that these learners provided each other with useful and grammatically correct feedback.

Interestingly, in a study conducted in the same context, with Thai EFL students, but using pairs working on a range of exercises outside class time in a self-access environment, McDonough and Sunitham (2009) found contradictory results to those found in McDonough's (2004) study discussed above. In responses to a questionnaire administered at the end of the study, McDonough and Sunitham found that most of the students (43 out of 48) reported that they preferred to work in pairs rather than alone on these activities. The main reason given was the assistance they felt they received from their peers on issues relating mainly to vocabulary. Yet a comparison of pre- and post-test results showed very little evidence of language learning. The post-test results showed that the learners were not successful in remembering the linguistic information they discussed with their peers. Thus how learners judge their experience of pair work may not necessarily be related to language learning gains evident in test scores, but rather to their own perceptions of those experiences, corroborating Green's (1993) survey results.

Thus the accumulated evidence on students' attitudes to group and pair work in general seems inconclusive. However, the findings about students' attitudes to group and pair work on grammar exercises are more uniform. They show that students do not believe that working in groups and pairs on grammar exercises is useful for L2 learning.

The Main Concerns About Group and Pair Work

The discussion on students' attitudes to group work has highlighted some of the concerns that students hold about group and pair work, particularly on grammar exercises. These concerns are often also expressed by language teachers and explain why teachers may be reluctant to implement group/pair work and collaborative writing tasks in their classes. In what follows, I discuss the two most frequently expressed concerns: The use of L1 and whether learners can provide valuable and correct feedback to each other. In discussing each concern, I begin with explaining the concern, and then consider the available empirical evidence to see whether the concern is justified.

Concern about using L1

One of the main concerns that is raised mainly by teachers and to some extent by students is the excessive use of L1 in group work. A number of researchers (e.g. Brooks & Donato, 1994; Carless, 2007, 2008; McDonough, 2004) have reported that teachers are sometimes reluctant to use group work in their language classes, particularly in foreign language classes where students share an L1, because of concerns that the students will use their L1 instead of the target language in such activities. Carless (2008), for example, based on interviews conducted with teachers and teacher educators in Hong Kong, noted that for these teachers the learners' tendency to use their L1 was considered the key challenge in decisions about whether or not to implement group work. These concerns are not without basis. Extensive use of L1 by learners working in groups has been reported in a number of studies. For example, Guk and Kellogg (2007) reported a large proportion of L1 use in a foreign language context (Korea) in learner–learner interactions (46.93% of the total learner–learner utterances). Studies eliciting learners' views concerning group and pair work also report on learners' expressed concerns about the amount of L1 that is used in such activities (e.g. Garrett & Shortall, 2002; Riley, 2009).

A number of reasons may explain why students revert to their L1 when working in small groups/pairs. Learners may use their L1 because they may have limited linguistic resources or because they do not have the requisite pragmatic and interactional competence required to participate in group/pair work. Sheen (1992), for example, considers it unlikely that students in foreign language classes, even after five to six years of language instruction, would have the linguistic resources necessary to complete the kind of group tasks often recommended in task-based approaches to L2 instruction. The study by Scott and de la Fuente (2008) showed that even advanced L2 learners had difficulties completing consciousness raising grammar tasks in pairs when they were not allowed to use their L1. Moreover, it seems that when discussion or problem-solving tasks are used, when students become very absorbed in the tasks, they are even more likely to use their L1 (Carless, 2008; de St Léger & Storch, 2009).

Another reason for the use of L1, particularly by learners in foreign language classes, is the sense of awkwardness of speaking to peers in an L2. Kang (2005) reported on learners' reluctance to speak in the L2 (English) in groups composed of fellow L1 (Korean) speakers. One participant commented about this 'unnatural' situation: 'I feel like I'm wearing a mask' (p. 284). Similar sentiments were expressed by some of our advanced French learners in a study (de St Léger & Storch, 2009) which sought to investigate learners' willingness to communicate in a range of classroom activities, including group and pair work. As Arushi, one of the students interviewed, explained:

> Small group discussion doesn't work, students always revert back to English, no matter how sincerely you try. I don't know if it's too embarrassing or just too awkward when you've got this relationship just as another uni student and suddenly now you are talking in French, it is a bit weird. (p. 279)

However, it should be noted that these findings and reports concerning L1 have come from studies where the tasks used were oral rather than writing tasks. Research on the use of L1 by students working in pairs on collaborative writing tasks, peer response, and language-focused written exercises has shown that generally the learners do not use the L1 excessively, and that when the L1 is used, it serves important task management and language learning functions. These studies have been conducted in a range of contexts including immersion (e.g. Swain & Lapkin, 2000), second language (e.g. Storch & Wigglesworth, 2003) and foreign language contexts (e.g. Anton & DiCamilla, 1998; Shehadeh, 2011; Storch & Aldosari, 2010). Furthermore, many of these researchers, informed by sociocultural theoretical perspectives, view a language, whether it be an L1 or an L2, as an important tool in cognitive development.

In the immersion context, where learners share an L1, Swain and Lapkin (2000) found that the learners do not use their L1 extensively when working on collaborative writing tasks. The researchers investigated the use of L1 (English) by students working in pairs in two Grade 8 French immersion classes. One class completed a jigsaw task; the other class completed a dictogloss task. The researchers found that less than 30% of total turns were in L1 across both tasks. Task type did not affect the amount of L1 use; rather there were considerable variations amongst pairs of students. Furthermore, the researchers found that the L1 served a number of important functions. One such function was task management. The shared L1 enabled the learners to establish a joint understanding of the task requirements and thus move the task along. The second function related to language learning. The shared L1 enabled the learners to search for vocabulary items, to assess alternatives, and to provide each other with information and explanations about grammatical rules and conventions. Swain and Lapkin argue that, if used judiciously, the L1 can be an important linguistic resource that L2 learners have at their disposal, and one that could be usefully harnessed in L2 learning.

In the L2 context students do not necessarily share an L1, and when they do and work in pairs on a writing task, they also seem to use the L1 sparingly. In a study we (Storch & Wigglesworth, 2003) conducted in an ESL context, we examined the dialogues of six pairs of intermediate and advanced ESL learners with a shared L1 as they completed two writing tasks, a data commentary and an argumentative essay. We found that most of the pairs used their L1 to a very limited extent, just odd words and occasional phrases. The main functions the L1 served, when it was used, was task management (e.g. decision regarding the scribe) and clarification of task instructions (e.g. clarification of the graphic prompt). In interviews, the learners attributed their reluctance to use their L1 to the context (ESL) where they felt that they were expected to use the L2, and to their language learning beliefs. They believed that using the L2 as much as possible would help to improve their L2. One student was also concerned that if he were to use his L1, this would adversely affect his L2.

In foreign language classes, the findings regarding L1 use are mixed and seem to be influenced by the writing task used. Some researchers report high use of L1 among their learners (e.g. Kuiken & Vedder, 2002; Malmqvist, 2005). However, in both studies, the dictogloss task was used. As discussed previously (Chapter 4), the dictogloss may be a difficult task for L2 learners. In contrast, researchers employing more meaning-focused tasks report on relatively low uses of L1 (e.g. Shehadeh, 2011; Storch & Aldosari, 2010). For example, in our study conducted in Saudi Arabia with EFL learners (Storch & Aldosari, 2010), discussed in Chapter 4, we investigated the effect of learner proficiency pairing (H–H, H–L and L–L) and task type on the amount of L1 (Arabic) used by these EFL learners. We found that there was a very modest use of the L1 in all pairs, including the L–L pairs. L1 words formed only 7% of the total number of words the learners uttered in their interactions, ranging from as low as 5% of total words to a high of 30% (found only in the case of one pair). L1 turns accounted for only 16% of the total number of turns. We also found that task type had a greater impact on the amount of L1 used than proficiency pairing. The L–L pairs used more L1 than the H–H and H–L pairs but mainly when working on the editing task. There was little difference in the amount of L1 used between the three proficiency pairings on the other two meaning-focused tasks (jigsaw and composition).

In our study we also found that when the L1 was used by these EFL learners, it served important functions, similar to those identified in other studies (Anton & DiCamilla, 1998; Swain & Lapkin, 2000; Villamil & de Guerrero, 1996). The shared L1 was used predominantly for the purpose of task management (45% of all L1 turns) and to facilitate deliberations over vocabulary (26% of all L1 turns), where learners provided each other with cross-linguistic equivalents as illustrated in the example below (see also Example 3 in Chapter 3). The excerpt in this example comes from a pair of relatively high-proficiency learners (Bareq and Kalid) working on a collaborative composition task (Storch & Aldosari, 2010: 369–370).

Example 1: Use of L1

87	Kalid:	Radiation from
88	Bareq:	Nuclear plant from the nuclear
89	Kalid:	From what?
90	Bareq:	Nuclear
91	Kalid:	What does
92	Bareq:	Nuclear *masane A shesman this asmah alamsaneA annwaw-eya (nuclear factories) esha'at (radiation)*

93	Kalid:	Radiation *esha'at (radiation)* from aaa
94	Bareq:	Nuclear plant yeah
95	Kalid:	Plant? What does plant?
96	Bareq:	*Masna'* (factory).
97	Kalid:	*Masna'* (factory) factory... nuclear factory.

As shown in this excerpt, Kalid sought the meaning of the words nuclear (turn 91) and plant (turn 95) and Bareq provided the L1 explanation, linking nuclear to factories and radiation (turn 92) and an L1 equivalent (turn 96) respectively. The assistance provided by Bareq enabled Kalid to learn new L2 vocabulary and produce the phrase nuclear factory (turn 97), a phrase he would not have been able to produce without the assistance provided by Bareq in the L1.

These results suggest that when learners engage in collaborative writing tasks, they may use their L1 more sparingly than is the case in oral tasks. Kim and McDonough (2011), who investigated the impact of pre-task modelling on the interaction of EFL high school learners in Korea on three tasks, a writing task (dictogloss) and two speaking tasks, observed little use of L1 among the learners on all three tasks. The researchers attributed their findings to the pre-task modelling.

More research is clearly needed to investigate and compare the amount and functions served by the L1 in writing versus oral tasks completed in pairs and groups. A more informed understanding of the role of the L1 in L2 learning may help to allay the concerns of both L2 teachers and learners about L1 use in classroom activities. In situations were L1 is used excessively, we need to consider the type of task, the L2 proficiency of the learners, and the instructional strategies that may reduce L1 use (e.g. pre-task modelling).

Concerns about the viability of peer feedback and learning from each other's mistakes

Another concern which is voiced by teachers and students about group/pair work, particularly on language-focused activities, is related to the ability of students, who are at a similar level of L2 proficiency, to provide each other with useful feedback on language. As research on peer response on L2 writing has shown (e.g. Carson & Nelson, 1996; Zhang, 1995), learners may have difficulties in providing feedback to their peers not only for cultural reasons, but also because they may feel inadequate in providing such feedback. They may also be uncertain about accepting feedback from a peer, a fellow non-expert.

Research has also shown that learners may not consider their peers to be a useful resource for language learning (Mackey *et al.*, 2001; McDonough,

2004; Williams, 1999) particularly peers who have a lower L2 proficiency. For example, in McDonough's (2004) study, conducted with Thai EFL learners following oral small group and pair work, only four of the 16 learners who participated in the study stated that talking to classmates was useful for learning language (vocabulary and grammar). In Kim and McDonough's (2008) study, which paired core learners once with a more advanced learner and the second time with a less advanced learner, most learners (six out of eight) stated that they preferred working with an advanced learner because they felt that they could learn more vocabulary and receive more grammar explanations from more proficient learners. They also felt more confident about getting the correct information from such learners. In contrast, when working with peers of similar L2 proficiency, they did not feel confident about resolving linguistic problems together.

A related concern is, in fact, whether learners will learn from each other's errors. Lightbown (1991: 208) notes that in EFL classrooms, L2 learners are exposed to 'masses of non-native input which will tend to confirm their own interlanguage hypotheses'. Sheen (1994) warns teachers against task-based group and pair work which may lead to the development of 'a classroom pidgin'. Students, too, have voiced concerns about learning 'the wrong grammar' from their peers (e.g. McDonough, 2004; Mishra & Oliver, 1998). There is in fact some evidence of the development of 'classroom dialects' (Tarone & Swain, 1995); however, this is usually the case in immersion contexts where learners have extensive contact with each other, inside and more so outside the class. Evidence from studies conducted on peer interaction shows little evidence that learners learn 'the wrong grammar'. Indeed large meta-analyses of studies investigating peer oral interactions, conducted in a range of contexts, have shown a positive relationship between interaction and second language learning (e.g. Keck *et al.*, 2006; Mackey & Goo, 2007). Jacobs's (1989) study, on the nature of peer feedback on writing, conducted with EFL learners in Thailand, found that the largest category of amendments was accurate corrections of incorrect forms (48% of corrections), followed by indication of uncertainty but without supplying the correct form (19%). Incorrect amendments of correct forms accounted for less than 10% of peer feedback marking.

Learning gains following collaborative writing tasks have also been documented in studies discussed in the previous chapter. These studies, whether using tailor made tests (e.g. Eckerth, 2008; Swain & Lapkin, 1998) or tracing for evidence of retention in subsequent learner performance (e.g. Donato, 1994; Storch, 2002; Watanabe & Swain, 2007), show a high proportion of retention of items that were discussed by the learners (i.e. LREs). However, because LREs can also be resolved incorrectly, retention may also be of 'the wrong grammar'. For example, in Swain and Lapkin's (1998) study, learners responded to over 70% of items on the tests in the same way as they were resolved in their previous LREs. That means that if the LREs were resolved incorrectly, this information was also retained. Thus an important consideration is what proportion of LREs are correctly resolved.

Research on collaborative writing shows that the majority of LREs are resolved correctly. Table 6.1 shows the proportion of correctly resolved LREs reported in studies conducted in a range of L2 contexts, expressed either as a proportion of total LREs found in the data, mean of correctly resolved LREs, or range to show variations between pairs and groups. Some studies also reported on the proportion of unresolved LREs.

As the table shows, regardless of context, whether learners worked in pairs or small groups, learners working collaboratively on writing and grammar tasks tend to resolve LREs correctly in the majority of cases. Lexical LREs show a higher proportion of correct resolution than grammatical LREs. Results concerning unresolved and incorrectly resolved LREs are mixed. Some studies show that learners are more likely to abandon LREs, leaving them unresolved, than to resolve them incorrectly (e.g. Kim, 2008; Leeser, 2004; Swain, 1998); whereas others show the opposite, with incorrectly resolved LREs forming a greater proportion than unresolved LREs (e.g. Fernández Dobao, forthcoming; Storch, 1997). Nevertheless, well over 50% of LREs are correctly resolved, even when pairs are composed of two relatively low-proficiency learners (see Leeser, 2004; Storch & Aldosari, 2013). The only task where learners seem to have difficulties resolving LREs correctly is the dictogloss task (e.g. Kim & McDonough, 2008; Malmqvist, 2005; Swain, 1998). This may be because the linguistic features targeted by the dictogloss may be beyond the learners' L2 knowledge.

Thus, these findings suggest that when learners work together, they tend to provide each other with correct information or they pool together their incomplete linguistic knowledge to reach, in the majority of cases, correct resolutions to deliberations about language. Eckerth's (2008) study, also discussed in the previous chapter, considered episodes in which learners expressed divergent opinions in their deliberations to examine the impact of such divergent opinions on performance on tailor made post-tests. The study found very little evidence of learners' reinforcing each other's incorrect L2 assumptions, as suggested by Sheen (1994). Furthermore, the study found that in 38% of negotiations, incorrect L2 knowledge was replaced by correct knowledge; that is, knowledge conforming to L2 norms. This correct knowledge was subsequently integrated into the learners' interlanguage as evident by their performance on immediate post-tests.

Although the data base is still relatively small, it nevertheless suggests that when learners work in pairs or small groups on writing tasks, learning

Table 6.1 Resolution of LREs

Study	Participants	Tasks	Correctly resolved LREs
Alegría de la Colina & García Mayo (2007)	N = 24 EFL Elementary Spain university Pairs	3 tasks: Jigsaw Dictogloss Text reconstruction	70% of all LREs Higher proportion of lexical than form-based LREs correctly resolved.
Fernández Dobao (forthcoming)	N = 110 L2 = Spanish Intermediate USA university 15 small groups (4 per group) 25 pairs	Jigsaw	Focused on lexical LREs Pairs: Correct LREs: 61% Incorrect: 26% Unresolved: 13% Groups: Correct LREs: 73% Incorrect: 15% Unresolved: 12%
Kim (2008)	N = 32 L2 = Korean Intermediate Korea, university 8 pairs and 16 individuals	Dictogloss	Focus on Lexical LREs Pairs: Correct: 53% Incorrect: 17% Unresolved: 30% Individuals: Correct: 39% Incorrect: 22% Unresolved: 39%

(continued)

Table 6.1 (Continued)

Study	Participants	Tasks	Correctly resolved LREs
Kim & McDonough (2008)	N = 24 EFL Korea university 8 intermediate paired once with fellow intermediate; another time with advanced learner	Dictogloss	Range for intermediate–intermediate pairs: 44%–60% Range for intermediate–advanced pairs: 64%–81%
Kim & McDonough (2011)	N = 44 (2 classes) EFL Korea middle school Class 1: pre-task modelling of talk Class 2: control All work in pairs	3 tasks (1 writing, 2 oral): Dictogloss Decision making Information gap	Pre-task modelling group mean = 0.75 Control group mean = 0.60 Distribution of correctly resolved (as well as unresolved and incorrectly resolved LREs) was consistent for all 3 tasks
Leeser (2004)	L2 = Spanish US university 8 pairs High–High (H–H) 9 pairs High–Low (H–L) 4 pairs Low–Low (L–L)	Dictogloss	H–H: 88% H–L: 64% L–L: 58% (in L–L pairs, 33.33% of LREs abandoned)
Malmqvist (2005)	N = 12 L2 = German, Mixed proficiency Sweden, university 4 groups of 3	Dictogloss	Range: 33.8%–75.9% (for 3 of 4 groups >66% correctly resolved)

Study	Participants	Task	Results
Niu (2009)	N = 16, EFL, upper interm China, university	Oral vs. Writing text reconstruction based on prior reading of a text	Oral task: 91.8% Writing task: 93.26%
Storch (1997)	N = 14, ESL Intermediate Australia, university, 4 pairs, 2 triads	Editing task	Grammatical LREs Correct: 65% Incorrect: 33% Unresolved: 1%
Storch (1998b)	N = 9, ESL Intermediate - Advanced Australia university, 3 pairs, 1 triad	3 grammar exercises (multiple choice, cloze, text reconstruction) + composition	Multiple choice: 86% Cloze: 74% (the lowest)
Storch (2007)	N = 66 (2 classes) ESL Intermediate Australia University, 21 pairs, 1 triad and 25 individuals	Editing task	Grammatical LREs Correct: 80% Incorrect: 13.7% Unresolved: 6.3%
Storch (2008)	N = 22, ESL Intermediate Australia University, Pairs	Text reconstruction	Correct: 79.65% Incorrect: 18.36% Unresolved: 2%

(continued)

Table 6.1 (Continued)

Study	Participants	Tasks	Correctly resolved LREs
Storch & Aldosari (2013)	EFL Saudi Arabia university 5 pairs each: High-High (H–H) High-Low (H–L) Low-Low (L–L)	Composition	H–H: 76% H–L: 77% H–L: 67%
Swain (1998)	N = 48 French immersion, Canada High School Pairs	Dictogloss	Correct: 54.7% Incorrect: 8% Unresolved: 19.5%

of 'correct language' (grammar and vocabulary) occurs more frequently than instances of learners learning 'incorrect language'. In such tasks, when learners have time to deliberate about language (more so than in speaking tasks, see Niu, 2009), they tend to resolve their language deliberations correctly by offering correct feedback or pooling their incomplete linguistic resources to reach generally correct resolutions. As such, L2 learners are a useful source of language learning for each other.

Learners' evaluation of collaborative writing

To date there are only four published studies that report on learners' evaluation of collaborative writing. One study (Storch, 2005) elicited learners' evaluation after they had engaged in one collaborative writing activity; the other three (Roskams, 1999; Shehadeh, 2011; Storch, 2004) are longitudinal studies where learners completed a number of collaborative writing tasks. These studies are discussed in turn. In this discussion, I include the learners' (using pseudonyms) verbatim responses to open-ended questions on questionnaires and in interviews in order to convey in their own words their perceptions and beliefs.

In one of a series of studies I conducted with high intermediate ESL students (Storch, 2005), I gave the students a choice to work individually or in pairs on a data commentary task. Of the 23 students who agreed to participate in the study, 18 chose to work in pairs and five chose to work individually. The students who worked in pairs were interviewed individually at the end of the study. Open-ended questions were used to elicit their attitudes to pair work in general as well as their reflections and perceptions about their experience of working collaboratively on the writing task.

The study found that most of the students were positive about group and pair work in general and most (16 of the 18 interviewed) were also positive about collaborative writing. Only two felt that group/pair work should be best relegated to oral rather than writing activities. However, of the 16 who held positive attitudes about collaborative writing, five (almost a third), expressed some reservations about the activity.

Of those that found the experience positive, most (12 students) felt that it helped them to compose ideas. They felt that collaborative writing enabled them to compare ideas and to learn from each other different ways of expressing their ideas. For example Angela said:

> Ah I think ... when I'm working in pairs we can get more ideas ... because different people have different ideas. So we can comparing the important ideas together that make a paragraph.

The students noted that such a pooling of resources provided opportunities to observe and to learn from each other. As Ed said:

> I see him writing and I ... in this situation oh writing in this way is good. I learn, I learn much so ... I learn from him and maybe he learn from me.

Shirley described the collaborative process of suggesting and evaluating each other's ideas as well as elaborating on each other's ideas that took place:

> Like sometimes she will say like um... start like the sentence, so I will think it's good idea, just write down. And then if I think maybe another idea so you can ... add to the sentence or delete.

A number of students (six) also felt that collaborative writing was helpful for improving the grammatical accuracy of the final text. They mentioned, for example, that it was easier to spot errors made by other writers than in their own writing. Students also commented on the benefits of collaborative writing in terms of exposure to new vocabulary. As Noriko explained:

> I just watch vocabulary or ... what vocabulary he was using, he used and ... Well if he used the vocabulary which I didn't know, I tried to use it for next time.

I gathered that for most of these students, collaborative writing was a fairly novel activity. This was confirmed in the interviews, when a number of the students mentioned that this was the very first time that they had ever co-authored a text. Yet, despite or perhaps because it was a novel activity, some students enjoyed it. As Howard said:

> This ... quite interesting because I never had that kind of activity before. Well, that's a pretty new idea for me, so I quite enjoy it.

However, some students had reservations about collaborative writing, reservations based largely on these students' own evaluation of their L2 proficiency. Two of the female students in this study reported that they were embarrassed to express their ideas because of low self-confidence in their writing skills. As mentioned in the discussion of learners' beliefs, self-concepts form an important element in these beliefs and may shape learners' attitudes and judgement of an activity.

There were also some concerns expressed about being critical of peers' work. Such concerns are often reported in the literature on peer response (see

Carson & Nelson, 1996; Nelson & Carson, 1998). This was expressed clearly by Maria:

> Yeah it's very hard because you can't say... I mean if I say something I ... I think... maybe she's no... I can't explain you... Maybe I think she'll ... she'll think that I will ... I want to be better than her ... You know, you can't just say stop you are wrong ... or maybe, maybe I am wrong. So it's hard to work in a group but it's very helpful.

Beliefs about writing also formed the basis for these learners' reservations about collaborative writing, beliefs that were shaped by the learners' prior writing experiences. Yong, for example, thought that collaborative writing was an enjoyable class activity. Nevertheless, he felt that writing was an individual endeavour, and thus expressed some reservations about writing collaboratively:

> I think ah ... discussing the idea is quite interesting and useful but ah ... Writing in pairs is ... only ... unbalanced. I think because the writing task is actually aimed at the individual's ability.

Writing was also perceived by another student as a process of focusing on a set of ideas and writing them down. Exposure to different ideas, and not knowing which were correct ideas, made the task harder for Noriko:

> Oh ... um ... I really did not like to work with somebody for writing task because sometimes it's going to be harder to concentrate with what, what I wanted to ... write or describe the chart or whatever. And sometimes really confused because ... when I thought about that one... but the people said the difference things and I will, I don't know which ... which is correct or not.

Thus the findings of the study showed that learners overall were favourably disposed to pair and group work, and that after writing for the first time in pairs, they enjoyed the activity and saw the benefits of the activity in terms of both writing processes and language learning. However, they still held some reservations about writing collaboratively, either because of a lack of confidence in their own L2 abilities or because they believed that writing is inherently a solitary activity. The main limitation of this study was that it elicited attitudes to collaborative writing after just one exposure to such an activity. The following studies investigated learners' attitudes to collaborative writing after the students had experienced the activity a number of times.

Shehadeh's (2011) longitudinal study, discussed earlier, also investigated learners' attitudes to collaborative writing, but did so after the learners had experienced writing together on 12 occasions (in a 16-week semester). In the study, the 18 EFL learners in the collaborative writing condition completed a questionnaire eliciting their perceptions of collaborative writing and any language learning gains. The study found that although these students had no prior experience of collaborative writing, the majority were very positive about their experiences. They felt that they gradually began to recognise the benefits of collaborative writing and also began to enjoy it. These perceptions had an impact on their behaviour, as they also stated that they gradually become more actively involved. Most of the students felt that the experiences enhanced their writing abilities, expressing opinions very similar to those expressed by my students in the 2005 study. For example, one of the students in Shehadeh's study wrote in response to an open-ended question on the survey: 'I learnt how to work with other students and learn from them. They have different ideas, different opinions, new words etc.' (p. 296). The students in Shehadeh's study also felt that their speaking skills and their confidence as writers improved as a result of writing collaboratively throughout the semester. Shehadeh admits that the limitations of his study were the use of surveys rather than interviews and requiring the learners to respond to the survey in the L2. These students' L2 proficiency was very low and thus their responses were quite brief.

Roskams' (1999) longitudinal study (over 10 weeks) employed two questionnaires, at the beginning and end of the study, and thus could gauge changes in students' attitudes to collaborative writing following their experiences rather than relying on students' retrospections. This was a large-scale study ($N = 217$) conducted with English for Academic Purposes (EAP) students enrolled in a Business Communication course in Hong Kong. The students were required to work in the same self-selected pairs for the duration of the term and on a range of tasks (oral and writing). These tasks formed the bulk of their assessment, contributing 80% to the total grade.

The study found that most of the students (80%) preferred working in pairs to working alone. They felt that their partners' comments helped to improve the text and that they had learned more by working with their partners than they would have by working alone. However, learning was mainly expressed in terms of mastery of content and general writing and speaking skills, rather than language skills (grammar and vocabulary). Moreover, the study found that attitudes to pair work remained entrenched. Those who preferred pair work at the beginning of the term had similar attitudes at the end of the term. Those who expressed a preference to work alone did not enjoy pair work and nor did they view it as a valuable learning experience. These findings corroborate to some extent the findings of my own study, discussed next.

In a longitudinal study (2004, 2009), which adopted a sociocultural theoretical perspective, I considered the trajectory in learners' attitudes to pair work as it unfolded over time and, more importantly, the relationship between these attitudes and action. The study was conducted over a semester (12 weeks). The students worked in the same self-selected pairs throughout the semester on three types of writing tasks: a composition, an editing exercise and then a text reconstruction. One version of each task was completed in pairs and another individually. All the pair talk was audio recorded. In order to collect data about the learners' attitudes to pair work, the students completed a modified version of Kinsella's (1996) Classroom Work Style survey at the beginning of the study. The survey elicited the students' preferences for individual, pair and small group work by providing them with a set of statements that they had to agree or disagree with (see Storch, 2009). The students were then interviewed on four occasions, after the completion of each task cycle and at the end of the study. The interview data together with the recordings of the pair talk provided a source of rich data about the interplay between attitudes and behaviour and changes in attitudes over time in the case of one learner. I focus here on the data of three participants: Mai and Charley who formed a collaborative relationship and Tanako who was the passive participant in a dominant/passive relationship she formed with Victor (see Storch, 2002, 2009).

Charley had positive attitudes to pair work from the outset. This was evident in his completed survey and his interviews. He stated in the first interview: 'Group working and many can share my opinions with others I think that's very good.' These positive sentiments were expressed in each of the subsequent interviews. Charley's views were shaped by his underlying beliefs about the best way of learning an L2. He believed that language is learnt via interaction:

> English cannot learn by by oneself by myself yes ... have to like consult with other people ...[Final interview]

Charley's responses on the survey show that he came to the activity with positive attitudes to pair work. These positive attitudes explain his behaviour. Charley engaged fully with the activities, offering opinions, counter opinions, and repairs (see Storch, 2002 and Chapter 4). The interview data show that his positive attitudes were reinforced by his experience of working collaboratively with Mai.

Mai, his partner in the pair work throughout the semester, also showed a preference for pair work over individual work on the survey. However, in her initial interview she expressed some reservations. Although she noted in her first interview (after the composition task) that group and pair work affords learners some benefits, she noted that such benefits depend on the partner in the pair work:

> I ... think it's better for us to work in pairs but sometime ... it depend on the individual between the two partners ... [Interview 1]

In the second interview she still expressed reservation about pair work, preferring to work alone despite recognising the benefits of pair work:

> I think it's ... it's better for me ... ah .. to discuss together but sometimes I like to do ... to do individually yeah.. [Interview 2]

However, in the final interview she expressed positive attitudes about pair work, noting that it is helpful for learning grammar:

> I like to work in pairs ... I think it's better, yeah ...it's better for me ... sometimes we have lack of grammar knowledge or ... some rule of grammar yeah ... so if we have in pair we can discuss together yeah .... [Final interview]

Unlike Charlie, Mai's attitudes towards collaborative writing changed over time. The survey, with its list of predetermined statements, did not reveal her reservations about group and pair work. The reservations became evident in the initial interview. However, her reservations were perhaps overcome by the positive experience of working with Charlie. She saw the benefits in terms of the suggestions he offered and perhaps in reflecting on what she had learnt. Thus her experience and her reflections on the experience of collaborative writing led to belief change.

Tanako, who worked with Victor, was a passive participant who contributed very little to the collaborative writing activities throughout the semester (see Storch, 2002, 2009). In the survey, Tanako showed a strong preference for individual work over group and pair work. During the course of the interviews, although Tanako mentioned some of the potential benefits of pair work, she continued to express a strong preference for individual work. She explained in the very first interview that she preferred to work alone because of her lack of confidence in her writing skills:

> because I don't know if I'm right or not and I'm a bit feel nervous writing in front of people as well because my spelling is might be bad or ... [Interview 1]

In all the subsequent interviews she reiterated her sense of lack of confidence and preference to work alone. Tanako's views concerning pair work simply became entrenched over time and her way of coping with working in a dispreferred mode (collaboration) was to simply disengage and contribute little to the activity. Gutiérrez and Stone (2000) refer to such actions as counterscripts: actions by students that contradict or resist the teacher's goals. As in Aragão's (2011) study, discussed previously, Tanako's beliefs about her own writing abilities affected her behaviour. At the same time, the dominant/passive relationship she formed with Victor perpetuated her beliefs.

Breen (1987) argues that if a task confronts a learner with psychological and social uncertainty, the learner will endeavour to reduce that uncertainty and restore personal equilibrium by whatever means possible. In this case, Tanako's passivity can be seen to represent an attempt to restore her equilibrium rather than expose her perceived deficiencies. Breen also notes that learners' assumptions about their own knowledge and ability may well diverge from external criteria such as test scores (see also Watanabe & Swain, 2008). In this dyad, although Victor was more fluent orally, his writing proficiency score was in fact lower than Tanako's.

Thus the study showed that learners' attitudes to pair work were related to their views concerning pair work in general, their beliefs about language learning as well as their estimation of their own L2 abilities. These beliefs and the actual experience of working in pairs shaped and reshaped their attitudes and could either lead to an entrenchment of these beliefs, or to changes over time. These findings show that the relationship between beliefs, attitudes and actions, as was noted in the previous discussion of language learning beliefs, is complex and unpredictable.

Clearly more research is needed about the attitudes of learners (and teachers) to collaborative writing in order to gain a better understanding of learners' observed behaviour and language learning outcomes of collaborative writing tasks. This research needs to be informed by current approaches to research on language learning beliefs in which beliefs are investigated in context, using a range of tools, beyond surveys, and which take into account the interaction between beliefs and actions. Attitudes towards collaborative writing may begin with individual beliefs shaped by prior educational experiences and/or beliefs about one's own abilities. However, attitudes, like beliefs are not stable. They are socially constructed and dynamic and as such we need to investigate how they evolve over time during and on reflection about collaborative writing activities. Such research is more likely to be able to capture the complex and dynamic nature of these attitudes and perceptions, and be sufficiently sensitive to measure any nuanced changes in the learners' language learning beliefs and attitudes over time, as learners experience collaborative writing activities.

7 Computer Mediated Collaborative Writing

Introduction

Thus far, the discussion of collaborative writing has focused on face-to-face collaboration. In this chapter I consider collaborative writing activities in computer mediated environments. The advent of the internet age and particularly developments in web applications have revolutionalised the way we create, communicate and share information with each other (McLoughlin & Lee, 2007; Myers, 2010; Warschauer & Grimes, 2007). First-generation web applications include emails, chat rooms and discussion boards. Second-generation web (Web 2.0) applications include podcasts, blogs, wikis and Google Docs as well as various social networking sites (e.g. Facebook, YouTube). The key distinction between these two web generations is that whereas earlier web applications allow publishing information; Web 2.0 applications also allow for more interactive participation in the creation and the sharing of information (Warschauer & Grimes, 2007). These web applications have received growing interest across all sectors of education (for an overview see McLoughlin & Lee, 2007; Parker & Chao, 2007) and across a diverse range of subject areas, including L2 classes. In L2 classes, computer mediated communication has been embraced because it is seen as providing learners with more opportunities to practice and to communicate in the L2 beyond the time constraints of the onsite classroom (Ortega, 2007).

Although various computer mediated communication (CMC) technologies have been employed in research with L2 learners since the mid 1990s (see review in Thorne, 2008), most of this research has been informed by the interaction hypothesis, with researchers examining the quantity of negotiation sequences, often comparing them to face-to-face negotiations to determine whether CMC facilitates more negotiations. The technologies used in these studies have tended to be first generation web applications, predominantly chat programmes, and the tasks used generally did not require the production of written texts (beyond the written chats). There is a relatively small body of research on CMC where L2 learners complete a collaboratively writing task and where their chats are analysed for the nature of languaging (LRE) episodes. The first section reviews this body of research.

The focus then shifts to the use of Web 2.0 technology, and in particular the use of wikis. Wikis are hailed as platforms for collaborative writing and hence form the main focus of this chapter. The second section provides information about the wiki, and the traits that make it a potentially useful tool for educational purposes, and particularly for group projects. This is followed by a review of research on wikis implemented in mainstream education classes. This review highlights some of the lessons that can be learnt from wikis implemented in this context in terms of learner contribution and engagement. The fourth section discusses empirical studies reporting on the implementation of wikis in L2 classes. This discussion considers not only learners' contributions and engagement with peers' contributions, but focuses in particular on the nature of languaging when learners collaborate on a wiki project. The concluding section draws on the research findings in both mainstream education and L2 contexts to suggest briefly how best to implement wiki collaborative writing projects in order to maximise the learning opportunities for learners. These recommendations, as well as areas that require additional investigation, are discussed in greater detail in the final chapter.

First-Generation Web Technology and L2 Collaborative Writing Tasks

Communication using first generation web applications can be synchronous (real time exchanges) or asynchronous (involving a time lag). The presumed advantage of these forms of computer mediated communication (CMC) for language learning stems from the fact that the interaction is text-based. This visual display of the learners' utterances is said to provide greater opportunities for conscious attention and reflection about language (Kern *et al.*, 2004). The visibility of the utterances (theirs and that of their peers) together with the additional processing time means that CMC communication can amplify the opportunities to notice errors, to offer repairs, to self-repair, and to negotiate about language. Furthermore, CMC is said to provide learners with additional time to contribute to a task thus reducing pressure, particularly on shy students, and encouraging all students to participate (Meyer, 2003).

There have been extensive investigations into the language learning potentials of computer mediated communication, including whether they do foster more negotiations (e.g. Blake, 2000; Lee, 2002; Pellettieri, 2000; Smith, 2003, 2005) and participation (e.g. Roed, 2003). These studies have produced conflicting results. A critical review of these studies by Ortega (2009a) concludes that despite the high expectations that CMC would foster high levels of negotiation for meaning, the mounting evidence suggests that this is not necessarily the case. Ortega points out that if the number of turns or time on task is taken into consideration, the number of negotiations in the reported studies often amounts to one or two negotiation sequences per pair for the entire time on task (e.g. see Blake, 2000; Fernández-Garcia & Martínez Arbelaiz, 2003; Lee, 2001). One reason that is offered to explain these low levels of negotiations in CMC is the non-sequential nature of CMC exchanges. For example, Lai and Zhao's (2006) study, conducted with six ESL dyads completing a spot the difference task in face-to-face and CMC modes, reported that in the CMC mode about half the recasts were delayed; provided three or four turns after the error. They were also difficult to notice because they were embedded in long turns. Furthermore, even when negative feedback was offered, it was not always taken up (i.e. repeated). Ortega (2009a) concludes that on the basis of the available empirical evidence, CMC is not necessarily a superior environment for interaction and attention to language than face-to-face interaction.

However, most of the studies on CMC reviewed by Ortega did not require learners to produce a joint or extended text. As such they are similar to investigations of interaction on oral tasks. As I argued in Chapter 2, writing tasks may in fact be a better modality for attention to language form. Studies which have required students to produce collaboratively written texts, using CMC, are relatively rare. Among the few exceptions are the studies by Tan et al. (2010), Zeng and Takatsuka (2009) and Shekary and Tahririan (2006). Each of these studies is discussed briefly. In these studies, informed by sociocultural theoretical perspectives, the focus was predominantly on the nature of the learners' dialogues (i.e. chats or written messages), analysed in terms of LREs.

Tan et al. (2010) investigated the patterns of interaction of the same pairs of learners in face-to-face and in computer mediated communication (CMC). In the study, six pairs of beginner learners of Chinese completed collaboratively two similar versions of seven writing tasks over a ten-week term. One task version was completed using pen and paper in a face-to-face mode in the regular classroom; the other in a computer mediated mode, using MSN messenger outside class time. The study found that most pairs displayed a different pattern in the two modes. However, some patterns were more prevalent in one mode of communication than another. Instances of dominant/passive and expert/novice patterns were more frequent in the face-to-face mode. Instances of a cooperative pattern were found only in the CMC mode. These findings were attributable to the tool used, MSN messenger, and its distinct asynchronous turn taking functions, encouraged cooperation (see Example 3 in Chapter 4), but at the same time discouraged asymmetrical relationships, where one learner contributed more than another (e.g. dominant/passive). Tan et al. (2006) also reported that although CMC may encourage equal participation, it may not necessarily encourage engagement with each other's contributions. In cooperative pairs, there was little evidence of collective scaffolding. The study did not investigate whether the different patterns impacted on language learning gains.

The studies by Zeng and Takatsuka (2009) and by Shekary and Tahririan (2006) investigated the nature of LREs generated by CMC as well as the impact on language learning, using tailor made immediate and delayed post-tests. In Zeng and Takatsuka's study, eight pairs of intermediate level EFL learners in China completed four collaborative writing tasks using the chat function of Moodle to communicate with each other. The learners' online chat logs were coded for LREs, noting the focus of these LREs and the nature of their resolution (successful vs. unsuccessful). The researchers reported a high occurrence of LREs, averaging 27 per pair. Discrete knowledge post-tests (e.g. fill-in-the blank, translation) were developed on the basis of these LREs. The researchers found that the immediate and delayed post-tests showed very high scores (over 70%), with test items that were successfully resolved in the LREs showing higher accuracy rates (well over 77%) on the post-tests. The researchers attributed the high test scores to the tool. They suggested that the text-based medium of communication (chats) amplified learners' attention to linguistic forms and facilitated collective scaffolding. Another important factor was the students' attitudes to the tasks and the mode of communication. The students' responses to a survey conducted at the end of the study showed that the students enjoyed the online collaborative writing experience, were willing to offer assistance to each other, viewed the text as a joint responsibility, and were satisfied with the co-authored work they submitted. An additional important factor that could explain both the large number of LREs found in the data and the evidence for language learning, not considered by the researchers, is that the task used was a collaborative writing task.

Shekary and Tahririan's (2006) study extended the investigation of the links between LREs and language learning gains by analysing LREs for a range of traits. The study was conducted with 16 Persian EFL learners of intermediate to advanced proficiency who were paired to yield mixed-proficiency pairs. The pairs completed three tasks: dictogloss, jigsaw and a free discussion task, using online chats. The authors do not specify whether the jigsaw required learners to complete a written text. Chat logs were analysed for LREs, but the analysis was quite detailed, beyond focus and nature of resolution. For example, the researchers analysed all LREs for length of LRE, how it was initiated, the complexity of the negotiations (whether it consisted of one or two moves or several moves), and whether there was evidence of uptake. The dyad specific tests, developed on the basis of the LREs, tested explicit knowledge (e.g. provide a definition, amend incorrect use).

The researchers found a large number of LREs in their chat data, averaging 90 per dyad, which they too attributed to the text-based nature of the chat interactions. It should be noted, however, that the number of LREs reported per dyad was for all three tasks. There was no mention of which of the tasks generated more LREs. In the immediate post-test, most learners remembered just over 70% of the linguistic items that they had discussed in their LREs. In the delayed post-test they remembered 56.7%. Correct resolution was found to be an important variable. A greater proportion of items that were correctly resolved in the LREs were also correctly remembered in the post-tests compared to linguistic items arising from incorrectly resolved or unresolved LREs. Using a series of regression analyses, the researchers found that the LRE trait that best predicted L2 learning in this context was successful uptake. Thus the researchers concluded that learning is most likely to take place when two conditions are fulfilled: the LRE is resolved correctly and the learner incorporates the correctly resolved form in their output (coded as uptake). These results conflict with the findings reported by Smith (2004, 2005) who found no relationship between uptake and gain scores in a study which analysed CMC interactions of ESL students on a jigsaw and a decision-making task.

Shekary and Tahririan (2006) provide little information about their study design. It is not clear what role writing had in their study, and whether the inclusion of a writing task, such as a dictogloss, encouraged uptake. The authors did observe that their learners were actively engaged with the tasks, and paid much attention to language; and that, for example, at the end of a task, sometimes learners commented on each other's errors. Again, it is hard to know whether the type of tasks used encouraged such attention to language.

The results of these studies accord with those reported in studies on face-to-face collaborative writing. They highlight the importance of factors such as the relationships learners form, the nature of LRE engagement, and in turn the importance of successful LRE resolution and level of engagement in reaching such resolutions for language gains. However, it is interesting to note that Zeng and Takatsuka (2009) and Shekary and Tahririan (2006) comment on the large number of LREs found in their studies, but compare these to LREs reported in studies using oral face-to-face activities (e.g. Williams, 1999), rather than studies employing collaborative writing tasks. Indeed, in all three studies, there is very little discussion on the potential impact that employing tasks requiring the production of a written text had on the LREs generated. There is also very little discussion in all three studies on the nature of the written text the learners produced. This absence may be because the technological tools used, such as chats, are tools of communication rather than tools designed for text creation. Web 2.0 tools, and especially wikis and Google Docs, are designed primarily to encourage collaborative text creation.

Second-Generation Technology (Web 2.0) and Collaborative Writing Tasks

Of all Web 2.0 technologies, wikis and blogs are arguably the most commonly used Web 2.0 tools in education. These two applications differ, however, in terms of authorship and readers (for an extended discussion of the main differences between wikis and blogs, see Elola & Oskoz, 2011; McLoughlin & Lee, 2007; Parker & Chao, 2007; Warschauer & Grimes, 2007). Briefly, a blog (web log) is typically authored by a single author and resembles a personal journal in which the author shares his/her views (or drafts of their papers) with a selected community. The most successful blogs tend to have a strong individual authorial voice (Warschauer & Grimes, 2007). Readers of the blog can read and comment on the blog, but cannot change the originally posted material. A wiki, on the other hand, is an application which has been principally established to enable a group of people to create a document (Leuf & Cunningham, 2001). Unlike the blog, it allows anyone to modify the content that has been placed on the wiki page and add new pages. As such it is the wiki that is the most relevant technology for collaborative writing and the main focus of this chapter.

Defining traits of wikis

The wiki is a special type of web page (or a collection of interlinked webpages) based on a hypertext system of storing and modifying information. A wiki allows multiple users to create and amend a jointly produced document (Leuf & Cunningham, 2001). The most well-known example of a collaboratively produced wiki is Wikipedia, an internet-based, user-generated encyclopaedia.

There are a number of different wiki sites (e.g. PBWiki.com, Wikispaces) and wiki engines (e.g. MediaWiki) which are available at low or no cost for educational (or non-profit) use. Although these sites and engines have some unique features that may make them more suitable for particular teaching environments (e.g. ability to upload images see Augar *et al.*, 2004), most seem to share a set of features which make them attractive for use in collaborative group projects. These features include an easily created and edited web page, a history log, and a discussion space.

Wiki pages can be created and edited from any web browser without any specialised technical knowledge or a programming language. The wiki is an asynchronous tool; that is, interaction between participants is delayed, and only one user can edit a page at any one time. However, all participants in a wiki project have equal access to the most recent version of the wiki page. Editing the wiki page can be open to the public (e.g. Wikipedia) or be limited to a select group of password-enabled users. In educational projects, the latter seems the preferred option.

The two other important features of wikis are the history log and discussion space. The history log tracks the time and content of contributions and edits, using different colour fonts to distinguish between deletions and insertions. It provides contributors the opportunities to review the evolution of the wiki page and to retrieve earlier versions if subsequent edits need to be undone. An equally important feature is the discussion space. This space is linked to each wiki page and enables users to post text-based messages about the page content and/or any revisions made. In this way, producing wikis can be accompanied by comments, discussion and annotations.

This combination of features suggests that wikis have the potential to facilitate collaborative online learning and this is certainly the claim made by a number of authors (e.g. Augar *et al.*, 2004; Godwin-Jones, 2003; McLoughlin & Lee, 2007). Godwin-Jones (2003: 15), for example, sees wikis as 'intensely collaborative'. The ease of posting and editing wiki pages is assumed to encourage contributions and engagement with each other's contributions (Wheeler *et al.*, 2008). Wikis are said to enhance writing skills and to encourage revisions (Chao & Lo, 2011). This is because participants in wiki projects are both authors and editors, reading critically the postings of their peers' contributions (see Matthew *et al.*, 2009), and also because their own texts become more publicly accessible. Wikis, designed for multiple users, are also seen by some (e.g. Jones, 2010; Osman-Schlegel *et al.*, 2011) as providing students with preparation for the kind of multiple-authored reports they are likely to encounter in the workplace.

Wikis also enable instructors to address one of the well-documented difficulties of group projects, that of unequal contributions (see Boud *et al.*, 2001; Johnson & Johnson, 1994; Slavin, 1992). The terms often used to describe this phenomenon is 'social loafing' or 'free riding', both imply that some members of a group do not contribute equally to the effort expanded, and yet get credit for the group effort. The history logs in a wiki, which provide an audit trail, can be a way of addressing the issue. By using the history logs, instructors can track and thereby assess each student's contributions to the wiki group project (see for example Elgort *et al.,* 2008).

There has been a growing literature on the implementation of wikis in the educational sector, and particularly higher education, since the early 2000s. There are reports on wiki projects in a diverse range of university courses (see Table 7.1), in distance learning courses (e.g. Augar *et al.,* 2004), as well as in hybrid courses which combine face-to-face and online components (e.g. Elgort *et al.,* 2008; Jones, 2010). In the school sector, a smaller number of accounts are available detailing the implementation of a wiki (e.g. Engstrom & Jewett, 2005; Grant, 2006). There has also been a growing awareness of the educational possibilities of wikis for L2 learning, with reports on how wikis can be incorporated into L2 classes (e.g. Ducate, *et al.,* 2011), and how they can be assessed (Elola & Oskoz, 2011).

In the following two sections I critically evaluate empirical research on the use of wikis in collaborative writing projects. I begin with research conducted in mainstream education (i.e. L1 context) across different subject disciplines. I then discuss in greater depth studies on wikis in the L2 context, focusing in particular on what we can learn about wiki collaborative writing as a tool for L2 learning.

Research on Wikis in Mainstream Education (L1 Context)

As noted in the previous section, wikis seem to hold much promise as collaborative learning platforms. However, empirical research in mainstream classes that can substantiate these promises is relatively scarce. Descriptive reports, based on teachers' and students' reflections on their experiences with wikis, are mixed. Rick and Guzdial (2006), for example, provide a detailed report on the varying success of implementing a range of wiki projects across different fields of study at their university. They report on very successful wiki projects implemented in architecture and English composition classes; but failed projects in engineering and mathematics classes, where students were prepared to accept a fail grade rather than participate in a wiki project.

Table 7.1 summarises information about 16 empirical studies on wiki collaborative writing projects that I refer to in this section. The information provided includes the context (e.g. type of course), tasks, and implementation conditions (where given). It includes details such as whether there was any

126 Collaborative Writing in L2 Classrooms

Table 7.1 Research on wiki collaborative writing projects in L1 contexts

Study	Context	Task and assessment	Implementation	Tools/Data
Alyousef & Picard (2011)	N = 6 (case study) Accounting	2 tasks in enquiry-based scenario: (i) response to questions (ii) report (both assessed)	Preparation: assessment criteria; students directed to You Tube clip Team: 6 students Duration: 5 wks	Discussion pages, Report, Surveys Interview (1 tutor and 1 student)
Bower et al. (2006)	N = 57 (2 classes) Info Tech	Class 1: response to questions Class 2: group project (both assessed)	Minimal training Class 1: whole class Class 2: teams of 2–5 Duration: semester	Surveys Interviews with academics Observation
Carr et al. (2007)	N = 174 Political Science	Essay: Intro & conclusion completed collaboratively, other parts individually	Introduction sessions + templates Teams: 4–6 Tutor allocated to ensure diversity Duration: 4 wks	Wiki logs + interviews (with students and staff) Observations
Cole (2009)	N = 75 Info Systems	Knowledge repository on set topics (materials posted used to create exam question)	Information on wikis incorporated into weekly classes Whole cohort Duration: 10 wks	Surveys and group interviews

Study	Participants	Task	Process	Data collection
Elgort et al. (2008)	N = 27, 2 courses in Info Managt	Course 1: report on 5 articles; Course 2: Web-based guide (both assessed)	Course 1: random allocation; Course 2: self-selected	Surveys; Lecturers' reflections
Grant (2006); Grant (2009): case study	3 high school classes (Year 9)	History-based research project	Intro on wiki software; Teams: 6–9; Teacher allocated; Duration: 3 wks	Focus gp Interviews, surveys; Wiki discussion logs and text
Hughes & Narayan (2009)	N = 19, 2 courses: Media	Course 1: cumulative key terms glossary; Course 2: Assignment archive of individual & small groups	Duration: semester	Survey
Jones (2010)	N = 68, Social work	Account of a major feature of a theory (assessed: including collab)	Guide to wikis posted on subject website; Trial wiki site – to provide practice; Teams: 6–7 (allocated – mixed campus and online students)	Observations; Discussion board logs (tools vague)

(continued)

Table 7.1 (Continued)

Study	Context	Task and assessment	Implementation	Tools/Data
Judd et al. (2010)	N = 772 Psychology	Scholarly summary of key concepts (assessed: individual contributions)	Introduce wiki via discussion board activities Teams: 20–30 Duration: 6 wks	Wiki discussion logs
Lin & Kelsey (2009)	N = 18 Education	Write or edit 5 articles	3 staged project: individual Collaboration Peer review Guidelines provided (2nd stage) Teams assigned by instructor to ensure heterogeneity	Interviews, surveys, reflective journals
Matthew et al. (2009)	N = 37 Teacher trainees	Amend existing wiki course content (assessed)	Introduced in lecture + handouts Teams: 2–3 self-selected Duration: semester	Wiki pages, diaries, Interviews Emails observations
Neumann & Hood (2009)	N = 52 wikis (n = 25); indiv(n = 27) Statistics	Reports (Not assessed)	Preparation: minimal (15 minutes) Teams: 4–6, self-selected Duration: 6 wks	Surveys Tests Wikis vs. individual reports

Osman-Schlegel et al. (2011)	N = 180 Archit.	Reports (Assessed: Individual grades based on contribution + peer & self-evaluation)	lecture on wikis Teams: 10 (1 member assigned as project manager) Duration: 10 wks	Surveys
Rick & Guzdial (2006)	4 disciplines (Archit, English, Science, Media) – focus on 2 cases	English composition: essays, summaries Engineering/Maths: evaluating simulations (both assessed)	Science/tech: 2 entire classes	Surveys
Witney & Smallbone (2011)	N = 153 Business	Group project (assessed)	Workshops on using wikis + guide available Team: 4	Surveys Observations Wiki postings

training of students prior to using wikis, whether the wiki projects were assessed, the size of the teams used and how they were set up, and the duration of the project. The table also lists the tools used by these studies to collect data. It should be noted that the studies listed are not, by any means, a comprehensive list of all studies on the use of wikis. However, they do seem to reflect the main findings reported in research on wikis. The table excludes accounts of wiki functionalities (e.g. Augur et al., 2004) and descriptive accounts of wiki implementations (e.g. Engstrom & Jewett, 2005). It also excludes studies where wikis were used only as a space to store individual assignments or only for peer editing activities (e.g. Wheeler et al., 2008).

The table shows that the emerging research on wikis has been conducted mostly with adult learners in the higher education sector. Studies on the use of wikis with adolescent learners in the school sector are still relatively rare (for exceptions see Grant, 2006). What stands out in reading these research reports is their diversity in terms of tasks and implementation conditions. This diversity makes comparison between studies difficult.

The tasks that have been used in the reported wiki projects include scholarly summaries (e.g. Judd et al., 2010), student generated glossaries of important terms (e.g. Hughes & Narayan, 2009); reports and course guides (e.g. Elgort et al., 2008); and amendments of existing documents (e.g. Matthew et al., 2009). Some reported wiki projects combined individual and team wiki pages. For example, in Carr et al. (2007), the political science students completed essays where only the introduction and conclusion were crafted collaboratively. In the Hughes and Narayan (2009) study, the glossary of important terms was based on cumulative individual postings.

Assessment practices also vary. In some studies, the group wikis were assessed with assessment rubrics emphasising the cohesiveness of the document (e.g. Elgort et al., 2008), in others students' individual contributions rather than the entire wiki were assessed (e.g. Alyousef & Picard, 2011; Judd et al., 2010) and in some other studies, the wikis were completed for practice only (e.g. Neumann & Hood, 2009). As noted later in this section, assessment practices may affect learners' motivation to contribute to a wiki project.

In terms of implementation, there are variations in the preparation provided prior to implementing wikis, the time given to complete the wikis, and the size of the groups. Preparations, particularly with Science and Information Technology students seem quite minimal (e.g. Bower et al., 2006), presumably because such students are assumed to be technologically savvy. In other studies, preparation and technical support is extensive, and includes practice sessions (e.g. Jones, 2010; Witney & Smallbone, 2011). The duration of the projects range from a few weeks (e.g. Carr et al., 2007; Grant, 2006) to semester long wiki projects (e.g. Matthew et al., 2009; Osman-Schlegel et al., 2011).

Group sizes (where reported) range from fairly large groups of 20 to 30 (e.g. Judd *et al.*, 2010) to middle size groups of about six students per group (e.g. Alyousef & Picard, 2011; Jones, 2010) to smaller groups composed of around three members (e.g. Matthew *et al.*, 2009). Large and middle size groups seem to predominate. One reason given for having large groups is that it mirrors 'the real world' writing situation, where teams responsible for producing a report can be quite large (Osman-Schlegel *et al.*, 2011). Allocation into groups in several studies (e.g. Carr *et al.*, 2007; Grant, 2006; Lin & Kelsey, 2009) was determined by the instructor with the expressed intent of ensuring within-group diversity, but in other studies, groups self-selected (e.g. Elgort *et al.*, 2008; Neumann & Hood, 2009). Group size and allocation practices may produce different group dynamics.

The studies vary in terms of research design and tools used to collect data. Most studies collect questionnaire data, but it is the more recent studies that supplement these data with an examination of the postings on the wiki discussion logs (e.g. Judd *et al.*, 2010) and learners' contributions to the wiki texts (e.g. Witney & Smallbone, 2011). There are two main strands in the extant body of research on wikis in mainstream education:

(i) students' perceptions of wiki projects;
(ii) contributions to wikis and engagement with each other's contributions.

A discussion of the key findings for each of these strands is presented below.

L1 students' perceptions of wiki projects

Students' perceptions, elicited via questionnaires and interviews, seem generally positive about the experience of working with wikis (e.g. Elgort *et al.*, 2008; Jones, 2010; Lin & Kelsey, 2009; Matthew *et al.*, 2009). As with any new technology, wikis are perceived by students as offering a welcome element of novelty (e.g. Elgort *et al.*, 2008), as well as posing some challenges. The students surveyed expressed some frustration with the technology (e.g. Jones, 2010) and confusion about what was expected of them in creating wiki documents (e.g. Lin & Kelsey, 2009). Although wikis are by design user-friendly, they still seem to require advanced levels of computer literacy (Osman-Schlegel *et al.*, 2011) as well as time to become familiar with the technology (Lin & Kelsey, 2009).

In surveys, students identify a number of benefits of wiki projects. For example, in Lin and Kelsey's (2009) study, the students noted that wikis afforded them the opportunities to exchange ideas and thus enhanced their creativity. In a study which elicited both students' and instructors' views about wikis, Elgort et al. (2008) found that the students found wikis useful for organising and for exchanging information, and the instructors found wikis useful in managing and marking group work.

However, not all researchers report such positive students' attitudes to wiki projects. In the study conducted by Carr et al. (2007), with political science students, only a small minority of students were positive about their wiki experience. A significant number of students in Osman-Schlegel et al.'s (2011) study commented that they found the wikis a difficult task, particularly owing to group dynamics and the large group size (10 per group). Elgort et al. (2008) reported that despite their students' positive views, when asked, many of the students indicated a preference to work alone rather than in groups. Witney and Smallbone (2011), who offered their business students an option to use wikis in their collaborative group assignment, found that most groups chose not to use wikis, and even those who did were not using them a great deal.

These attitudes may be shaped to some extent by the level and nature of contributions of peers to the wiki projects (discussed below), as well as more general views about collaborative writing and group work per se (see discussion in Chapter 6).

Contributions and engagement

Given that wikis are touted as collaborative writing platforms which encourage contributions and engagement, of greater interest are studies reporting on the frequency of contributions to wiki projects, and on the level of engagement with peers' contributions. In studies that elicited students' reflections on their wiki project via surveys and interviews, learners admitted to being reluctant to post contributions and to engage with each other's contributions, particularly in the early stages of the wiki project (e.g. Lin & Kelsey, 2009). Furthermore, even when learners contributed, contributions were not evenly distributed among group members (e.g. Carr et al., 2007; Elgort et al., 2008; Neumann & Hood, 2009). For example, in the Elgort et al. (2008) study, only half of the students surveyed felt that all members of their group contributed equally to their wiki project. However, as Jones (2010) points out, uneven contribution is a common problem in group projects, regardless of whether or not technology is utilised.

This body of research also suggests that engagement with each other's contributions is rare. For example, in a survey conducted by Hughes and Narayan (2009), the students admitted that they never viewed their peers' contributions, nor did they review their own contributions once posted and were thus unaware of whether their contributions had been edited by their peers. The majority of the learners claimed to have edited their peers' contributions on very few occasions (one to three occasions) throughout the semester-long project.

Given that many of the studies reporting on students' contributions and engagement are perception-based studies (e.g. Hughes & Narayan, 2009; Jones, 2010; Matthew et al., 2009; Neumann & Hood, 2009); that is, based on participants' self reports elicited via questionnaires and interviews (see Table 7.1), it could be argued that they do not necessarily reflect accurately the students' frequency of contributions and level of engagement. However, studies which supplemented questionnaire and interview data with a systematic analysis of wiki postings confirm that peer editing is rare (e.g. Carr et al., 2007; Elgort et al., 2008; Grant, 2006, 2009; Judd et al., 2010). For example, in a large scale study ($N = 174$), Carr et al. (2007) found that a minority of the students (less than 30%) were responsible for most of the edits and comments found in the log files, despite all students being encouraged to comment on each other's contributions. In another large scale study ($N = 772$), Judd et al. (2010) found that a relatively small number of their students created most of the wiki content. The researchers found that only 10% of the students were very productive, contributing over 40% of the total texts. The researchers also found that many of the editing comments (29%) were superficial, resulting in no or little changes to the content.

Furthermore, peer editing when it does occur, is not necessarily welcome. Grant (2006), reporting on a wiki project implemented in a high school in the UK, found that the one instance when a student edited another site, the editing was met with hostility, and the original authors reinstated their original text. Older students may display similar sentiments. In Wheeler et al.'s study (2008), university students in education, who used wikis as a site for peer editing, admitted that they were willing to contribute to a wiki, but were averse to having their contributions amended by other group members.

Whether students utilise the discussion function of the wikis is rarely mentioned in research reports. Judd et al. (2010) mentioned that there were very few comments posted on the discussion pages. Communication between participants using the discussion function of the wiki seems more likely when such communication is explicitly specified in the assignment instructions. For example, Osman-Schlegel et al.'s (2011) students were explicitly encouraged to use the discussion page to discuss, exchange ideas or make suggestions before choosing as a group what to include in their submitted wiki assignment. In the surveys, many students commented positively on this form of communication. However, it should be noted that in this project, group members also met face-to-face and the discussions that occurred in the face-to-face format was then uploaded into the discussion page, to enable those who were unable to meet to be informed of what was discussed. Witney and Smallbone (2011) reported that the students' preferred means of communication when working on group projects were face-to-face, mobile phones, and emails.

Thus it seems that the affordances provided by wiki to co-construct a wiki text are not necessarily taken advantage of. Reluctance to contribute and to engage with each other's contributions, whether by editing the pages or communicating via the discussion page, has been attributed to a number of affective factors such as lack of confidence and motivation (e.g. Cole, 2009). There were also more pragmatic factors reported such as timing. A number of authors found that students completed their wiki projects at the last minute (e.g. Alyousef & Picard, 2011; Carr et al., 2007; Judd et al., 2010), and thus there was very little time or opportunity to engage with each other's contributions.

The nature of the task and how the task is assessed can also explain lack of contribution and engagement in wiki projects. Tasks such as whole class response to questions (e.g. Bower et al., 2006) or the creation of a glossary of terms (e.g. Hughes & Narayan, 2009) lack authenticity as group projects, and thus do not seem to be well disposed to a collaborative effort. Assessment practices are also an important consideration. Studies where students are graded on their individual contribution seem to encourage a division of labour rather than co-construction (e.g. Alyousef & Picard, 2011; Judd et al., 2010).

Rick and Guzdial (2006) highlight the importance of the wider educational context for the success of wiki projects. In their report, the failure of wiki projects in mathematics and engineering classes was attributed to the nature of assessment tasks and class culture. In courses where assessment tends to be based on single answer assignments, and where competition and individual rather than collective effort are strongly promoted, introducing wiki collaborative projects is unlikely to succeed. An educational system which promotes and rewards individual effort cultivates notions of individual text ownership and intellectual property. Such notions can explain students' reluctance to amend their peers' postings, as well as displeasure at having their own postings amended. Individual postings are viewed as individual property, out of bounds for uninvited peer amendments. Grant's study (2006, 2009) provided clear evidence of the hostility students felt towards amendments made to their postings. Thus, despite the fact that wikis are designed to promote a sharing and co-construction of texts, these design features cannot overcome deeply entrenched notions of individual text ownership.

The size of the group may also affect notions of shared ownership. In Judd et al.'s study (2010), groups contained 20–30 students; in Cole's (2009) and in Rick and Guzdial's (2006) studies, entire classes formed the teams working on the wiki. In such relatively large groups, notions of ownership may be very diffused. In the Osman-Schlegel *et al.* (2011) study, where groups of 10 students were assigned to work on wiki projects, led by a project manager, a significant number of the students commented that the groups were too large to work effectively. However, even in projects utilising smaller groups of four to six members (e.g. Carr *et al.*, 2007; Neumann & Hood, 2009), co-construction did not necessarily occur. Neumann and Hood (2009) in fact recommended using large wiki groups, so as to lessen the impact of a lack of participation by one or two students.

Contributions and engagement, however, may increase over time, as learners become more familiar with each other and thus develop trust. For example, Lin and Kelsey's (2009) study, conducted with graduate education students, identified three distinct phases in the life of a wiki project. The phases were entitled: Exploration (a crisis of authority), Adaptation (a crisis of relationship), and Collaboration (a resolution of crisis).

The first phase (Exploration) was characterised by confusion about what was expected and lack of comfort with peer editing, tied to notions of individual text ownership. In this early phase, the participants did not share a sense of joint ownership that would permit them to edit each other's contributions. They felt territorial about their own contributions, and respectful of the boundaries of others' work. The initial product was a text composed of distinct individual contributions, reflecting a cooperative enterprise rather than a collaborative enterprise. After the first wiki was submitted and the work was found to be of poor quality, the instructor provided more guided instructions on how to co-construct a wiki. In the phase that followed (Adaptation), participants began to communicate more effectively in both face-to-face and online modes. The participants also reported increased comfort in using the technology and more willingness to edit each other's contributions. However, peer editing was still scarce. During the final stage (Collaboration), once the participants had the opportunity to build a trusting relationship, they reported (in interviews, surveys and reflective journals) that they were more comfortable with peer editing. The frequency of communication and of co-authoring increased.

Conclusion on L1 studies

Although wikis include features that are designed to facilitate collaboration, the research findings suggest that their use does not necessarily encourage collaborative learning behaviour; that is, the co-construction of ideas. As Hughes and Narayan (2009), among many others (e.g. Jones, 2007;

Neumann & Hood, 2009) point out, a wiki may be a collaborative writing platform, but unless it is enacted collaboratively, it may become merely a static information collection tool.

In order to improve the level of contribution and engagement in wiki group projects some scholars recommend paying careful attention to the wiki task design, the size of the groups, and the assessment rubrics. A number of researchers also call for longer projects and training students for such projects (e.g. Grant, 2006, 2009; Neumann & Hood, 2009). However, as Judd *et al.* (2010) point out, careful design and training may help to improve levels of contributions, but are unlikely to resolve students' underlying reluctance to collaborate. Research suggests that the bigger challenge for educators wishing to implement wikis in their instructional programmes is how to ensure that the collaboration promoted by wikis aligns with the underlying classroom culture.

As noted in the section that follows, many of the findings reported in studies conducted with L2 students are similar to those reported in L1 studies. Thus the recommendations made by L1 researchers are just as relevant to instructors wishing to implement successful wiki writing projects in their L2 classes.

Wikis in L2 Classes

The earliest reports on the potential of wikis for use in L2 classes appeared in 2005 (e.g. Thorne & Payne, 2005), with a larger number of studies published since 2010. Table 7.2 summarises 18 published empirical studies reporting on the use of wiki collaborative writing projects with L2 students. As in the case of Table 7.1, the list of studies included in the table is not comprehensive. It includes the most often cited studies. It excludes stance papers or overviews of research (e.g. Elola & Oskoz, 2010b, 2011; Li, 2012; Wang & Vásquez, 2012). The table provides information about the context, including the students' L2 proficiency, tasks, implementation, and types of data collected. In many of these studies, these details are omitted, particularly details about pre-task preparation and assessment.

As the table shows, research on wikis in L2 contexts is still quite limited in scope. Many of the published reports are exploratory small-scale studies (e.g. Elola & Oskoz, 2010a; Kost, 2011; Li & Zhu, 2011), often focusing on a single case study (e.g. Bradley *et al.*, 2010; Lee, 2010; Mak & Coniam, 2008). Data collected include surveys and interviews (with only some of the participants), as well as analysis of the archived wiki pages.

As in the case of studies on wikis in L1 contexts, most of the L2 studies have been conducted with university learners. Studies conducted with school

Table 7.2 Research on wiki collaborative writing projects in L2 contexts

Study	Context	Task and assessment	Implementation	Data/tools
Arnold et al. (2009)	N = 54 (3 classes) L2 = German Interm USA, university	Create a resource (on a novel)	Class 1: unguided, teams of 3 Class 2 and 3: guided, teams of 2–4	Survey Archived wiki pages
Bradley et al. (2010)	N = 56 (focus on 1 CS) ESP (Engineering), advanced Sweden, university	4 assignments (exchange ideas, 2 joint texts, peer feedback, (not assessed)	Rationale explained Teams: 2–3 Duration: 7 wks	Archived wiki pages
Chao & Lo (2011)	N = 51 EFL (English majors) Taiwan, university	Staged story script: gp planning, indiv writing, peer review, indiv publishing (assessed: collaboration and contribution)	Sts had prior wiki experience Teams: 4–5 self-selected and elected leader Various means of communication Duration: 5 wks	Surveys
Ducate et al. (2011)	N = 30, from 3 universities A: French B: Spanish C: German 10 sts in each Intermediate USA, university	A: Micropedia of a French book B: Interactive children's book (sub tasks) C: Synthesis of historical and cultural terms from a German novel (sub tasks) All assessed	1 hr training + model task A: teams 2–3 (over 2 months) B: teams 4–5, one designated leader (2 weeks) C: teams 3–4 (6 weeks)	Surveys

(continued)

Table 7.2 (Continued)

Study	Context	Task and assessment	Implementation	Data/tools
Elola & Oskoz (2010a)	N = 8 L2 = Spanish Advanced USA, university	Argumentative essay	Training session for wikis and chats (voice and text) Pairs- assigned similar prof Duration: 15 days	Surveys Chats Essays
Kessler (2009) See also Kessler & Bikowski (2010)	N = 40 EFL Pre-service teachers Mexico, university	A class wiki reflecting on what has been learnt about a key term (culture)	Training session Entire group Duration: 16 wks	Interviews Portions of wikis edited
Kessler et al. (2012)	N = 38 (CSs: 3 groups) EAP Advanced	Research project (using Google docs)	Training Teams: 3–4 Self-selected Duration: 3 wks	Portion of documents contributed
Kost (2011)	N = 8 L2 = German Canada, university	Essays (narrative and expository) (assessed: pair grade)	Pairs (self-selected)	Wiki pages Discussion logs
Kuteeva (2011)	N = 14 EFL Sweden, university	Staged essay: Indiv writing, peer review then posted as group wiki (assessed)	Groups assigned according to topic Duration: 3 wks	Surveys Essays Observations

Lee (2010)	N = 35 (focus: 1 CS) L2 = Spanish Beginners USA, university	4 tasks (story, description, travel plan, letter). Each task staged: drafting, revising, editing publishing (and focusing on the use of certain structures) Assessed (for text quality and collaboration)	Brief training, You Tube video + practice Team: 4–5 Assigned (each team had a high-proficiency learner) Duration: 2–3 wks per stage	Interviews Surveys Wiki pages
Li & Zhu (2011)	N = 9 EFL Intermediate China, university (experimental)	3 tasks: narration, exposition, argument (not assessed)	3 hours training Team: 3 Self-selected Duration: 5 wks	Interviews Archives of wiki pages
Lund (2008) (see also Lund & Smørdal, 2006)	N = 31 EFL Norway, high school (classroom study)	Task based on collective perceptions of USA	Introduction Groups: 2–3 Duration: 2 wks	Videos of classes Surveys Wiki pages
Mak & Coniam (2008)	N = 24 (focus on 1 CS) EFL Low prof. Hong Kong, Middle school	Section of school brochure (assessed)	Training Team: 4 assigned Duration: 6 wks	Wiki pages

(continued)

Table 7.2 (Continued)

Study	Context	Task and assessment	Implementation	Data/tools
Miyazoe & Anderson (2010)	N = 61 EFL Upper interm Japan, university	Wiki tasks: Translation	Blended: simultaneous use of indiv blogs, online forums & wikis Duration: 15 wks	Surveys Interviews Completed tasks, forums
Oskoz & Elola (2012)	N = 16 L2 = Spanish Advanced USA, university	Expository text	Training Means of communication: face to face, chats (text and voice), discussion board and wikis Pairs (on wikis) –assigned Discussion board: bigger groups (4) Duration: 3 wks	Surveys Online journals Chats, discussion board, wiki pages
Zorko (2009)	N = 40 (focus on 1 CS) ESP (Sociology) Advanced Slovenia, university	Research report on problem-solving task	Team: 3	Interviews

age L2 learners are relatively rare (for exceptions see Lund, 2008; Mak & Coniam, 2008). Furthermore, most have been conducted with learners of English as a second or foreign language (see also meta-analysis in Wang & Vásquez, 2012). Studies on the use of wikis with learners of languages other than English have been predominantly with learners of European languages such as Spanish (e.g. Elola & Oskoz, 2010a; Lee, 2010), German (e.g. Arnold et al., 2009; Kost, 2011), and French (e.g. Ducate et al., 2011).

A diversity of tasks and implementation conditions is evident in these studies. Meaning-focused tasks predominate, and choice of task seems to depend very much on the L2 proficiency of the learners. Unlike the tasks that have been used in face-to-face collaborative writing activities, when using wikis the tasks tend to resemble the kind of assessment tasks used in content classes. Hence, whereas in face-to-face collaborative writing, the time given to complete the tasks averages 30 minutes (see Chapter 4), in wiki collaborative writing, the time given is two to three weeks or longer. Argumentative essays and research-based reports have been used with advanced learners (e.g. Elola & Oskoz, 2010a; Kessler et al., 2012; Zorko, 2009) whereas narratives and story scripts with intermediate learners (e.g. Chao & Lo, 2011; Ducate et al., 2011). Some of the tasks have a more explicit focus on language and tend to be used with learners of lower L2 proficiency. For example, Lee (2010), in a study conducted with elementary learners of Spanish, used a number of tasks which required the use of particular grammatical structures or lexical items (e.g. two forms of the Spanish past tense, preterit and imperfect, to produce a narrative). Miyazoe and Anderson (2010), in a study with intermediate EFL learners in Japan, used translation tasks of passages taken from the course book. Assessment information is often not mentioned, or when mentioned, it is quite vague.

In some studies, the wiki task is carefully staged (e.g. Chao & Lo, 2011; Ducate et al., 2011; Lee, 2010), or adopts a mixed approach, allowing individual and group efforts as well as synchronous and asynchronous exchanges via various means of communication, not just the wiki discussion pages (e.g. Chao & Lo, 2011; Oskoz & Elola, 2012). For example, in Chao and Lo's (2011) study, with EFL students in Taiwan, the wiki task (a story script) had five distinct stages: collaborative planning, individual drafting, peer revision (for content) followed by peer editing (for language and mechanics) and finally individual publishing. Furthermore, in the planning stage, which took place either in face-to-face meetings, by phone, MSN messaging or wiki discussion pages, members of the group decided how to divide the story, with each member of the group being responsible for drafting one part of the whole story script. In the publishing stage, each member combined all the individual sections and made them into a complete story. Thus the collaborative aspects of this task were relegated to the planning and editing stages, rather than to the entire writing process. In Lund's (2008) study, with EFL high school learners in Norway, the learners first worked in small groups (of two to three learners) and then posted their contributions to the collective class wiki (about their perception of the USA). Thus the sequencing was from small group face-to-face activity to a larger group wiki activity.

However, in several studies (e.g. Kessler, 2009; Lund, 2008; Mak & Coniam, 2008) the assigned wiki task is totally unstructured, giving students full autonomy in all decisions concerning how to complete the wiki task. For example, in Kessler's (2009) study, the entire class of 40 pre-service EFL students produced a collective definition of the term culture, with little input from the instructor apart from some brief instructions and periodic reminders to contribute and produce an accurate text. In other studies, the content (and staging) is controlled. For example, in Lee's (2010) study, the four wiki assignments had a specified genre (e.g. letter, narrative) and each wiki assignment had four stages (draft, revise, edit, publish), to be completed by a set date. Although the topics were open-ended, the tasks required students to use particular linguistic structures (e.g. an advice letter required students to use the present subjunctive).

Group sizes also vary, although on the whole they tend to be medium-sized teams of around four to six members (e.g. Chao & Lo, 2011; Lee, 2010; Mak & Coniam, 2008) or more commonly small groups comprising two or three members (e.g. Bradley *et al.*, 2010; Elola & Oskoz, 2010a, 2011; Kost, 2011; Li & Zhu, 2011). It is interesting to note that in studies using medium-sized teams, there is a leader assigned by the teacher (e.g. Lee, 2010) or elected by the group (e.g. Chao & Lo, 2011). There are very few reports on the use of wikis with large teams in L2 classes (for an exception see Kessler, 2009).

Five main strands can be identified in this volume of research:

(i) L2 learners' perceptions of wiki-based projects;
(ii) the nature of learners' contributions and engagement;
(iii) focus on language;
(iv) patterns of interaction;
(v) the quality of the collaboratively produced text.

The following sub-sections discuss the main findings of these research strands.

L2 learners' perceptions of wiki projects

L2 Learners' perceptions of wiki collaborative projects is the topic which has received the most research attention to date. As in the case of studies with students in mainstream classes, interview and questionnaire data show that the majority of L2 learners involved in wiki projects are positive about their experience (e.g. Arnold *et al.*, 2009; Chao & Lo, 2011; Ducate *et al.*, 2011; Elola & Oskoz, 2010a; Kost, 2011; Lee, 2010; Lund, 2008; Oskoz & Elola, 2012; Zorko, 2009). Miyazoe and Anderson (2010), who compared learners' attitudes to wikis, blogs and discussion forums, all of which were implemented concurrently, reported that the students preferred wikis to the other two technological tools. Reasons for such positive attitudes include not only the novelty value of the technology (Ducate *et al.*, 2011; Miyazoe & Anderson, 2010), but also the peer assistance available in wiki projects (e.g. Elola & Oskoz, 2010a; Lee, 2010; Lund, 2008; Miyazoe & Anderson, 2010). In a number of studies, students identified access to the wiki pages created by other groups as particularly beneficial (e.g. Kuteeva, 2011; Lund, 2008; Zorko, 2009). This access enabled them to compare their own text with that of others and learn from it.

However, it should be noted that even in studies reporting high student satisfaction with wiki projects, when asked or given the choice, a number of students stated a preference to work on wikis individually rather than in groups (e.g. Ducate, *et al.*, 2011; Elola & Oskoz, 2010a; Lee, 2010). Students in Elola and Oskoz's (2010a) study, who completed one of their assignments individually and another in pairs using wikis, claimed that working individually was preferred because it provided them with an opportunity to develop their own writing style and to work at their own pace. The main causes of students' reported frustrations in wiki projects seem to be unequal and late contributions from other group members (e.g. Ducate *et al.*, 2011; Lee, 2010).

Contributions and engagement

A number of researchers investigating L2 learners' contributions to wiki texts report on unequal contributions by group members (e.g. Ducate *et al.*, 2011; Kessler & Bikowski, 2010; Mak & Coniam, 2008; Oskoz & Elola, 2012). For example, Kessler and Bikowski (2010), in a reanalysis of the data collected by Kessler (2009), found that the majority of their learners (22 out of 40) contributed minimally to the wiki and that the contribution of these learners occurred just before the due date, clearly for compliance purposes. Such late contributions mean that there is very little opportunity for other group members to react to the posting. Unequal contributions and involvement may relate to the size of the group. Large groups (e.g. Kessler & Bikowski, 2010) may experience a greater incidence of what has been termed in the literature on group work 'social loafing'. When wikis are implemented with smaller groups or pairs, unequal contribution seems to be less of an issue (e.g. Kessler et al., 2012; Kost, 2011).

Research on wikis in L2 contexts has tended to analyse much more closely learners' revisions of the wiki text than is the case with research on wikis in L1 (e.g. Arnold et al., 2009; Kessler, 2009; Kessler & Bikowski, 2010; Mak & Coniam, 2009). For example, Arnold et al. (2009) adapted Faigley and Witte's (1981) taxonomy to analyse revisions learners made to the wiki pages. The taxonomy distinguished between three types of changes: formal or surface level changes (e.g. grammatical and lexical revisions, changes to formatting), meaning-preserving changes (minor additions, deletions, substitutions, reordering), and meaning-developing changes (significant content additions and deletions). The researchers found that the majority of revisions were meaning-changing revisions to content followed by surface-level editing. Kessler (2009) analysed the nature of revisions, distinguishing between revisions that focused on content or form. Form-based revisions were further analysed for the type of error corrected, whether the revisions were accurate, and whether they also included some alteration to content. The results of this analysis are discussed in the next sub-section. In the follow-up study, Kessler and Bikowski (2010) focused more closely on revisions to meaning, and categorised these revisions for the type of act: additions, deletions, clarifications/elaborations, synthesis, and additions of links. The researchers reported infrequent synthesis and addition of links.

Reluctance to amend the postings made by peers, reported in research with mainstream students, is also reported in wiki projects with L2 learners, and for the very same reasons. As in Grant's study (2006), conducted with high school learners, the EFL high school students in Lund and Smørdal's (2006) study seemed willing to expand on the contributions of others, rather than improve or amend classmates' contributions. Where amendments occurred, they were mainly in the form of minor linguistic editing rather than amending content. Reporting on the same project, Lund (2008) found that the students also expressed some unhappiness when other students edited or deleted their personal contributions. Lund explains that these attitudes attest to entrenched notions of ownership and individual accountability, notions which are grounded in school assessment practices which promote and reward individual efforts. Such reluctance to revise peers' contributions is not restricted to wikis implemented with high school students. Lee's (2010) study, with EFL adult learners, also found that some students were reluctant to change their peers' ideas without gaining permission from the author of the posting.

Some researchers suggest that a willingness to make changes to the contributions of peers requires the group to develop a sense of text co-ownership.

This sense of co-ownership needs to be given time to develop. For example, Mak and Coniam (2008), in a study conducted with ESL students in Hong Kong over a two month period, noted that initially (in Week 1) the learners simply added ideas to the text posted by a peer. However, over time, as the project progressed, contributions took the form of reorganising and elaborating on each other's postings, thus producing longer texts than these students generally produced in their individual assignments. Similarly, Kessler and Bikowski (2010) identified different phases in the contributions to a wiki over a 16-week period, with each phase reflecting a growing comfort with the wiki. The first phase, entitled build and destroy, was one where contributions took the form of wholesale deletions and additions. It is not clear whether the deletions and additions were made following a careful reading and evaluation of the peers' contributions. This phase occurred in the first two weeks of the project. In the second phase, labelled full collaboration and lasting 10 weeks, there was evidence of elaborations and additions rather than large scale deletions. However, only a minority of students participated in the first two phases of the wiki (13 out of 40). The third phase was when the students engaged in informal reflection on the course, and used the wiki more like a discussion board. It was only in this late phase that 18 students made postings for the first time. However, the researchers noted that the final document did not show evidence of synthesis nor of cohesion. Thus, although time may encourage some form of contribution, it may not necessarily encourage co-construction of the wiki.

Focus on language

In research on wikis with L2 students, it is amendments made to language use which are of particular interest. In order to determine whether wiki collaborative writing is conducive for L2 learning, we need empirical evidence which shows that wikis encourage learners to engage in languaging. That is, we need to see evidence of learners deliberating and reflecting about language use, providing positive as well as corrective feedback, and pooling their linguistic resources to resolve uncertainties about language use, be it vocabulary, grammar or mechanics.

Studies on whether wikis encourage learners to focus on language have in the main only considered whether learners self or other correct. Research on whether students engage in languaging such as asking for confirmation about the use of a particular structure or word, providing explanations for amendments made, which may occur in the discussion/chat pages of the wiki, are relatively rare. Kost (2011) noted that the learners in her study used the pages to discuss ideas, ask grammatical questions, request editing help and provide each other with encouragement. However, the researcher did not analyse these comments for frequency or distribution. Lund and Smørdal (2006) observed that metacomments seemed sparse and usually made by one primary author. Elola and Oskoz (2010a) and Oskoz and Elola (2012), who examined the discussion pages (text-based chats), reported that learners chatted mainly about content issues rather than about language. In the interview data (Elola & Oskoz, 2010a), it was revealed that the chats were not perceived by the students as a suitable vehicle to discuss and improve their grammar; rather they were perceived as beneficial for exchanging ideas about the content (what arguments and evidence to include) and structure of their essay.

Studies investigating peer revisions for language use in wiki pages have produced mixed results. Some studies (e.g. Elola & Oskoz, 2010a; Kessler, 2009; Mak & Coniam, 2008) found relatively few instances of learners correcting their own or their peers' linguistic errors. For example, Kessler's (2009) study, conducted with advanced EFL learners, found that although the participants collaborated on the content of the page, they often ignored grammatical errors. The vast majority of revisions (54%) dealt with content, followed by attention to fairly superficial features of the collective text (e.g. spacing, font size). These revisions for style formed a greater proportion of total revisions (27%) than revisions for linguistic accuracy and word choice (17% of all revisions). Many grammatical errors were overlooked. Furthermore, follow up interviews with the participants revealed that the absence of editing was not related to lack of knowledge of grammatical rules. Similar findings were reported by Kessler *et al.* (2012), where EAP students were composing a joint research report using Google Docs (which has similar functionalities to wikis). The researchers found that most of the attention to language form was on spelling and punctuation, with least attention given to errors in grammatical structures (e.g. verb tenses). It is unlikely that these advanced EAP students avoided correcting for accuracy owing to lack of grammatical knowledge. Mak and Coniam's (2008) study, mentioned earlier, also reported that their learners paid very little attention to the grammatical accuracy of the collaboratively produced wiki. However, the students in the Mak and Coniam study were relatively young (age 11) and of low L2 proficiency.

In contrast, other researchers (e.g. Arnold *et al.*, 2009; Kost, 2011; Lee, 2010) have reported that learners do provide each other with feedback on language in wiki projects. For example, Arnold *et al.* (2009) found that their students revised wiki pages for grammatical and lexical errors (termed surface level revisions). Furthermore, most (75%) of the revisions were correct. Lee (2010) also reported that as the semester progressed, the learners engaged in more revisions, including editing for language. Nevertheless, 40% of the students remained reluctant to edit their peers' writing because of a lack of confidence in their own writing, and also preferred their instructor's feedback to that of their peers. This is perhaps not surprising given that these were elementary learners of Spanish.

A number of factors may explain these divergent findings. These factors are indeed similar to those identified in research on face-to-face collaborative writing (see discussion in Chapter 4). They include the type of task, the size and composition of the groups assigned to work on wiki projects, the role of the instructor, and the learners' goals and perceptions. In terms of tasks, as research on face-to-face collaboration has shown (e.g. Alegría de la Colina & García Mayo, 2007; Storch, 2001a), structured language-focused tasks encourage a greater focus on form than meaning-focused tasks. Lee (2010), for example, who reported evidence of learners correcting for accuracy, used tasks that required students to use specific grammatical structures. Researchers who reported very little attention to accuracy in wiki projects have tended to use unstructured, open-ended tasks. For example, in Kessler's study (2009), the students had to compose a collective definition of the term *culture*. In Mak and Coniam's (2008) study, the learners composed a brochure describing some aspects of their school.

Group size and composition may also impact on whether learners engage in other correction. Very large groups may discourage learners from providing each other with feedback because perhaps there is a diffused sense of responsibility for the wiki produced. Kessler (2009) had a very large group (40 students) working on the wiki page. Studies which reported more frequent peer editing (e.g. Arnold *et al.*, 2009) used small groups (three to four students per group) or pairs (e.g. Kost, 2011). Whether students have an assigned or elected leader in medium size groups may also be a factor. For example, in Lee's (2010) study the instructor assigned students to groups (of four to five learners) ensuring that each group had a relatively high-proficiency learner. The role of that learner was to assist the others in the group in the revision process.

Another factor that may impact on the incidence of corrective feedback in wiki projects is the role of the instructor. Thus, whereas in Kessler's (2009) and Mak and Coniam's (2008) studies the learners worked autonomously; in Lee's (2010) study, the instructor played a key role, drawing learners' attention to linguistic errors during the revision phase of the project. Arnold *et al.*'s (2009) study compared the editing behaviour of wikis implemented in teacher-guided and unguided classes. Although students in both classes corrected wiki pages for language use (coded as surface level revisions), there were significantly more such corrections in the teacher-guided classes. In Ducate *et al.*'s (2011) study, students initially were uncomfortable with editing their peers' work, but following additional instructor guidance on editing and peer interaction, the students became more engaged and more interactive in the task, as well as more comfortable with editing their peers' work.

A range of affective factors, such as learners' goals, attitudes and perceptions may also explain learners' reluctance to edit each other's postings for accuracy. These individual factors are shaped by context (culture) and language learning history, as discussed in the previous chapter. For example, Mak and Coniam's study (2008), conducted with young EFL learners in Hong Kong, attributed their learners' reluctance to provide each other with corrective feedback to local cultural and educational factors. The researchers suggested that their Chinese background learners were reluctant to offer corrective feedback because they were averse to causing their peers to lose face by having their errors exposed (see also research on peer response, e.g. Carson & Nelson, 1996). Furthermore, according to Mak and Coniam, in Hong Kong students apparently spend little time on proofreading and correcting their own work. The adult L2 Spanish learners in Elola and Oskoz's study (2010a) also stated in the surveys that they thought it was inappropriate to correct their partners because such corrections may be perceived as criticisms and thus threaten the establishment of a good working relationship.

Learners' perception of the task may differ to that of the teacher or researcher and thus affect task behaviour. In Kessler's (2009) study, the interview data revealed that the learners perceived the wiki task as a meaning-focused rather than language-focused activity. Therefore they were more tolerant of errors, particularly when they felt that the errors did not impede comprehension. Oskoz and Elola (2012) also noted that although all learners in their study wanted to complete the essay, how they used the various means of communication to achieve this goal was affected by their own interpretation of the writing activity.

One other factor that may explain the nature of learners' engagement with each other's contributions, including editing for language use, is the type of relationships learners form when working on a wiki. The following section discusses the findings of a small number of studies that have looked more closely at the patterns of interaction students form when working on wiki projects.

Patterns of interaction

To date very few studies have considered the type of relationships learners form when working in groups on wiki projects. In studies on wikis in mainstream classes, there is reference to group dynamics (e.g. Carr *et al.*, 2007; Osman-Schlegel *et al.*, 2011; Witney & Smallbone, 2011), to cooperation rather than collaboration and to social loafing, but little in-depth analysis of the different approaches groups may adopt to working on wikis. In research on wikis with L2 students, there are now a few studies (e.g. Bradley *et al.*, 2010; Kost, 2011; Li & Zhu, 2011) that have examined more closely the different patterns of interaction of groups working on wiki projects. These studies show that, as in the case of research on face-to-face collaborative writing, these patterns affect how learners develop the content of wiki pages (Bradley *et al.*, 2010), how they revise such pages, including revisions for grammatical accuracy and expression (Bradley *et al.*, 2010; Kost, 2011), as well as the students' perceptions about any learning gains arising from these wiki writing activities (Li & Zhu, 2011).

The study by Bradley *et al.* (2010) provides perhaps the clearest evidence of the effect of patterns of interaction on learners' contributions to the wikis. The study was conducted with 54 English for Specific Purposes (Engineering) students in Sweden, working on four wiki projects. The learners formed 25 small groups (mainly pairs). The researchers analysed the archived wiki pages the learners produced and identified three distinct patterns of contributions and revisions. Of the 25 groups investigated, five groups showed no interaction in the creation of their wiki pages. Another five groups showed primarily a cooperative approach, and the majority (15 groups) showed a collaborative approach.

In the no interaction pattern, one member of the group composed the entire wiki page, with no visible contributions from peers. In the cooperative groups, contributions were in the form of text updates, with very distinct individual contributions. Often tasks were divided between members of the group (e.g. each student composing one side of the argument). The following example of a wiki page, reproduced from Bradley *et al.*'s study (p. 256), shows the nature of the contributions to the wikis in groups adopting a cooperative orientation. The unshaded text shows an existing text, the shaded text an added text.

> People that are looking for IT-related subjects will probably find wikis, such as Wikipedia very useful. Since the information about IT is so computer-based, most of the experts in those subjects will have access to internet and Wikipedia, so many experts can change the information. When looking for information about some subject further away from computer you might find it being less correct as less experts can contribute to the pages.
>
> [...] We believe that it depends on the field, some fields are more subjective than others. For example, whether or not electromagnetical

> fields causes cancer is a subject that is somewhat controversial and there are not yet clear evidence for it. Because of this, different authors may have radically different views on the subject and therefore their articles may be more an expression of their personal opinion than an objective truth.

What the excerpt suggests, as was reported by Tan et al.'s (2010) study, is that in the cooperative approach each member of the group read the previously posted text and then added to the topic. Although the learners clearly perceived the text as a joint production, there was no evidence of co-construction, or of a focus on language form. The wiki page produced was simply a text composed of consecutive texts produced by each of the learners. In Kost's study (2011), one pair (out of four pairs) also adopted a cooperative approach, with one learner taking on the role of the writer, the other (more proficient learner) accepting the role of the editor.

The nature of contributions and revisions evident in groups adopting a collaborative approach in Bradley et al.'s study was very different to that in cooperative groups. In collaborative groups learners engaged in co-constructing the wiki page by reading, evaluating, and refining ideas posted by their peers. In such texts, it was no longer possible to separate the contributions of individual members, as the members became the joint owners of the entire text (cf. definition of collaboration in Chapter 1). The following excerpt, reproduced from the study (p. 258), shows this collaborative effort. The excerpt shows a paragraph added to an originally posted paragraph and the subsequent revisions (shaded texts show additions/rephrasing, strike through texts show deletions) to this paragraph by the two other peers.

> This might lead towards all spare time we got is dedicated towards watching movies or TV shows or listening to music because of the easy acccss to download the ~~video or audio.~~ audio and video. If you go back 10 years it was a lot different. At home when a specific tv-show was on t all gather in the sofa to watch the show together. In some way it was a kind of family quality time. Nowadays everything ~~is stressed up, the list~~ it's different. Not only the lists of movies and tv-shows are a lot longer but there are still only 24 hours. also the playtime. People ~~watches movies or tv-show~~ watch movies or tv-shows if they have time when it airs on tv, or they download it and ~~whats~~ watch it when they have some ~~time to spare~~ sparetime.

The collaborative effort evident in this excerpt entailed not only additions and elaborations to the content, but also revisions for language use. Although not all errors were amended, the text shows improvement in terms of phrasing and spelling errors. The researchers also noted that in collaborative groups, the learners often included explicit comments and questions (e.g. what do you think?) next to the posted text. Such comments invited peers to share and contribute their ideas to the text. Collaborative groups were found to produce more revised versions of the wikis and with a higher number of edits than wikis produced by the other non-collaborative groups.

Bradley *et al.*, attributed the findings that the majority of the small groups (15 out of 25) were found to work collaboratively to the inherently collaborative nature of wikis. However, this does not explain why a sizeable proportion of the groups (10 out of 25) did not adopt a collaborative approach. Interviews with the learners, had they been used in the study, may have shed light on why some learners formed collaborative relationships and others did not.

Li and Zhu's (2011) small-scale study, conducted with EFL students in China, also investigated the patterns of wiki group interactions but used not only wiki page archives, but also discussion pages data and interviews. Together these sources of data provide insights into the students' revision behaviour as well as perceptions of their learning experiences. The data of nine students (forming three groups of three), working on three non-assessed writing tasks (one task per week), were used in the study. Based on an analysis of posts on the discussion boards and informed by my model of dyadic interaction (Storch, 2002, 2009), three patterns of interaction were identified: collectively contributing/mutually supportive, authoritative/responsive, and dominant/withdrawn. These patterns are similar to the collaborative, expert/novice, and dominant/passive patterns identified in my model (see Chapter 4).

Li and Zhu reported that in the collectively contributing/mutually supportive pattern, all members of the group acted as a collective, contributing to the wiki task and engaging with each other's ideas. There was evidence of collective scaffolding as members pooled their linguistic resources to solve deliberations about language use. The learners were fully engaged with each other not only in the discussion pages but also in constructing their wiki-based essay focusing on the ideas to include as well as how to best express these ideas. There was evidence in the discussion pages of learners building on each other's ideas by elaborating and explaining points raised by their peers, by deliberating about linguistic choices, and by editing their text. The history page showed evidence that all three members of the group were actively involved in revising and editing their wiki.

In the authoritative/responsive pattern, one member of the group took on a leading role, but actively encouraged the other two members to contribute to the task. The other two members acknowledged and accepted the authority of their leader. The authoritative learner played an active role not only in contributing to the wiki page but also in monitoring the progress of the assignment, and in suggesting solutions to problems that arose. Moreover, in this group there was also evidence of a pooling of linguistic resources to solve language problems. Nevertheless, the writing process resembled a cooperative rather than collaborative effort, with the final text being a combination of the individual learners' contributions.

In the dominant/withdrawn pattern, two members contributed to the wiki and one member was relatively passive, contributing very little to the activity. In the group displaying this pattern, there was little evidence of collective scaffolding. Suggestions made by the two more active participants did not encourage engagement. Ideas suggested were often ignored. There was very little evidence of revision for language errors in the text created, as the participants seemed to invest very little in the text created. In one instance, revisions made were subsequently reverted to the initial author's version.

The study found that each of the three groups displayed a distinct and consistent pattern. Task type and passage of time did not alter the patterns formed. The study also found that these distinct patterns affected the learners' perception of their experiences of wikis. The learners who formed the collective/supportive pattern and the authoritative/responsive pattern found the experience interesting, enjoyable and beneficial for their language leaning. In contrast, the learners who formed the dominant/withdrawn pattern felt that they did not gain from their experience of working on the wikis. As discussed in Chapter 6, learners' actual experiences of participating in an activity is likely to influence their evaluation of the activity in terms of any language learning gains. However, the researchers did not investigate why the learners may have formed such distinct patterns of group interaction nor their attitudes towards group work.

More research is needed to investigate the nature of group relationships, given that these relationships impact on the level and nature of contributions and the revision behaviour of wiki group members. It also affects the participants' perceptions about working with wikis and learning gains. Such research will need to investigate and explain why learners form such distinct patterns. Findings from such studies will help to inform instructors on how to best design and implement wiki projects that foster greater collaboration among the groups.

The quality of the collaboratively produced text

Research investigating whether writing collaboratively using wikis leads to an improved written text, or when used with L2 writers to language learning, is relatively scarce. Mak and Coniam (2008), in their study with EFL young learners in Hong Kong, reported that their learners produced longer texts and used more complex language in their wiki projects than they did in regular assignments. However, this evaluation was based on observations rather than a systematic analysis of texts produced individually and collaboratively in wikis.

Elola and Oskoz (2010a) is one of the few studies that investigated the impact of wikis on the written product more systematically. In this small scale study ($N = 8$), advanced learners of Spanish produced one set of argumentative essays collaboratively in pairs and the subsequent essay individually. In both formats students produced the essays using wikis. Using a range of measures of fluency, accuracy and complexity, the researchers found no significant differences between the essays produced in the two modes. Using the wiki logs enabled the researchers to also examine the students' approaches to writing and report on some observed differences. When producing essays in pairs, it seems that the pairs established the structure of the essay and then wrote and revised their essays throughout the composing process. When writing individually, the structure was constantly revised, but editing was only done in the final draft. The authors noted however, that in both modes, many errors were ignored.

It should be noted that research on the impact of wikis on L1 writing development is also scarce; and what evidence exists does not show that wikis lead to improved writing. For example, Neumann and Hood's (2009) study, conducted in a mainstream statistics course, compared two approaches to report writing. In five classes, learners produced a report using a wiki and in the other five classes the students wrote individually. Although those in the wiki classes attended classes more regularly and in the surveys gave a higher rating on engagement with producing the report than students who wrote individually, post-tests did not show an advantage for wikis. The post-tests, which tested students' explicit knowledge of report writing, found that both approaches improved the students' explicit knowledge of what report writing entails. Furthermore, there were no differences between the groups in terms of grades on subsequent reports produced by students individually for assessment. Thus the authors concluded that wikis may enhance engagement but not necessarily performance (the written product). It should be noted, however, that the majority of the group reports were incomplete, perhaps because they were not assessed.

Additional research on the impact of wikis on L2 learning and on writing development of L2 writers (and for that matter, L1 writers) is imperative, given the growing use of wikis in these contexts. The longitudinal nature of wiki projects and the fact that wiki logs record learners' contributions and revisions provide researchers with access to a potentially rich data source. These data could be used to trace the long-term impact of computer mediated collaborative writing on the text produced, the composing processes, and on any observed gains.

Conclusion

The research reviewed in this chapter, both in mainstream and L2 learning contexts, has shown that although wikis may provide learners with a potentially ideal environment for collaboration, they do not necessarily guarantee collaboration. Various recommendations have been made about how to promote participation, collaboration, and engagement.

The need to train learners has been identified as crucial in both contexts. Engstrom and Jewett (2005), in a report based on a large scale wiki project conducted with 400 middle school students and 11 teachers, emphasised that training participants to use the wiki was one of the most important components of the project and that both teachers and students needed to be trained. Several researchers suggest that effective training should cover not only the technical skills needed, but also how to provide peer feedback (e.g. Arnold et al., 2009).

The need for alignment between the pedagogical aims of the wiki, the type of wiki activity, and the assessment criteria have also been identified as important in promoting successful wiki projects. As in the implementation of any educational programme, educators need to ensure that there are clear and logical connections between the intended outcome of a learning activity and what it is hoped the students will achieve (Biggs, 2003). In terms of using wikis, what this means is that instructors need to make informed decisions about issues such as the type of wiki task, the size and composition of the group, how the activity is implemented, including the role of the instructor and the length of the project, and the assessment criteria. These decisions are discussed in greater detail in the next chapter. The chapter also points to areas in need of additional investigation, areas noted briefly in this as well as preceding chapters.

8 Conclusion: Pedagogical Implications and Research Directions

Introduction

In this final chapter, I begin by presenting an overview of the main themes covered in this book. This first section reiterates the theoretical and pedagogical rationale for collaborative writing activities in L2 writing classes. It then summarises the main findings of empirical research regarding the potential language learning gains that such activities afford learners, the factors that may impact on the success of such activities, and available evidence of language learning gains arising in and as a consequence of participating in collaborative writing.

I then focus on pedagogy. The second section discusses some of the key decisions that teachers need to make when planning to use collaborative writing tasks in their L2 classes, whether face-to-face or using wikis. The third section discusses some of the challenges that teachers may face when implementing collaborative writing activities. Based on the available research literature as well as on my own experience of implementing and researching collaborative writing activities with L2 learners, I offer some suggestions that may address these challenges. Section Four identifies some of the aspects of collaborative writing that need further exploration.

Overview of the Main Themes

Collaborative writing combines interaction (orally or electronically in wiki environments) between authors as they engage in the production of a joint text, and over which the authors share responsibility. When implemented in L2 classes, collaborative writing tasks require learners to agree not only on what to say, but also how to say it, thus pushing them to deliberate about their language choices. Theories of second language acquisition, whether from a psycholinguistic or sociocognitive theoretical orientation, view such deliberations as potential sites for language learning.

From a psycholinguistic theoretical perspective, second language learning arises from the negotiations about language form that learners engage in while being oriented to meaning making (Long, 1996). From a sociocognitive theoretical perspective, drawing on Vygotsky's (1978) sociocultural theory, deliberations about language are viewed as socially situated processes where knowledge is co-constructed and is then available for the individual to internalise. This may be new knowledge (e.g. new vocabulary) or extension and reinforcement of existing linguistic knowledge. Swain (2000) refers to such deliberations as languaging. Languaging is using language to direct thinking when attempting to solve a problem. When engaging in collaborative writing, languaging can take two forms: self-directed (private speech) and other directed speech (collaborative dialogue). In collaborative writing, both forms of speech are vocalized, audible and available for further deliberation. The problem-solving task is composing a text in the L2 that expresses the writers' intended meaning accurately and appropriately.

In their deliberations about language, learners engage in important cognitive processes. They verbalise gaps in their interlanguage, formulate and test hypotheses, assess alternatives, self- or other correct. These processes occur not necessarily because there is a breakdown in communication, but because writing is a more natural task to encourage learners to pay attention to form than tasks which require only oral interaction. Furthermore, in these deliberations about language, learners draw on their collective linguistic resources and generally reach correct resolutions to their deliberations.

Collaborative writing activities also accord with the main tenets of communicative and task-based approaches to L2 instruction. Studies which have examined the dialogues that occur during collaborative writing tasks, particularly when implemented in the face-to-face mode, show that these tasks, whether meaning- or language-focused, also provide learners with opportunities to practice using the L2 for a range of functions. When completing these tasks, learners offer opinions and counter opinions, debate their ideas, explore alternative vocabulary and ways of expressing their ideas, explain grammatical conventions, ask for and received help, correct both themselves and each other.

Thus studies that have investigated the nature of learner talk during collaborative writing activities show evidence that these activities are replete with occasions for second language learning and language use. We now also have some evidence that L2 learners composing collaboratively tend to produce texts that are more accurate and of better quality than texts produced by learners writing individually. More importantly, we have evidence supplied by researchers using different research designs, including tailor made post-tests or a process-product approach, that learners retain much of the knowledge they co-construct in collaboration with their peers; however, the nature of their engagement in the knowledge co-construction process is an important variable.

Studies investigating collaborative writing, predominantly in the face-to-face mode, employ detailed microgenetic analysis that provides insights into how and why learning may or may not take place during collaborative work. These studies have also identified a number of factors that may impact on the quantity and quality of learners' deliberations about language, operationalised as language-related episodes (LREs). These factors include, among others, the tasks used, the learners' L2 proficiency, and the relationship learners form when working in pairs. These factors are often interrelated. Thus, the impact of task type depends also on the L2 proficiency of the learners and on their attitudes towards the assigned tasks, pair work, and working with a specific partner. Perceived L2 proficiency, language learning beliefs, and the goals of each pair or group member are likely to influence relationships formed. Learners may form different types of relationships when working with their peers, but it is a collaborative relationship, where there is a high degree of equality and mutuality, which has been found to be the most conducive to language learning.

Although learners (and teachers) may have some reservations about writing collaboratively – reservations based on previous experiences and beliefs concerning language learning – when learners actually experience collaborative writing and are questioned about it, they generally express positive attitudes towards collaborative writing. These students recognise that working with peers exposes them to different ideas, enables them to pool their different linguistic expertise, and to learn from each other. The concerns that both L2 learners and teachers have about group work, and by implication collaborative writing; namely, extensive use of L1 and the inability of learners to provide each other with useful feedback, are not borne out by studies on collaborative writing which have investigated the nature and outcomes of learners' deliberations about language (LREs).

Research on collaborative writing in more recent times has focused on wiki collaborative projects. The features of wikis make them a potentially ideal platform for collaborative writing. They also extend the opportunities to collaborate and interact in the L2 outside the physical confines of the classroom. However, research on wiki projects to date, in general education and L2 classes, shows that although learners seem fairly positive about the experience of working in groups on wiki projects, they do not always contribute nor engage with each other's ideas in the production of the wiki texts. An additional concern revealed by research on wikis in L2 contexts is learners' reluctance to other-correct for language use. Such reluctance may dissipate over time as learners become more familiar and comfortable about working with each other and with using the wiki site. However, it seems that in the online mode, learners are less likely to engage in deliberations about language choice; that is, to language, unless computer mediated collaboration complements other forms of communication and the instructor plays a more active role.

Despite the potential benefits that collaborative writing activities afford L2 learners, whether in face-to-face or computer mediated mode, implementing such activities is not without its challenges. Teachers wishing to implement successful collaborative writing activities need to plan carefully and make some informed decisions. In the next section I discuss these decisions and the challenges as well as some recommendations.

Decisions to Make When Implementing Collaborative Writing Tasks

Before implementing collaborative writing tasks, whether in face-to-face or online mode, L2 instructors need to make a number of important decisions. In this section, I focus on three of these decisions. The first decision to be made is which task to choose. Once a task is chosen, the instructor also needs to determine whether it will be graded, and if so, how. Another important decision relates to student allocation into pairs and small groups, and in the case of groups, the size of the group. Each of these decisions is discussed in turn, including some of the advantages and disadvantages of various options and strategies available to teachers.

Task type

The choice of tasks to be used for collaborative writing activities needs to take cognisance of the learners' L2 proficiency and the instructor's pedagogical goals. The choice is between meaning-focused or language and grammar-focused tasks. Research on face-to-face collaborative writing activities has shown that meaning-focused tasks (e.g. jigsaw, data commentary text) may elicit fewer LREs than language- (e.g. dictogloss) and grammar-focused tasks (e.g. editing, cloze), and fewer grammatical than lexical LREs.

However, meaning-focused tasks are more likely to draw learners' attention to form-meaning connections, and as such generate a greater depth of engagement with language choices.

In contrast, grammar- and language-focused tasks seem successful in eliciting attention to form, particularly the forms targeted by the tasks, but the quality of the languaging may be superficial. Superficial engagement may not lead to language learning and/or consolidation of explicit linguistic knowledge. The dictogloss, the most frequently used task in research on collaborative face-to-face writing, seems to draw learners' attention to a range of grammatical forms, beyond those targeted by the task. As such it seems a suitable collaborative writing task, if the aim is to maximise learners' attention to language. However, the findings of a number of studies suggest that the dictogloss is a difficult task for learners, and may not be suitable for lower proficiency L2 learners. Thus researchers who employ a dictogloss task now tend to include not only a practice session but also model (e.g. using a video clip) the desired quality of languaging. There is some empirical evidence to suggest that such modelling encourages learners to collaborate.

In wiki collaborative writing, the choice of tasks may be even more critical. A number of researchers (e.g. Lee, 2010; Lund, 2008; Mak & Coniam, 2008) argue that it is the nature of the task, more than the technology itself, that will influence the level of engagement and collaboration in the wiki environment. Unlike the tasks used in face-to-face collaborative writing activities, wikis are completed outside the confines of the class time, and tend to be group projects which require extensive writing (e.g. argumentative essays, research-based reports, glossaries). However, for such tasks to encourage all members of the small group to participate, they need to be authentic group projects (see O'Donnell & Hoy, 2002). That is, they should require a team effort for successful completion. Essays and glossaries of key terms, tasks that have been used in wiki projects, are authentic writing tasks, but do not necessarily require a team effort for successful completion. This may explain the observed lack of contributions by all members of a group in such tasks. Research-based projects, with a clear purpose and outcome that are relevant and meaningful to the students, such as the school brochures project used by Mak and Coniam (2008), are more likely to encourage participation. At the same time, it is equally important to use tasks that do not easily lend themselves to a division of labour so that learners collaborate rather than cooperate. For example, large reports with a number of sub-sections, or stories which develop different scenarios, the kind of tasks used in a number of recently reported L2 wiki projects, are more likely to be divided among members of a group than a text that requires learners to present a unified stance on an issue, or a problem-solving task that has only one allowable solution.

However, such meaning-focused tasks may not encourage a focus on language. Research suggests that learners are reluctant to other-correct for language use. In studies which have reported that students did amend each other's contributions, the instructors played an active role, explicitly encouraging the learners to focus on language choice. Moreover, in wiki projects learners rarely seem to use the discussion space available on wiki pages, and when the discussion space is utilised, it is used mainly for deliberations about content rather than language. Thus, when composing wiki pages, it seems that languaging is no longer externalised and hence no longer available for further inspection. One factor that can explain this phenomenon is the lack of social presence and immediacy inherent in wikis.

In order to encourage externalised forms of languaging, wikis need to be augmented to compensate for the lack of co-presence, audibility and simultaneity. One strategy is to use a blended approach, combining more familiar and more immediate forms of communication, such as class face-to-face interaction and emails, with the asynchronous wiki form of communication. Recent research suggests that such hybrid forms of implementation encourage a greater focus on language use (see Zorko, 2009) and are reported by students to be the preferred means of communication (Witney & Smallbone, 2011). Alternatively, wikis could be supplemented with synchronous web-based voice applications such as the commercial tools *Skype*, *Skype TM*, or *Voice Direct* (see Oskoz & Elola, 2011; Sykes *et al.*, 2008) thus combining, as in face-to-face collaboration, oral and written language output. This combination may enhance the collaborative value of the wiki by facilitating greater interaction between learners. The use of various means of communication replicates collaborative writing scenarios in the professional world (Brown & Adler, 2008).

Grading

Another decision instructors need to make is whether the collaborative writing tasks should be graded, and if so how. Classroom-based studies reporting on collaboratively completed activities in the face-to-face mode, including writing tasks, grammar exercises and tests, suggest that even when there is no grade attached to the task, most learners contribute actively to the activity. Ewald's study (2005), for example, on Spanish L2 learners' interaction in small group quizzes, found many instances in the data of collective scaffolding, despite the fact that the quizzes only constituted about 2% of the students' final course grade. In my own longitudinal classroom-based study (Storch, 2009), of the ten pairs observed, the majority (six) formed collaborative relationships, contributing and engaging with each other's contributions. The tasks the students completed were not assessed. Thus it seems that grading of relatively short collaborative writing tasks of the type used in face-to-face activities is not necessary. Such tasks can form part of classroom practice.

However, in the case of wikis, the collaborative writing projects tend to be longer and more substantial and thus tend to be graded. One of the contentious issues discussed in the literature on collaborative and cooperative learning is whether to assign group projects a group grade or individual grades. The debate about grading is often related to notions of interdependence. There is some disagreement among scholars over whether students who work on group assignments should receive the same grade or whether they should be graded individually on the basis of their contribution. The assumption underlying awarding the same grade to all members of the group is that it would promote what has been termed in the literature positive interdependence; that is, where students feel more accountable to the group and thus contribute to the task (O'Donnell & Hoy, 2002; Pfaff & Huddleston, 2003).

However, others argue that this may be unfair, rewarding the social loafers or the so-called free-riders; those not contributing very much to the task yet receiving the same grade as those who do contribute. There may also be some reluctance among teachers to assign a group grade because such a grade may not reflect accurately an individual student's language ability. These concerns can be dealt with in wiki projects more easily than in face-to-face group assignments.

Wikis provide a conspicuous advantage over face-to-face collaboration because the wikis provide a written record of the interactions between students. This makes each member's contributions more transparent enabling instructors to trace, and if necessary, to assess individual contributions to the joint product. Assessment that rewards students not only for the quantity of individual contributions but also the quality of such contributions and for the level of engagement with the contributions of other members of the group may go some way towards encouraging collaboration. Thus assessment criteria need to reward both the process and the product, the quality of individual contributions as well as the quality of the co-constructed text (see Trentin, 2009). In the case of L2 learners, in order to encourage a focus on language, assessment criteria need to place some weighting on the linguistic quality of the text produced.

Macdonald (2003) describes a number of models of assessing online collaborative group projects that rely to varying degrees on individual and group marks. A particularly effective strategy reported was to include a reflective exercise where students, following their first collaborative online assignment, were asked to reflect on the process and suggest strategies they may adopt in future collaborations. Such reflection was found to have a positive impact on the outcome of collaboration in later collaborative assignments.

Group size and allocation

In face-to-face collaborative L2 writing, students generally tend to work in pairs. In wiki projects the groups in L2 contexts tend to be small to medium sized, certainly smaller than in L1 contexts. The decision whether to use pairs or groups in collaborative writing tasks needs to be based on pedagogical considerations.

The advantages of pairs over groups is that pairs are more likely to feel a stronger sense of text ownership and hence there may be greater individual contributions to the decision-making process. Research on face-to-face group work has shown that when working in groups on oral or writing tasks, some learners may not feel any pressure to contribute (see Fernández Dobao, 2012; Foster, 1998). Research on wiki collaborative projects in L1 contexts has shown that in groups, particularly large groups, the sense of text ownership is more diffused, and hence some learners contribute very little to the task, contribute late in the life of a project or engage superficially with the text co-created. Furthermore, when working in pairs, each learner has more opportunities to participate and to practice their language skills. Thus a number of researchers using wikis with L2 students advocate the use of pairs, arguing that pair work is more conducive to interaction and hence to language learning (e.g. Elola & Oskoz, 2010a; Kost, 2011; Kuteeva, 2011).

However, there are also cogent arguments in support of using group rather than pair work in collaborative writing tasks, whether face-to-face or wikis. Fernández Dobao (2012) argues that there are more knowledge sources to draw on in small groups than pairs, and as shown in her study, learners deliberate about language and resolve these deliberations correctly more often when working in small groups than when working in pairs. Thus potentially, small group work creates more L2 learning opportunities for learners than pairs. Although Fernández Dobao observed that in some small groups not all students contributed to the activity, in a subsequent study (Fernández Dobao, forthcoming), it was found that even those who did not overtly engage benefitted from the activity (see also Ewald, 2005). The extent of these gains, however, needs to be investigated further.

An argument in support of larger groups is that such larger groups emulate the team work learners are likely to encounter in the work environment. For more advanced L2 learners, this may be a valid argument. The optimal size for such collaborative writing projects seems to be three to four (see review in Pfaff & Huddlestone, 2003). In larger groups, assigning a group leader is another way of encouraging group member participation. In the workplace, teams are often assigned a group manager.

A related matter is that of group/pair formation, and whether it is the teacher who assigns students to pairs or small groups or whether students are allowed to self-select their partners in the pair or small group. The advantage of self-selection is that students choose to work with peers with whom they are familiar, and this means that they may be more comfortable and willing to challenge each others' suggestions and to offer other-repairs (see Dale, 1997; Ewald, 2005). In my research (e.g. Storch, 2005, 2007, 2009; Storch & Wigglesworth, 2007), I let students self-select their partners. Despite this self-selection process, not all pairs form collaborative relationships. In Shehadeh's (2011) longitudinal classroom-based study, students were required to change partners every two to three weeks. In the interviews, most said that they liked changing partners. In wiki projects, research suggests that the nature and duration of the projects require teams to work together to develop group trust and cohesion. Changing partners mid project is not feasible nor advisable, but perhaps changing partners for different wiki projects may be a worthwhile strategy.

The advantage of teacher assignment is that the teacher can decide about the mix of proficiency levels. The main quandary for teachers is whether to assign L2 learners to work in similar or different proficiency pairs, and the optimal placement of relatively low-proficiency learners. The little available research suggests that when low-proficiency learners work with fellow low-proficiency learners, they may not generate many LREs and they may not be able to resolve many of their LREs. However, low–low pairs tend to form collaborative relationships with both learners engaging in the task, and both having the opportunity to use the L2 for a range of functions (Storch & Aldosari, 2013). In foreign language settings, where learners' opportunity to use the L2 is minimal, this may be an important consideration when pairing students. In contrast, in mixed-proficiency pairs, the lower proficiency learner may gain from exposure to more instances of languaging (i.e. more LREs), but such pairs are likely to form asymmetrical relationships where the lower proficiency learner assumes a more passive role, contributing little to the task. Dominant/passive relationships are not conducive to language learning. Thus, determining the ideal proficiency mix of pairs and small groups depends on the pedagogical aims of the collaborative writing activity, whether it is L2 practice or exposure to more linguistic resources.

It should be noted that studies on the impact of similar and mixed-proficiency grouping have to date focused only on pairs. There is very little research on the effect of similar and mixed proficiency of learners in groups, and whether, for example, assigning a group leader impacts on group dynamics, on learners' contributions, and on the quantity and quality of languaging. Given the tendency to use small groups in wiki collaborative writing tasks, such research is needed in order to enable teachers to make more informed decisions about the optimal grouping of learners.

Challenges and Suggested Strategies

Despite the strong theoretical and pedagogical reasons for implementing collaborative writing tasks in the L2 classroom, collaborative writing activities, whether implemented in face-to-face or computer mediated form, may not always succeed. In this section I discuss two of the challenges that teachers may face: students' reluctance to take part in collaborative writing activities (see Chapter 6), and the patterns of interaction they form when working on such tasks, given that some patterns are not conducive to learning (see Chapter 5). I also put forward a number of suggestions about dealing with these challenges.

Resistance

One of the first challenges that may confront teachers wishing to implement collaborative writing activities is resistance from students. Such resistance may stem from underlying language learning beliefs, including beliefs about writing as a solitary activity, beliefs which may have been reinforced or shaped by previous unhappy experiences of working on group projects (Chisholm, 1990; Pfaff & Huddleston, 2003). Resistance may also be attributable to lack of familiarity with a new approach to instruction. Faced with such resistance, what should teachers who wish to implement collaborative writing activities do?

Leki and Carson (1994) provide some sound advice. Writing about the mismatch they found between students' and teachers' thoughts about approaches to L2 writing instruction, the authors warn instructors not to simply change their approach to teaching in order to match students' expressed desires nor to simply assume that they need to convince their students that they, the instructors, know best what students need for the development of their academic literacy. Rather, they suggest that teachers need to carefully consider the nature of the mismatch and how best to address it. In what follows I provide various suggestions that may address resistance to collaborative writing activities.

(1) *Becoming aware of students' attitudes to collaborative writing*
First and foremost, it is important for teachers to become aware of their students' attitudes towards and concerns about collaborative writing, as is the case with any newly introduced instructional practice. One strategy recommended by a number of scholars (e.g. Horwitz, 1985, 1988; Kinsella, 1996) is to use a short questionnaire to elicit students' attitudes and to use the responses from the questionnaire as a springboard for classroom discussion before implementing the activity. The questionnaire raises teachers' awareness of their students' attitudes and of the beliefs shaping these attitudes. The discussion that ensues may challenge existing opinions and serve to increase receptivity to new activities.

If using collaborative writing activities on more than one occasion, it may be worthwhile revisiting that discussion briefly, after students have experienced the activity. As the studies which elicited learners' views following their experience of collaborative writing show, learners may become aware of the benefits of collaborative writing once they have experienced such activities.

(2) *Giving students a choice*
I also believe that learners should be given a choice about whether to participate in collaborative writing activities, particularly so in the case of adult learners who are more likely to have strongly held preferences. That choice, however, should be offered not only when first implementing collaborative writing but throughout the term or semester, to allow students to reconsider their choices, after observing other students participating in such activities and hearing about their experiences.

(3) *Explaining the rationale for collaborative writing*
The introduction of collaborative writing activities should be preceded with an explanation provided by teachers about the potential benefits of such collaboration for language learning as well as for future professional pursuits. When an activity is new and unfamiliar, teachers need to clearly explain the purpose and rationale for such an activity. If students are convinced that the activity is worthwhile, they are more likely to have a positive attitude towards it.

Patterns of interaction

Another challenge relates to the patterns of interaction learners form when working in pairs or groups, and specifically their contribution and engagement with each other's contributions. Research on face-to-face collaborative writing and wiki projects has shown that simply assigning learners to work together in pairs or small groups on writing tasks does not necessarily mean that learners will collaborate in the creation of the text or the wiki respectively. Research (discussed in Chapter 5) shows that it is the collaborative pattern that is most beneficial for language learning.

Various strategies have been proposed in the literature to encourage the formation of collaborative relationships including modelling collaborative interaction, providing practice sessions, the latter being particularly relevant for wiki collaborative writing tasks, and monitoring the nature of learners' interactions. These and the need to take a broader look at the classroom culture and assessment practices are discussed in turn in the following sub sections.

(1) *Modelling collaborative interaction*
The use of pre-task modelling of collaborative dialogue before implementing collaborative writing tasks has been mentioned in a number of studies on collaborative face-to-face writing. The modelling can be in the form of a short video clip or the researcher/teacher modelling collaborative dialogues. Such modelling has been shown to encourage learners to adopt a collaborative pattern of interaction, in L2 contexts with adult learners (Kim & McDonough, 2011), as well as in L1 contexts with young learners (Dale, 1994b). For example, in Dale's (1994b) study, with 9th graders, the researcher and teacher modelled co-authoring behaviour, including how to deal with disagreements and debate the merits of alternative ideas. Dale reported evidence of ensuing successful collaboration among her students. Researchers employing wiki projects, in both L1 and L2 contexts, often mention pre-task training, but there is rarely mention of pre-task modelling of collaborative talk (e.g. Ducate et al., 2011). Yet the study by Lin and Kelsey (2009), conducted with L1 education students, found that it was only after the researchers provided more guided instructions to their participants about how to co-author a wiki that participants began to communicate with their group members more effectively.

(2) *Training/practice*
There seems to be a general consensus amongst researchers that students need to be trained to become familiar with wikis. Merely assigning students to work in groups on wiki tasks may provide them with the experience of different group dynamics but does not guarantee that they will know how to handle such dynamics effectively or collaborate. To encourage collaboration, pre-task training should go beyond acquainting students with the functions of wikis. As mentioned above, the training

should also include pre-task modelling of collaboration as well as some training on providing peer feedback (Arnold *et al.*, 2009). Students may also need training to develop skills such as team work, task management and how to negotiate roles and responsibilities (Dovey, 2006).

The development of such skills requires not only training but also practice. Students need to experience collaborative writing activities on more than one occasion. Macdonald (2003), for example, describes a number of online collaborative projects, and suggests that successive tasks may lead to greater success. Working in groups over a period of time also enables students to develop trust in each other and group cohesion – important factors in the success of group projects.

(3) *Monitoring*

Teachers need to monitor interaction, whether it is in face-to-face or online mode. In the face-to-face mode, where the writing activity is of a relatively short duration, the teacher may encourage all students to change partners regularly (see Shehadeh, 2011). Changing partners should also happen if the teachers observe that the pair (or small group) dynamics warrant it.

Monitoring of students' patterns of interaction is easier in wiki environments. However, the project duration tends to be longer, and changing partners frequently may not be a viable option. Kessler (2009), among others, suggests that in wiki projects instructors should play a more active role throughout the life of the project, prompting students to participate, and even joining group online discussions. Such careful monitoring and early intervention may mean that potential problems related to group dynamics are dealt with early in the life of the project.

(4) *Taking stock of the bigger picture*

Pre-task training and informing students about the merits of collaborative writing, however, may still not be sufficient to encourage students to engage in the task, to offer each other feedback, to collaborate. These strategies may be by themselves insufficient to counteract implicit messages students receive from the instructional practises they experience. Research on face-to-face collaborative writing has shown that the classroom culture and the teaching style (see DiNitto, 2000) affect how students behave in group work. A number of studies on wiki collaborative projects, in both L1 and L2 contexts, have shown the impact of the wider educational context, and particularly the nature of assessment tasks and assessment practices, on students' behaviour in wiki projects and ultimately the success of the collaborative wiki projects (e.g. Rick & Guzdial, 2006). Collaboration may be more difficult to achieve when co-authoring activities are implemented as add-ons to courses which otherwise encourage competition and reward individual efforts.

Thus, to encourage collaboration, a sharing of ideas and the provision of feedback to each other may require a re-conceptualisation of classroom teaching and assessment practices. As Macdonald (2003) points out, students are more likely to contribute to a collaborative task if the task is assessed on the basis of the collaborative effort (see discussion in previous section) and if students are involved in a number of such activities rather than the collaborative assignment being an isolated incident in an otherwise individually assessed course. Collaborative writing tasks also need to be integrated into regular class work and form part of regular assessment tasks. For example, perhaps one reason why in Zorko's (2009) study the wiki projects were successful, is because they were used in a context of blended, problem-based learning where students worked in small groups on all their assessment tasks. The wiki was simply an additional environment that facilitated the existing problem-based learning approach, rather than a new instructional strategy.

Research Directions

The implementation of collaborative writing in L2 contexts is still in its infancy, as is the available research. Future research needs to extend the existing research base and delve further into some of the issues investigated in only a small number of studies to date. Given the rapid developments of Web 2.0 technology, we are likely to see more uses of collaborative writing tools, such as wikis and Google Docs, in L2 writing classes. Although there is a growing body of research reporting on the use of wikis, in L1 and L2 contexts, we need further investigations to fully explore the learning opportunities afforded by these tools.

The review of the available research on collaborative writing, in face-to-face and in the computer mediated environment, has shown that to date most of the research has focused on the teaching of English (as a second or foreign language) with adult L2 learners. This research needs to be extended into a wider range of language learning contexts. As a number of scholars have pointed out (e.g. Manchón, 2009, 2011a, 2011b; Ortega, 2009b), we cannot assume that findings of studies conducted in ESL/EFL contexts can be unquestioningly generalised to all L2 contexts.

Furthermore we need longitudinal, qualitative studies. Such research can have greater explanatory powers than studies that are of relatively short duration. Detailed microgenetic investigations of what transpires during collaborative writing activities can provide researchers with insights into how learning is happening and why learning may or may not happen during collaborative work. Such insights can be used to inform instructors on how to implement collaborative writing activities more effectively and thus improve learning outcomes.

In the previous two sections, I discussed some of the decisions and challenges that face instructors who wish to implement collaborative writing tasks in their L2 classes. A number of pedagogical strategies were suggested such as utilising periodic student reflections on their experience of collaborative writing, more active teacher intervention in wiki projects, the combination of face-to-face and computer mediated interactions. Future research needs to investigate the impact of these strategies on learners' willingness to engage and the nature of their engagement in collaborative writing activities.

Another area that needs to be investigated is the learning outcomes of collaborative writing activities. To date, there has been very little research on the outcomes of collaborative L2 writing in the face-to-face mode (see Chapter 5), and even less on computer mediated collaborative writing (see Chapter 7). What research exists has tended to focus on short-term gains (following the implementation of one collaborative writing activity) and on improvements in linguistic accuracy. Clearly more research needs to be undertaken on the impact of collaborative writing on L2 learning as well as L2 writing. When writing collaboratively, learners may be exposed to new ways of thinking about a topic, new ways of presenting and organising ideas, and new ways of approaching a writing task. Thus future research on the outcomes of collaborative writing needs to adopt a broader definition of gains, one that considers improvement in linguistic accuracy and complexity and in writing quality as well as in composing processes and confidence. Such investigations need to be longitudinal, because the impact on the writer may not become evident immediately or necessarily after a single collaborative writing experience. They also need to examine both the outcomes and the processes in tandem. Investigating only the outcomes or only the processes provides only half the picture.

There has been some research on the nature of the relationships learners form when writing in pairs in the face-to-face mode. This research has indicated that relationships formed affect the opportunities for learning affording by such writing activities. There are emerging studies on the nature of small group relationships in wiki projects, and the impact such relationships have on learners' contributions and engagement with each other's postings. This is an area that needs additional investigation. We need to gain a greater understanding of why learners form different types of relationships. Two related areas that merit closer exploration are learners' attitudes and notions of text ownership.

Research on learners' beliefs and the attitudes they shape has shown that beliefs and attitudes may predispose learners towards certain kinds of behaviour. I use the term *may* intentionally because as the discussion in Chapter 6 shows, the relationship between beliefs, attitudes and behaviour is complex and not always predictable. Nevertheless, a relationship between attitudes and behaviour is undeniable. To date researchers have investigated mainly learners' attitudes towards group and pair work, per se, rather than attitudes to collaborative writing. Research on learners' attitudes to collaborative writing may provide us with a better understanding of learners' observed behaviour in collaborative writing tasks. This research needs to be informed by current approaches to research on language learning beliefs in which beliefs are investigated longitudinally and in context, using a range of tools, beyond surveys, and which take into account the interaction between beliefs and actions.

Another important and related topic for further investigation, particularly in group projects with multiple authors, as in the case of wiki collaborative writing, is the notion of text ownership. A sense of a shared ownership of the text produced is one of the defining traits of collaborative writing (see definition in Chapter 1). Research on wiki writing projects has uncovered learners' reluctance to amend each other's postings, as well as aversion to having one's own postings amended. This behaviour has been attributed to the perception cultivated in our Western educational system of text as individual property. Hunter's (2011) study, based on the discourse analysis of discussion pages in a FanFiction wiki created by voluntary online writing groups, shows that a collaboratively produced wiki is one where members of the group are willing to relinquish author centric notions of text ownership. In a formal educational context, a collective notion of text ownership may take time to develop. Among the strategies proposed in the previous section to encourage the development of a collaborative orientation is the use of well-designed assessment criteria and providing learners with successive (and presumably successful) experiences of collaborative writing projects. Whether these assessment practices and experiences do lead to the development of more collective notions of text ownership need to be investigated. In such research we need to analyse not only what learners say in interviews and surveys, but also employ discourse analysis of their postings, as in Hunter's study. Such research tools may provide us with greater insights into learners' perceptions of authorship and text ownership.

Concluding Remarks

Collaborative writing, the co-authoring and co-ownership of a text, is not a frequently used activity in L2 classes, as writing is usually perceived to be a solitary, individual activity. However, this may well change given the latest developments in Web 2.0 technology, a technology that makes it easier than ever before for students to write together. The argument put forward in this book is that collaborative writing tasks, whether implemented in face-to-face, computer mediated, or a hybrid mode, if carefully designed and implemented, may provide optimal opportunities for language learning. They provide opportunities for authentic communication among learners, encouraging learners to deliberate about language while engaged in meaningful text production.

Beyond these opportunities for language learning, collaborative writing activities may provide learners with opportunities to develop their L2 writing. Thorne and Reinhardt (2008) argue that in a technology driven world, advanced level L2 literacies need to include familiarity with new and emerging computer mediated writing tools. Incorporating wiki collaborative writing projects thus provides L2 learners with opportunities to become acquainted with new and evolving computer mediated means of communicating and of composing. They also offer a way of adding real world relevance to class activities. The latter may be of even greater relevance in the foreign language class, where, according to Manchón (2011a), learners often see no real need or purpose in learning to write in the foreign language.

However, it is important to note that despite the benefits that collaborative writing can confer on L2 learners, I am not advocating that collaborative writing tasks should displace individual writing. Rather, I believe that both forms of writing can complement each other to expand the writers' writing experience. The judicious integration in L2 classes of collaborative writing, in the face-to-face and/or computer mediated mode in L2 classes, can assist learners to become more active participants in their language learning process whereby, through collaboration they acquire the linguistic and writing conventions of the L2. Web 2.0 technology, such as wikis and Google Docs, creates a space for such activities beyond the confines of the traditional classroom setting.

This book set out to achieve two aims. The first aim was to present a theoretical and pedagogical rationale as well as empirical evidence in support of collaborative writing. I hope that the discussion and evidence presented encourages language teachers to include collaborative writing activities in their classes. I also hope that the discussion and suggestions made in this book can assist teachers to make informed decisions about how to best implement such activities in their teaching context.

The implementation of collaborative writing needs to be in tandem with more investigations of such activities. The second, and related aim of this book, was to encourage researchers to build on the existing body of research. I hope that this book will encourage researchers to pursue some of the topics outlined above, and in their pursuit adopt innovative research methodologies, which investigate simultaneously writing processes and products in well-designed longitudinal studies. In this way, we as a community of writing instructors and scholars will become better informed about the learning potentials of collaborative writing.

References

Abadikhah, S. (2012) The effect of mechanical and meaningful production of output on learning English relative clauses. *System* 40(1), 129–143.

Adams, R. (2003) L2 output, reformulation, and noticing. Implications for IL development. *Language Teaching Research* 7(3), 347–376.

Adams, R. (2006) L2 tasks and orientation to form: A role for modality? ITL: *International Journal of Applied Linguistics* 152 (1), 7–34.

Adams, R. (2007) Do second language learners benefit from interacting with each other? In A. Mackey (ed.) *Conversational interaction in SLA* (pp. 29–51). Oxford: Oxford University Press.

Adams, R. and Ross-Feldman, L. (2008) Does writing influence learner attention to form? In D. Belcher and A. Hirvela (eds) *The Oral-literate Connection* (pp. 243–266). Ann Arbor MI: The University of Michigan Press.

Aldosari, A. (2008) The influence of proficiency levels, task type and social relationships on pair interaction: An EFL context. Unpublished PhD dissertation, University of Melbourne, Australia.

Alegría de la Colina, A. and García Mayo, M.P. (2007) Attention to form across collaborative tasks by low-proficiency learners in an EFL setting. In M.P. García Mayo (ed.) *Investigating Tasks in Foreign Language Learning* (91–116). Clevedon: Multilingual Matters.

Aljaafreh, A. and Lantolf, J.P. (1994) Negative feedback as regulation and second language learning in the zone of proximal development. *The Modern Language Journal* 78(4), 465–483.

Alvarado, C.S. (1992) Discourse styles and patterns of participation on ESL interactive tasks. *TESOL Quarterly* 26(3), 589–593.

Alyousef, H.S. and Picard, M.Y. (2011) Cooperative or collaborative literacy practices: Mapping metadiscourse in a business students' wiki group project. *Australasian Journal of Educational Technology* 27(3), 463–480.

Anton, M. and DiCamilla, F. (1998) Socio-cognitive functions of L1 collaborative interaction in the L2 classroom. *Canadian Modern Language Review* 54(3), 314–342.

Aragão, R. (2011) Beliefs and emotions in foreign language learning. *System* 39(3), 302–313.

Arnold, N., Ducate, L. and Kost, C. (2009) Collaborative writing in wikis: Insights from a culture project in a German class. In L. Lomicka and G. Lord (eds) *The next generation: Social networking and online collaboration in foreign language learning* (pp. 115–144). San Marcos, TX: CALICO.

Augar, N., Raitman, R. and Zhou, W. (2004) Teaching and learning online with wikis. In R. Atkinson, C. McBeath, D. Jonas-Dwyer and R. Phillips (eds) *Beyond the comfort zone: Proceedings of the 21st ASCILITE Conference* (pp. 95–104). Perth, 5–8 December. http://www.ascilite.org.au/conference/perth04/procs/augar.html.

Bachman, L.F. (1990) *Fundamental considerations in language testing*. Oxford: Oxford University Press.

Barcelos, A.M.F. (2003) Researching beliefs about SLA: a critical review. In P. Kalaja and A.M.F. Barcelos (eds) *Beliefs about SLA: New research approaches* (pp. 7–33). Dordrecht: Kluwer Academic Press.

Barcelos, A.M.F. and Kalaja, P. (2011) Introduction to beliefs about SLA Revisited. *System* 39(3), 281–289.

Bejarno, Y. (1987) A cooperative small-group methodology in the language classroom. *TESOL Quarterly* 21(3), 483–501.

Benson, P. and Lor, W. (1999) Conceptions of language and language learning. *System* 27(4), 459–472.

Bereiter, C. and Scardamalia, M. (1982) From conversation to composition: The role of instruction in the developmental process. In R. Glaser (ed.) *Advances in instructional psychology* (pp. 1–64). Hillsdale, NJ: Erlbaum.

Bernat E. and Gvozdenko, I. (2005) Beliefs about language learning: Current knowledge, pedagogical implications and new research directions. *TESL EJ* 9(1), 1–21.

Biggs, J. (2003) *Teaching for quality learning at university: What the student does*. (2nd edn). Buckingham: Society for Research into Higher Education: Open University Press.

Birdsong, D. (1989) *Metalinguistic performance and interlinguistic competence*. New York: Springer.

Blake, R. (2000) Computer-mediated communication: A window on L2 Spanish interlanguage. *Language Learning and Technology* 4(1), 120–136.

Borg, S. (2003) Teacher cognition in language teaching: A review of research on what language teachers think, know, believe, and do. *Language Teaching* 36(2), 81–109.

Boud, D., Cohen, R. and Sampson, J. (2001) *Peer learning in higher education: Learning from and with each other*. London: Kogan Page

Bower, M., Woo, K., Roberts, M. and Watters, P. A. (2006) Wiki pedagogy – A tale of two wikis. *Proceedings of the 7th International Conference on Information Technology Based Higher Education and Training* (pp. 187–198), Sydney, Australia.

Bradley, L., Lindström, B. and Rystedt, H. (2010) Rationalities of collaboration for language learning in a wiki. *ReCALL* 22(2), 247–265.

Breen, M. (1987) Learner contribution to task design. In C. Candlin and D.F. Murphy (eds) *Language learning tasks* (pp. 23–46). London: Prentice Hall International.

Breen, M. (2001) Introduction: Conceptualization, affect and action in context. In M. Breen (ed.) *Learner contributions to language learning: New directions in research* (pp. 1–11). Harlow: Pearson Education.

Bremner, S. (2010) Collaborative writing: Bridging the gap between the textbook and the workplace. *English for Specific Purposes* 29(2), 121–132.

Brooks, D.B. and Donato, R. (1994) Vygotskian approaches to understanding foreign language learner discourse during communicative tasks. *Hispania* 77(2), 262–274.

Brooks, L. and Swain, M. (2009) Languaging in collaborative writing: Creation and response to expertise. In A. Mackey and C. Polio (eds) *Multiple perspectives on interaction in SLA* (pp. 58–89). Mahwah, NJ: Lawrence Erlbaum.

Brown, A.V. (2009) Students' and teachers' perceptions of effective foreign language teaching: A comparison of ideal. *The Modern Language Journal* 93(1), 46–90.

Brown, S. and Adler, R.P. (2008) Minds on Fire: Open education, the long trail, and learning 2.0 *Educause Review* 43(1) 16–32. Retrieved on 20 August 2012 from http://www.educause.edu/ero/article/minds-fire-open-education-long-tail-and-learning-20
Bruffee, K.A. (1980) *A short course in writing*. Boston: Little, Brown.
Bruffee, K.A. (1984) Collaborative learning and the 'conversation of mankind'. *College English* 46(7), 635–652.
Butler, Y.G. (2011) The implementation of communicative and task-based language teaching in the Asia-Pacific Region. *Annual Review of Applied Linguistics* 31, 36–57.
Bygate, M., Skehan, P. and Swain, M. (eds) (2001) *Researching pedagogical tasks, second language learning, teaching and testing*. Harlow: Longman.
Camps, A., Guasch, O., Millan, M. and Ribas, T. (2000) Metalinguistic activity: The link between writing and learning to write. In A. Camps and M. Milan (eds) *Metalinguistic activity in learning to write* (pp. 103–124). Amsterdam: Amsterdam University Press.
Canale, M. (1983) From communicative competence to communicative language pedagogy. In J.C. Richards and R.W. Schmidt (eds) *Language and communication* (pp. 2–27). London: Longman.
Canale, M. and Swain, M. (1980) Theoretical bases of communicative approaches to second language teaching and testing. *Applied Linguistics* 1(1), 1–47.
Carless, D. (2007) The suitability of task-based approaches for secondary schools: Perspectives from Hong Kong. *System* 35(4), 595–608.
Carless, D. (2008) Students' use of the mother tongue in the task-based classroom. *ELT Journal* 62(4), 331–338.
Carr, T., Morrison, A., Cox, G. and Deacon, A. (2007) Weathering wikis: Net-based learning meets political science in a South African university. *Computers and Composition* 24(3), 266–284.
Carson, J.G. and Nelson, G.L. (1994) Writing groups: Cross-cultural issues. *Journal of Second Language Writing* 3(1), 17–30.
Carson, J.G. and Nelson, G.L. (1996) Chinese students' perceptions of ESL peer response group interaction. *Journal of Second Language Writing* 5(1), 1–19.
Chang, G. and Wells, G. (1988) The literate potential of collaborative talk. In T. Maclure, T. Phillips and A. Wilkson (eds) *Oracy Matters* (pp. 95–109). Stony Stratford, England: Open University Press.
Chao Y-C. and Lo, H-C. (2011) Students' perceptions of wiki-based collaborative writing for learners of English as a foreign language. *Interactive Learning Environments* 19(4), 395–411.
Chenoweth, N.A. and Hayes, J.R. (2001) Fluency in writing. Generating texts in L1 and L2. *Written Communication* 18(1), 80–98.
Chi, M.T.H., Bassok, M., Lewis, M.W., Reimann, P. and Glaser, R. (1989) Self explanations: how students study and use examples in learning to solve problems. *Cognitive Science* 13(2), 145–182.
Chi, M.T.H., Leeuw, N.D., Chiu, M. and Lavancher, C. (1994) Eliciting self explanations improves understanding. *Cognitive Science*, 18(3), 439–477.
Chisholm, R.M. (1990) Coping with the problems of collaborative writing. *The Writing Across the Curriculum Journal* 2, 90–108. Retrieved August 15, 2012 from http://wac.colostate.edu/journal/vol2/chisholm.pdf
Cole, M. (2009) Using wiki technology to support student engagement: Lessons from the trenches. *Computers and Education* 52, 141–146.
Colen, K. and Petelin, R. (2004) Challenges in collaborative writing in the contemporary corporation. *Corporate Communication* 9(2), 136–145.

Connor, U. and Asenavage, K. (1994) Peer response groups in ESL writing classes: How much impact on revision? *Journal of Second Language Writing* 3(3), 257–276.

Coughlan, P. and Duff, P. (1994) Same task, different activities: Analysis of SLA task from an activity theory perspective. In J.P. Lantolf and G. Appel (eds) *Vygotskian approaches to second language research* (pp. 173–191). Norwood, NJ: Ablex.

Cumming, A. (1989) Writing expertise and second language proficiency. *Language Learning* 39(1), 81–141.

Cumming, A. (1990) Metalinguistic and ideational thinking in second language composing. *Written Communication* 7(4), 482–511.

Daiute, C. (1986) Do 1 and 1 make 2? Patterns of influence by collaborative authors. *Written Communication* 3(3), 382–408.

Daiute C. and Dalton, B. (1993) Collaboration between children learning to write: Can novices be masters? *Cognition and Instruction* 10(4), 281–333.

Dale, H. (1994a) Collaborative research on collaborative writing. *The English Journal* 83(1), 66–70.

Dale, H. (1994b) Collaborative writing interaction in one ninth-grade classroom. *Journal of Educational Research* 87(6), 334–344.

Dale, H. (1997) *Co-authoring in the Classroom. Creating an Environment for Effective Collaboration*. Urbana Illinois: National Council of Teachers of English.

Damon, W. and Phelps, E. (1989) Critical distinctions among three approaches to peer education. *International Journal of Educational Research* 58(2), 9–19.

de Guerrero, M.C.M. and Villamil, O.S. (2000) Activating the ZPD: Mutual scaffolding in L2 peer revision. *The Modern Language Journal* 84(1), 51–68.

de St Léger and Storch, N. (2009) Learners' perceptions and attitudes: implications for willingness to communicate in an L2 classroom. *System* 37(2), 269–285.

Dewey, J. (1938/1970) *Experience and Education*. New York: Macmillan.

Dias, P., Freedman, A., Medway, P. and Pare, A. (1999) *Worlds apart: Acting and writing in academic and workplace contexts*. Mahwah, NJ: Lawrence Erlbaum.

DiCamilla, F.J. and Anton, M. (1997) Repetition in the collaborative discourse of L2 learners: A Vygotskian perspective. *The Canadian Modern Language Review* 53(4), 609–633.

Dillenbourg, P. (1999) Introduction: What do you mean by 'collaborative learning'? In P. Dillenbourg (ed.) *Collaborative Learning: Cognitive and Computational Approaches* (pp. 1–19). Amsterdam: Pergamon.

Dillenbourg, P., Baker, M., Blaye, A. and O'Malley, C. (1996) The evolution of research on collaborative writing. In P. Reimann and H. Spada (eds) *Learning in Humans and Machine: Towards an Interdisciplinary Learning Science* (pp. 189–211). Oxford, Elsevier.

DiNitto, R. (2000) Can collaboration be unsuccessful? A sociocultural analysis of classroom setting and Japanese L2 performance in group tasks. *Journal of the Association of Teachers of Japanese* 34(2), 179–210.

DiPardo, A. and Warshauer Freedman, S. (1988) Peer response groups in the writing classroom: Theoretic foundation and new directions. *Review of Educational Research* 58(2), 119–149.

Donato, R. (1988) Beyond group: A psycholinguistic rationale for collective activity in second-language learning. Unpublished doctoral dissertation, University of Delaware, Newark.

Donato, R. (1994) Collective scaffolding in second language learning. In J.P. Lantolf and G. Appel (eds) *Vygotskian Approaches to Second Language Research* (pp. 33–56). Norwood, NJ: Ablex.

Dörnyei, Z. and Kormos, J. (2000) The role of individual and social variables in oral task performance. *Language Teaching Research* 4(3), 275–300.
Dovey, T. (2006) What purposes, specifically? Re-thinking purposes and specificity in the context of the 'new vocationalism'. *English for Specific Purposes* 25, 387–402.
Ducate, L., Lomicka, L. and Moreno, N. (2011) Wading through the world of wikis: An analysis of three wiki projects. *Foreign Language Annals* 44(3), 495–524.
Duff, P.A. (1986) Another look at interlanguage talk: Taking task to task. In R.R. Day (ed.) *Talking to learn: Conversations in second language acquisition* (pp. 147–181). Rowley, MA: Newbury House.
Dunn, A. (1993) Dictogloss - When the words get in the way. *TESOL in Context* 3(2), 2–23.
Eckerth, J. (2008) Investigating consciousness-raising tasks: Pedagogically targeted and non-targeted learning gains. *International Journal of Applied Linguistics* 18(2), 121–145.
Ede, L. and Lunsford, A. (1990) *Singular texts/plural authors*. Carbondale: Southern Illonois University Press.
Elbow, P. (1973) *Writing without teachers*. Oxford: Oxford University Press.
Elbow, P. and Belanoff, P. (1989) *Sharing and responding*. New York: Random House.
Elgort, I., Smith, A. and Toland, J. (2008) Is wiki an effective platform for group course work? *Australasian Journal of Educational Technology* 24(2), 195–210.
Ellis, R. (1994) *The study of second language acquisition*. Oxford: Oxford University Press.
Ellis, R. (2003) *Task-based language learning and teaching*. Oxford: Oxford University Press.
Ellis, R., Basturkmen, H. and Loewen, S. (2001) Learner uptake in communicative ESL lessons. *Language Learning* 51(2), 281–318.
Elola, I. and Oskoz, A. (2010a) Collaborative writing: Fostering foreign language and writing conventions development. *Language Learning and Technology* 14(3), 51–71.
Elola, I. and Oskoz, A. (2010b) A social learning approach to writing in the FL classroom: Adopting new pedagogical approaches through the use of online components. In G. Levine and A. Phipps (eds) *Critical and intercultural theory and Language Pedagogy* (pp. 185–201). Boston, MA: Heinle and Heinle.
Elola, I. and Oskoz, A. (2011) Writing between the lines. Acquiring the presentational mode through social tools. In N. Arnold and L. Ducate (eds) *Present and future promises of CALL: From theory and research to new directions in language teaching* (pp. 171–210). San Marcos, TX: CALICO.
Emig, J. (1971) *The composing processes of twelfth graders*. Urbana, IL: National Council of Teachers of English.
Engstrom, M. and Jewett, D. (2005) Collaborative learning the wiki way. *Tech Trends* 49, 12–15.
Ewald, J.D. (2005) Language-related episodes in an assessment context: A 'small group quiz'. *The Canadian Modern Language Review* 61(4), 565–586.
Faigley, L. and Witte, S. (1981) Analysing revision. *College Composition and Communication* 32(4), 400–414.
Fernández Dobao, A. (2012) Collaborative writing tasks in the L2 classroom: Comparing group, pair, and individual work. *Journal of Second Language Writing* 21(1), 40–58.
Fernández Dobao, A. (forthcoming) Vocabulary learning in collaborative tasks: a comparison of pair and small group work. *Language Teaching Research*.
Fernández-Garcia, M. and Martínez Arbelaiz, A. (2003) Learners' interactions and the negotiation of meaning: A comparison of oral and computer-assisted written conversations. *ReCALL* 15(1), 113–136.
Ferris, D. and Hedgcock, J. (2005) *Teaching ESL composition: Purpose, process, and practice*. Mahwah, NJ: Lawrence Erlbaum.

Flower, L. (1979) Writer-based prose: A cognitive basis for problems in writing. *College English* 41(1), 19–37.
Flower, L. and Hayes, J.R. (1981) A cognitive process theory of writing. *College Composition and Communication* 32(4), 365–388.
Fortune, A. (2005) Learners' use of metalanguage in collaborative form-focused L2 output tasks. *Language Awareness* 14(1), 21–38.
Fortune, A. and Thorp, D. (2001) Knotted and entangled: New light on the identification, classification and value of language related episodes in collaborative output tasks. *Language Awareness* 10(2–3), 143–160.
Foster, P. (1998) A classroom perspective on the negotiation of meaning. *Applied Linguistics* 19(1), 1–23.
Foster, P. and Ohta, A. (2005) Negotiation for meaning and peer assistance in second language classrooms. *Applied Linguistics* 26(3), 402–430.
Fotos, S. and Ellis, R. (1991) Communicating about grammar: A task-based approach. *TESOL Quarterly* 25(4), 605–628.
Freire, P. (1970) *Pedagogy of the Oppressed*. (Trans. M.B. Ramos) New York: Continuum.
García Mayo, M.P. (2002a) The effectiveness of two form-focused tasks in advanced EFL pedagogy. *International Journal of Applied Linguistics* 12(2), 156–175.
García Mayo, M.P. (2002b) Interaction in advanced EFL pedagogy: A comparison of form-focused activities. *International Journal of Educational Research* 37(3-4), 323–341.
Garrett, P. and Shortall, T. (2002) Learners' evaluations of teacher-fronted and student-centred classroom activities. *Language Teaching Research* 6(1), 25–57.
Gass, S. (1997) *Input, interaction, and the second language learner*. Mahwah, NJ: Erlbaum.
Gass, S. (2003) Input and interaction. In C. Doughty and M.H. Long (ed) *The handbook of second language acquisition* (pp. 224–255). Oxford, UK: Blackwell.
Gass, S. and Mackey, A. (2007) *Data elicitation for second and foreign language research*. Mahwah, NJ: Lawrence Erlbaum.
Gass, S., Mackey, A. and Ross-Feldman, L. (2011) Task-based interactions in classroom and laboratory settings. *Language Learning*, 61: Suppl. 1, 189–220.
Godwin-Jones, R. (2003) Emerging technologies. Blogs and wikis: environments for online collaboration. *Language Learning and Technology* 7(2), 12–16.
Gollin, S. (1999) 'Why? I thought we'd talked about it before': Collaborative writing in a professional workplace setting. In C. Candlin and K. Hyland (eds) *Writing: Texts, processes and practices* (pp. 267–290). London: Longman.
Graham, S. (2006) A study of students' metacognitive beliefs about foreign language study and their impact on learning. *Foreign Language Annals* 39(2), 296–309.
Grant, L. (2006) Using wikis in schools: A case study. *Futurelab*. Retrieved 24 August 2012 from http://www2.futurelab.org.uk/resources/publications-reports-articles/discussion-papers/Discussion-Paper258
Grant, L. (2009) 'I don't care do ur own page!' A case study of using wikis for collaborative work in a UK secondary school. *Learning, Media and Technology* 32(2), 105–117.
Green, J.M. (1993) Student attitudes toward communicative and non-communicative activities: Do enjoyment and effectiveness go together? *The Modern Language Journal* 77(1), 1–10.
Guk, H. and Kellogg, D. (2007) The ZPD and whole class teaching: Teacher-led and student-led interactional mediation of tasks. *Language Teaching Research* 11(3), 281–299
Gutiérrez, K.D. (1994) How talk, context, and script shape contexts for learning: A cross-case comparison of journal sharing. *Linguistics and Education* 5(3-4), 335–365.

Gutiérrez, K.D. and Stone, L.D. (2000) Synchronic and diachronic dimensions of social practice. In C.D. Lee and P. Smagorinsky (eds) *Vygotskian perspectives on literacy research* (pp. 150–164). Cambridge: Cambridge University Press.

Gutiérrez, X. (2008) What does metalinguistic activity in learners' interaction during a collaborative L2 writing task look like? *The Modern Language Journal* 92(4), 519–537.

Hall, J.K. and Walsh, M. (2002) Teacher–student interaction and language learning. *Annual Review of Applied Linguistics* 22, 186–203.

Hanaoka, O. (2007) Output, noticing, and learning: An investigation into the role of spontaneous attention to form in a four-stage writing task. *Language Teaching Research* 11(4), 459–479.

Harklau, L. (2002) The role of writing in classroom second language acquisition. *Journal of Second Language Writing* 11(4), 329–350.

Harley, B. and Swain, M. (1984) The interlanguage of immersion students and its implications for second language teaching. In A. Davies, C. Criper and H. Howatt (eds) *Interlanguage* (pp. 291–311). Edinburgh: Edinburgh University Press.

Harris, J. (1994) Definition of collaborative writing. In J.S. Leonard, C.E. Wharton, R. M. Davis and J. Harris (eds) *Authority and textuality. Current views of collaborative writing* (pp. 77–84). West Cornwall, CT: Locus Hill Press.

Hayes, J.R. (1996) A new framework for understanding cognition and effect in writing. In C.M. Levy and S. Randsdell (eds) *The science of writing: Theories, methods, and individual differences and applications* (pp. 1–27). Mahwah, NJ: Lawrence Erlbaum.

Hillebrand, R.P. (1994) Control and cohesion: Collaborative learning and writing. *English Journal* 83(1), 71–74.

Hirvela, A. (2007) *Connecting reading and writing in second language writing instruction*. Ann Arbor: The University of Michigan Press.

Horwitz, E.K. (1985) Using student beliefs about language learning and teaching in the foreign language methods course. *Foreign Language Annals* 18(4), 333–340.

Horwitz, E.K. (1987) Surveying student beliefs about language learning. In A. Wenden and J. Rubin (eds) *Learner strategies in language learning* (pp. 119–132). New York: Prentice Hall.

Horwitz, E.K. (1988) The beliefs about language learning of beginning university foreign language students. *The Modern Language Journal* 72(3), 283–294.

Hughes, J.E. and Narayan, R. (2009) Collaboration and learning with wikis in post-secondary classrooms. *Journal of Interactive Online Learning* 8(1), 63–82.

Hunter, R. (2011) Erasing 'property lines': A collaborative notion of authorship and textual ownership on a fan wiki. *Computers and Composition* 28(1), 40–56.

Hyde, M. (1993) Pair work – A blessing or a curse? An analysis of pair work from pedagogical, cultural, social and psychological perspectives. *System* 21(3), 343–348.

Ives, D. (2004) Three NS–NNS upper primary school pairs. A case study. *Australian Language and Literacy Matters* 1(4), 11–16.

Iwashita, N. (2001) The effect of learner proficiency on interactional moves and modified output in nonnative–nonnative interaction in Japanese as a foreign language. *System* 29(2), 267–287.

Izumi, S. (2002) Output, input enhancement, and the noticing hypothesis: An experimental study in ESL relativisation. *Studies in Second Language Acquisition* 24(4), 541–577.

Izumi, S. and Bigelow, M. (2000) Does output promote noticing and second language acquisition? *TESOL Quarterly* 34(2), 239–278.

Izumi, Y. and Izumi, S. (2004) Investigating the effects of oral output in the learning of relative clauses in English: Issues in the psycholinguistic requirements for effective output tasks. *The Canadian Modern Language Review* 60(5), 587–609.

Jacobs, G. (1989) Miscorrection in peer feedback in writing class. *RELC Journal* 20(1), 68–76.

Jacoby, S. and Gonzales, P. (1991) The constitution of expert-novice in scientific discourse. *Issues in Applied Linguistics* 2(2), 149–181.

Johnson, D.W. and Johnson, R.T. (1979) Conflict in the classroom: Controversy and learning. *Review of Educational Research* 49(1), 51–70.

Johnson, D.W. and Johnson, R.T. (1994) Cooperative learning in the culturally diverse classroom. In R.A. DeVillar, C.J. Faltis and J.P. Cummings (eds) *Cultural diversity in schools: From rhetoric to practice* (pp. 57–73). New York: State University of New York Press.

Jones, P. (2007) When a wiki is the way: Exploring the use of a wiki in a constructively aligned learning design. In *ICT: Providing choices for learners and learning. Proceedings ascilite Singapore 2007* (pp. 460–466). http://www.ascilite.org.au/conferences/singapore07/procs/jones-p.pdf.

Jones, P. (2010) Collaboration at a distance: Using a wiki to create a collaborative learning environment for distance education and on-campus students in a social work course. *Journal of Teaching in Social Work* 30, 225–236.

Judd, T., Kennedy, G. and Cropper, S. (2010) Using wikis for collaborative learning: Assessing collaboration through contribution. *Australasian Journal of Educational Technology* 26(3), 341–354.

Kalaja, P. and Barcelos, A M.F. (eds) (2003) *Beliefs about SLA: New research approaches* (pp. 1–4). Dordrecht: Kluwer Academic Press.

Kang, S. (2005) Dynamic emergence of situational willingness to communicate in a second language. *System* 33(2), 277–292.

Keck, C.M., Iberri-Shea, G., Tracy-Ventura, N. and Wa-Mbaleka, S. (2006) Investigating the empirical link between task-based interaction and acquisition: a meta-analysis. In J. Norris and L. Ortega (eds) *Synthesizing research on language learning and teaching* (pp. 91–131). Amsterdam: John Benjamins.

Kern, R. (1995) Students' and teachers' beliefs about language learning. *Foreign Language Annals* 28(1), 71–91.

Kern, R., Ware, P. and Warschauer, M. (2004) Crossing frontiers: New directions in online pedagogy and research. *Annual Review of Applied Linguistics* 24, 243–260.

Kessler, G. (2009) Student-initiated attention to form in wiki-based collaborative writing. *Language Learning and Technology* 13(1), 79–95.

Kessler, G. and Bikowski, D. (2010) Developing collaborative autonomous learning abilities in computer mediated language learning: attention to meaning among students in wiki space. *Computer Assisted Language Learning* 23(1), 41–58.

Kessler, G., Bikowski, D. and Boggs, J. (2012) Collaborative writing among second language learners in academic web-based projects. *Language Learning and Technology* 16(1), 91–109.

Kim, Y. (2008) The contribution of collaborative and individual tasks to the acquisition of L2 vocabulary. *The Modern Language Journal* 92(1), 114–130.

Kim Y. and McDonough, K. (2008) The effect of interlocutor proficiency on the collaborative dialogue between Korean as a second language learners. *Language Teaching Research* 12(2), 211–234.

Kim Y. and McDonough, K. (2011) Using pretask modelling to encourage collaborative language learning opportunities. *Language Teaching Research* 15(2), 183–199.

Kinsella, K. (1996) Designing group work that supports and enhances diverse classroom work style. *TESOL Journal* 6(1), 24–30.
Kost, C. (2011) Investigating writing strategies and revision behaviour in collaborative writing projects. *CALICO Journal* 28(3), 606–620.
Kowal, M. and Swain, M. (1994) Using collaborative language production tasks to promote students' language awareness. *Language Awareness* 3(2), 73–93.
Krashen, S.D. (1981) *Second language acquisition and second language learning.* Oxford: Pergamon Press.
Krashen, S.D. (1982) *Principles and practice in second language acquisition.* Oxford: Pergamon Press.
Krashen, S.D. (1985) *The input hypothesis: Issues and implications.* London: Longman.
Kuiken, F. and Vedder, I. (2002) The effect of interaction in acquiring the grammar of a second language. *International Journal of Educational Research* 37(3-4), 343–358.
Kumaravadivelu, B. (2003) *Beyond methods: Macrostrategies for language teaching.* New Haven, CT: Yale University Press.
Kumaravadivelu, B. (2006) TESOL methods: Changing tracks, challenging trends. *TESOL Quarterly* 40(1), 59–81.
Kuteeva, M. (2011) Wikis and academic writing: Changing the writer–reader relationship. *English for Specific Purposes* 30(1), 44–57.
Lai, C. and Zhao, Y. (2006) Noticing and text-based chat. *Language Learning and Technology* 10(3), 102–120.
Lantolf, J.P. (2000) Introducing sociocultural theory. In J.P. Lantolf (ed.) *Sociocultural theory and second language learning* (pp. 1–26). Oxford: Oxford University Press.
Lantolf, J.P. (2005) Sociocultural theory and L2 learning: An exegesis. In E. Hinkel (ed.) *Handbook of research in second language teaching and learning* (pp. 335–354). Mahwah, NJ: Erlbaum.
Lantolf, J.P. (2006) Sociocultural theory and L2. State of the art. *Studies in Second Language Acquisition* 28(1) 67–109.
Lantolf, J.P. and Thorne, S. (2006) *The sociogenesis of second language development.* Oxford: Oxford University Press.
Lantolf, J.P. and Yañez-Prieto, C. (2003) Talking yourself into Spanish: Intrapersonal communication and second language learning. *Hispania* 86(1), 97–109.
LaPierre, D. (1994) Language output in a cooperative learning setting: Determining its effects on second language learning. Unpublished master's thesis, Ontario Institute for Studies in Education. University of Toronto, Ontario, Canada.
Lay, M.M. and Karis, W.M. (eds) (1991) *Collaborative writing in industry: investigations in theory and practice.* Farmingdale, NY: Baywood.
Lee, L. (2001) Online interaction: Negotiation of meaning and strategies used among learners of Spanish. *ReCALL* 13(2), 232–244.
Lee, L. (2002) Synchronous online exchanges: A study of modification devices on non-native discourse. *System* 30(2), 275–288.
Lee, L. (2010) Exploring wiki-mediated collaborative writing: A case study in an elementary Spanish course. *CALICO Journal* 27(2), 260–276.
Leeser, M.J. (2004) Learner proficiency and focus on form during collaborative dialogue. *Language Teaching Research* 8(1), 55–81.
Leki, I. (2001) 'A narrow thinking system': Nonnative-English-speaking students in group projects across the curriculum. *TESOL Quarterly* 35(1), 39–68.
Leki, I. and Carson, J. (1994) Students' perceptions of EAP writing instruction and writing across the disciplines. *TESOL Quarterly* 28(1), 81–101.

Leonard, J.S., Wharton, C.E., Davis, R.M. and Harris, J. (eds) (1994) *Author-ity and textuality. Current views of collaborative writing*. West Cornwall, CT: Locust Hill Press.

Leow, R. (1997) Attention, awareness, and foreign language behaviour. *Language Learning* 47(3), 467–505.

Leuf, B. and Cunningham, W. (2001) *The wiki way: Quick collaboration on the web*. Boston, MA: Addison-Wesley Longman.

Li, M. (2012) Use of wikis in second/foreign language classes: A literature review. *CALL-EJ* 13(1), 17–35.

Li, M. and Zhu, W. (2011) Patterns of computer-mediated interaction in small writing groups using wikis. *Computer Assisted Language Learning* 24(1), 1–22.

Lightbown, P. (1991) What have we here? Some observations on the influence of instruction on L2 learning. In R. Phillipson, E. Kellerman, L. Selinker, M. Sharwood Smith and M. Swain (eds) *Foreign/Second language pedagogy: A commemorative volume for Claus Faerch* (pp. 197–212). Philadelphia: Multilingual Matters.

Lin, H. and Kelsey, K. (2009) Building a net- worked environment in wikis: The evolving phases of collaborative learning in a wikibook project. *Journal of Educational Computing Research* 40(2), 145–169.

Little, D. and Singleton, D. (1990) Cognitive style and learning approach. In R. Duda and P. Riley (eds) *Learning styles* (pp. 11–19). Nancy, France: University of Nancy.

Littlewood, W. (2010) Chinese and Japanese students' conceptions of the 'ideal English lesson'. *RELC Journal* 41(1), 46–58.

Littlewood, W. (2011) Communicative language teaching. An expanding concept for a changing world. In E. Hinkel (ed.) *Handbook of research in second language teaching and learning*, Vol. 2. (pp. 541–557). New York: Routledge.

Lockhart, C. and Ng, P. (1995) Analyzing talk in ESL peer response groups: Stances, functions and content. *Language learning* 45(4), 605–655.

Loewen, S. (2005) Incidental focus on form and second language learning. *Studies in Second Language Acquisition* 27(3), 361–386.

Loewen, S. and Philp, J. (2006) Recasts in the adult English L2 classroom: characteristics, explicitness, and effectiveness. *Modern Language Journal* 90(4), 536–56.

Long, M.H. (1983) Native speaker/non-native speaker conversation and the negotiation of comprehensible input. *Applied Linguistics* 4(2), 126–141.

Long, M.H. (1985) Input and second language acquisition theory. In S.M. Gass and C.G. Madden (eds) *Input in second language acquisition* (pp. 377–393). Rowley, NA: Newbury House.

Long, M.H. (1991) Focus on form: A design feature in language teaching methodology. In K. de Bot, R.B. Ginsberg and C. Kramsch (eds) *Foreign language research in a cross-cultural perspective* (pp. 39–52). Amsterdam: Benjamins.

Long, M.H. (1996) The role of the linguistic environment in second language acquisition. In W.C. Ritchie and T.K. Bhatia (eds) *Handbook of language acquisition. Vol. 2: Second language acquisition* (pp. 413–468). New York: Academic Press.

Long, M. (2000) Focus on form in task-based language teaching. In R.D. Lambert and E. Shohamy (eds) *Language policy and pedagogy: Essays in honor of A. Ronald Walton* (pp. 179–192). Amsterdam: John Benjamins.

Long, M.H. (2007) *Problems in SLA*. New York: Lawrence Erlbaum.

Long, M.H. and Crookes, G. (1992) Three approaches to task-based language teaching. *TESOL Quarterly* 26(1), 27–56.

Long, M.H. and Porter, P.A. (1985) Group work, interlanguage talk, and second language acquisition. *TESOL Quarterly* 19(2), 207–227.

Long, M.H. and Robinson, P. (1989) Focus on form: Theory, research and practice. In C.J. Doughty and J. Williams (eds) *Focus on form in classroom second language acquisition* (pp. 15–41). Cambridge: Cambridge University Press.

Louth, R., McAllister, C. and McAllister, H.A. (1993) The effects of collaborative writing techniques on freshmen writing and attitudes. *The Journal of Experimental Education* 61(3), 215–224.

Lund, A. (2008) Wikis: a collective approach to language production. *ReCALL*, 20(1), 35–54.

Lund, A. and Smørdal, O. (2006) Is there space for the teacher in a wiki? In: *Proceedings of the 2006 International Symposium on Wikis* (WikiSym '06) (pp. 37–46). Odense, Denmark: ACM Press.

Macdonald, J. (2003) Assessing online collaborative learning: process and product. *Computers and Education* 40(4), 377–391.

Mackey, A. (2007) Interaction as practice. In R. DeKeyser (ed.) *Practice in a second language: Perspectives from applied linguistics and cognitive psychology* (pp. 85–110). New York: Cambridge University Press.

Mackey, A. and Goo, J. (2007) Interaction research in SLA: A meta-analysis and research synthesis. In A. Mackey (ed.) *Conversational Interaction in Second Language Acquisition: A Collection of Empirical Studies* (pp. 407–452). Oxford: Oxford University Press.

Mackey, A., McDonough, K., Fuji, A. and Tatsumi, T. (2001) Investigating learners' reports about the L2 classroom. *IRAL* 39(4), 285–307.

Mackey, A., Oliver, R. and Leeman, J. (2003) Interactional input and the incorporation of feedback: An exploration of NS–NNS and NNS–NNS adult and child dyads. *Language Learning* 53(1), 35–66.

Mackey, A., Philp, J., Egi, T. and Tatsumi, T. (2002) Individual differences in working memory, noticing interactional feedback and L2 development. In P. Robinson (ed.) *Individual differences and instructed language learning* (pp. 181–209). Philadelphia: Benjamins.

Mak, B. and Coniam, D. (2008) Using wikis to enhance and develop writing skills among secondary school students in Hong Kong. *System* 36(3), 437–455.

Malmqvist, A. (2005) How does group discussion in reconstruction tasks affect written language output? *Language Awareness* 14(2-3), 128–141.

Manchón, R.M. (2009) Introduction: Broadening the perspective of L2 writing scholarship: The contribution of research on foreign language writing. In R. Manchón (ed.) *Writing in foreign language contexts: Learning, teaching, and research* (pp. 1–22). Clevedon, UK: Multilingual Matters.

Manchón, R. (2011a) The language learning potential of writing in foreign language contexts: Lessons from research. In T. Cimasko and M. Reichelt (eds) *Foreign language writing instruction. Principles and practices* (pp. 44–64). Anderson, South Carolina: Parlor Press.

Manchón, R. (2011b) Writing to learn the language: Issues in theory and research. In R. Manchón (ed.) *Learning-to-write and writing-to-learn in an additional language* (pp. 61–84). Amsterdam/Philadelphia: John Benjamins.

Manchón, R.M., Roca de Larios, J. and Murphy, L. (2009) The temporal dimension and problem-solving nature of foreign language composing processes. Implications for theory. In R.M. Manchón (ed.) *Writing in foreign language contexts. Learning, teaching, and research* (pp. 102–129). Bristol, UK: Multilingual Matters.

Matsuda, P.K. (2003) Process and post-process: A discursive history. *Journal of Second Language Writing* 12, 65–83.

Matthew, K.I., Felvegi, E. and Callaway, R.A. (2009) Wiki as a collaborative learning tool in a language arts methods class. *Journal of Research on Technology in Education* 42(1), 51–72.

McCarthey, S.J. and McMahon, S. (1992) From convention to invention: Three approaches to peer interactions during writing. In R. Hertz-Lazarowitz and N. Miller (eds) *Interaction in cooperative groups. The theoretical anatomy of group learning* (pp. 17–35). Cambridge: Cambridge University Press.

McDonough, K. (2004) Learner–learner interaction during pair and small group activities in a Thai EFL context. *System* 32(2), 207–224.

McDonough, K. and Sunitham, W. (2009) Collaborative dialogue between Thai EFL learners during self-access computer activities. *TESOL Quarterly* 43(2), 231–254.

McLoughlin, C. and Lee, M.J.W. (2007) Social software and participatory learning: Pedagogical choices with technology affordances in the Web 2.0 era. In ICT: Providing choices for learners and learning. *Proceedings of Ascilite Singapore 2007*, pp. –675. http://www.ascilite.org.au/conference/singapore07/procs/mcloughlin.pdf

Mercer, S. (2011) Language learner self-concept: complexity, continuity and change. *System* 39(3), 335–346.

Meyer, K.A. (2003) Face-to-face versus threaded discussions: the role of time and higher-order thinking. *Journal of Asynchronous Learning Networks* 7(3), 55–65.

Mirel, B. and Spilka, R. (eds) (2002) *Reshaping technical communication: New directions and challenges for the 21st century.* Mahwah, NJ: Lawrence Erlbaum.

Mishra, S. and Oliver, R. (1998) Secondary school ESL learners' perceptions of pair work in Australian classrooms. *TESOL in Context* 8(2), 19–23.

Miyazoe, T. and Anderson, T. (2010) Learning outcomes and students' perceptions of online writing: Simultaneous implementation of a forum, blog, and wiki in an EFL blended learning setting. *System* 38(2), 185–199

Myers, G. (2010) *Discourse of blogs and wikis.* London: Continuum.

Nakahama, Y., Tyler, A. and van Lier, L. (2001) Negotiation of meaning in conversational and information gap activities: A comparative discourse analysis. *TESOL Quarterly* 35(3), 377–406.

Nassaji, H. and Swain, M. (2000) Vygotskian perspective on corrective feedback in L2: The effect of random vs. negotiated help on the learning of English articles. *Language Awareness* 9(1), 34–51.

Nassaji, H. and Tian, J. (2010) Collaborative and individual output tasks and their effects on learnng English phrasal verbs. *Language Teaching Research* 14(4), 397–419.

Navarro, D. and Thornton, K. (2011) Investigating the relationship between belief and action in self-directed language learning. *System* 39(3), 290–301.

Negueruela-Azarola, E. (2011) Beliefs as conceptualizing activity: a dialectical approach for second language classroom. *System* 39(3), 359–369.

Nelson, G.L. and Carson, J.G. (1998) ESL students' perceptions of effectiveness of peer response groups. *Journal of Second Language Writing* 7(2), 113–131.

Nelson, G.L. and Murphy, J.M. (1993) Peer response groups: do L2 writers use peer comments in writing their drafts? *TESOL Quarterly* 27(1), 135–142.

Neumann, D. and Hood, M. (2009) The effects of using a wiki on student engagement and learning of report writing skills in a university statistics course. *Australasian Journal of Educational Technology* 25(3), 382–398.

Niu, R. (2009) Effect of task-inherent production modes on EFL learners' focus on form. *Language Awareness* 18(3-4), 384–402.

Nobuyoshi, J. and Ellis, R. (1993) Focused communication tasks and second language acquisition. *English Language Teaching Journal* 47(3), 203–210.

O'Donnell, A.M., Dansereau, D.F., Rocklin, T., Lambiotte, J.G., Hythecker, V.I. and Larson, C.O. (1985) Cooperative writing: Direct effects and transfer. *Written Communication* 2(3), 307–315.
O'Donnell, A.M. and Hoy, A.W. (2002) Promoting thinking through peer learning. *Theory Into Practice* 41(1), 2–4.
Ohta, A.S. (1995) Applying sociocultural theory to an analysis of learner discourse: Learner–learner collaborative interaction in the zone of proximal development. *Issues in Applied Linguistics* 6(2), 93–121.
Ohta, A.S. (2000) Rethinking interaction in SLA: Developmentally appropriate assistance in the zone of proximal development and the acquisition of L2 grammar. In J.P. Lantolf (ed.) *Sociocultural theory and second language learning* (pp. 51–78). Oxford: Oxford University Press.
Ohta, A.S. (2001) *Second language acquisition processes in the classroom. Learning Japanese.* Mahwah, NJ: Lawrence Erlbaum
Oliver, R. (1995) Negative feedback in child NS–NNS interactions. *Studies in Second Language Acquisition* 18(4), 459–481.
Ortega, L. (2007) Meaningful L2 practice in foreign language classrooms: A cognitive-interactionist SLA perspective. In R.M. DeKeyser (ed.) Practice in a second language. *Perspectives from applied linguistics and cognitive psychology* (pp. 180–207). Cambridge: Cambridge University Press.
Ortega, L. (2009a) Interaction and attention to form in L2 text-based computer-mediated communication. In A. Mackey and C. Polio (eds) *Multiple perspectives on interaction. Second language research in honour of Susan Gass* (pp. 226–253). New York: Routledge.
Ortega, L. (2009b) Studying writing across EFL contexts: Looking back and moving forward. In R. Manchón (ed.) *Writing in foreign language contexts: Learning, teaching, and research* (pp. 232–255). Clevedon: Multilingual Matters.
Oskoz, A. and Elola, I. (2011) Meeting at the wiki: The new arena for collaborative writing in foreign language courses. In M. Lee and C. McLaughlin (eds) *Web 2.0-based e-learning: Applying social informatics for tertiary teaching* (pp. 209–227). Hershey, PA: IGI Global.
Oskoz, A. and Elola, I. (2012) Understanding the impact of social tools in the FL writing classroom: Activity theory at work. In G. Kessler, A. Oskoz and I. Elola (eds) *Technology across writing contexts and tasks* (pp. 131–153). San Marcos, Texas: CALICO.
Osman-Schlegel, L., Fluker, G. and Cheng, S.T. (2011) Working collaboratively in a group assignment using a Mediawiki for an architecture and construction management undergraduate unit. In *Proceedings ASCILITE 2011. Changing demands, changing directions* (pp. 947–957). Hobart, Australia.
Pajares, F.M. (1992) Teachers' beliefs and educational research: Cleaning up a messy construct. *Review of Educational Research* 62(3), 307–332.
Palmeri, J. (2004) When discourses collide: A case study of interprofessional collaborative writing in a medically oriented law firm. *Journal of Business Communication* 4(1), 37–65.
Paribakht, T.S. and Wesche, M. (1997) Vocabulary enhancement activities and reading for meaning in second language vocabulary acquisition. In J. Coady and T. Huckin (eds) *Second language vocabulary acquisition: A rationale for pedagogy* (pp. 174–200). Cambridge: Cambridge University Press.
Parker, K.R. and Chao, J.T. (2007) Wiki as a teaching tool. *Interdisciplinary Journal of Knowledge and Learning Objects* 3, 57–72.
Peacock, M. (2001) Pre-service ESL teachers' beliefs about second language learning: A longitudinal study. *System* 29(2), 177–195.

Pellettieri, J. (2000) Negotiation in cyberspace: The role of chatting in the development of grammatical competence. In M. Warschauer and R. Kern (eds) *Network-based language teaching: Concepts and practice* (pp. 59–86). New York: Cambridge University Press.

Peng, J.E. (2011) Changes in language learning beliefs during a transition to tertiary study: the mediation of classroom affordances. *System* 39(3), 314–324.

Perl, S. (1980) Understanding composing. *College Composition and Communication* 31(4), 363–369.

Petrovsky, A.V. (1983a) Toward a construction of a social psychological theory of the collective. *Soviet Psychology* 21(2), 3–21.

Petrovsky, A.V. (1983b) The new status of psychological theory concerning groups and collectives. *Soviet Psychology* 21(4), 57–78.

Pfaff, E. and Huddleston, P. (2003) Does it matter if I hate teamwork? What impacts student attitudes toward teamwork. *Journal of Marketing Education* 25(1), 37–45.

Philp, J. and Mackey, A. (2010) Interaction research: what can socially informed approaches offer to cognitivists (and vice versa)? In R. Batstone (ed.) *Sociocognitive perspectives on language use and language learning* (pp. 210–228). Oxford: Oxford University Press.

Pica, T. (1992) The textual outcomes of native speaker/non-native speaker negotiation: what do they reveal about second language learning? In C. Kramsch and S. McConnell-Ginet (eds) *Text and context: cross disciplinary perspectives on language study* (pp. 198–237). Lexington, MA: D. C. Heath.

Pica, T. (1994) Review article: Research on negotiation: What does it reveal about second language learning conditions, processes, and outcomes? *Language Learning* 44(3), 493–527.

Pica, T. (1996) The essential role of negotiation in the second language classroom. *JALT Journal* 78(2), 241–68.

Pica, T. and Doughty, C. (1986) Input and interaction in the communicative language classroom: A comparison of teacher-fronted and group activities. In S. Gass and C. Madden (eds) *Input and second language acquisition* (pp. 115–132). Rowley, MA: Newbury House.

Pica, T. and Doughty, C. (1988) Variations in classroom interaction as a function of participation pattern and task. In J. Fine (ed.) *Second language discourse. A textbook of current research* (pp. 41–58). Norwood, NJ: Ablex.

Pica, T., Kanagy, R. and Falodun, J. (1993) Choosing and using communication tasks for second language instruction and research. In G. Crookes and S. Gass (eds) *Task and Language Learning* (pp. 9–34.) Clevedon: Multilingual Matters.

Pica, T., Lincoln-Porter, F., Paninos, D. and Linnel, J. (1996) Language learners' interaction: How does it address the input, output and feedback needs of L2 learners? *TESOL Quarterly* 30(1), 59–83.

Pienemann, M. (1989) Is language teachable? Psycholinguistic experiments and hypotheses. *Applied Linguistics* 10(1), 52–79.

Polio, C. and Gass, S.M. (1998) The role of interaction in native speaker comprehension of nonnative speaker speech. *The Modern Language Journal* 82(3), 308–319.

Purpura, J. (2004) *Assessing grammar*. Cambridge: Cambridge University Press.

Qi, D.S. and Lapkin, S. (2001) Exploring the role of noticing in a three-stage second language writing task. *Journal of Second Language Writing* 10(4), 277–303.

Reichelt, M. (2009) A critical evaluation of writing teaching programmes in different foreign language settings. In R.M. Manchón (ed.) *Writing in foreign language contexts. Learning, teaching, and research* (pp. 183–208). Bristol: Multilingual Matters.

Reid, J.M. (1987) The learning style preferences of ESL students. *TESOL Quarterly* 21(1), 87–111.

Reinders, H. (2009) Learner uptake and acquisition in three grammar-oriented production activities. *Language Teaching Research* 13(2), 201–222.

Richards, J.C. and Rogers, T.S. (2001) *Approaches and methods in language teaching* (2nd edn). Cambridge: Cambridge University Press.

Rick, J. and Guzdial, M. (2006) Situating CoWeb: A scholarship of application. *International Journal of Computer-Supported Collaborative Learning* 1(1), 89–115.

Riley, P. (2009) Shifts in beliefs about second language learning. *RELC Journal* 40(1), 102–124.

Roca de Larios, J., Manchón, R.M. and Murphy, L. (2006) Generating text in native and foreign language writing: A temporal analysis of problem solving formulation processes. *The Modern Language Journal* 90(1), 100–114.

Roed, J. (2003) Language and learner behavior in a virtual environment. *Computer Assisted Language Learning* 16(2-3), 155–172.

Roskams, T. (1999) Chinese EFL students' attitude to peer feedback and peer assessment in an extended pairwork setting. *RELC Journal* 30(1), 79–123.

Rulon, K.A. and McCreary, J. (1986) Negotiation of content: Teacher-fronted and small-group interaction. In R.D. Richard (ed.) *Talking to learn: Conversation in second language acquisition* (pp. 182–199). Rowley, Mass: Newbury House.

Samuda, V. and Bygate, M. (2008) *Tasks in second language learning*. New York: Palgrave Macmillan.

Savignon, S.J. (1983) *Communicative competence: Theory and classroom practice*. Reading, MA: Addison-Wesley.

Savignon, S.J. (2005) Communicative language teaching: strategies and goals. In E. Hinkel (ed.) *Handbook of research in second language teaching and learning* (pp. 635–651). Mahwah, NJ: Erlbaum.

Schmidt, R. (1983) Interaction, acculturation, and the acquisition of communicative competence: A case study of an adult. In N. Wolfson and E. Judd (eds) *Sociolinguistics and second language acquisition* (pp. 137–174). New York: Newbury House.

Schmidt, R. (1990) The role of consciousness in second language learning. *Applied Linguistics* 11 (2), 192–196.

Schmidt, R. (1994) Deconstructing consciousness in search of useful definitions for applied linguistics. *AILA Review* 11(1), 11–26.

Schneider, B. and Andre, J. (2005) University preparation for workplace writing: An exploratory study of the perceptions of students in three disciplines. *Journal of Business Communication* 42(2), 195–218.

Schrage, M. (1994) Writing to collaborate; collaborating to write. In J.S. Leonard, C.E. Wharton, R.M. Davis and J. Harris (eds) *Authority and textuality. Current views of collaborative writing* (pp. 17–24). West Cornwall, CT: Locus Hill Press.

Scott, V.M. and de la Fuente, M.J. (2008) What's the problem? L2 learners' use of the L1 during consciousness-raising form-focused tasks. *The Modern Language Journal* 92(1), 100–113.

Sheen, R. (1992) Problem solving brought to task. *RELC Journal* 23(2), 44–59.

Sheen, R. (1994) A critical analysis of the advocacy of the task-based syllabus. *TESOL Quarterly* 28(1), 127–151.

Shehadeh, A. (2011) Effects and student perceptions of collaborative writing in L2. *Journal of Second Language Writing* 20(4), 286–305.

Shekary, M. and Tahririan, M.H. (2006) Negotiation of meaning and noticing in text-based online chat. *The Modern Language Journal* 90(4), 557–573.

Skehan, P. (2003) Task-based instruction. *Language Teaching* 36(1), 1–14.

Slavin, R.E. (1992) When and why does cooperative learning increase achievement? Theoretical and empirical perspectives. In R. Hertz-Lazarowitz and N. Miller (eds) *Interaction in cooperative groups. The theoretical anatomy of group learning* (pp. 145–173). Cambridge: Cambridge University Press.

Smith, B. (2003) Computer-mediated negotiated interaction: An expanded model. *The Modern Language Journal* 87(1), 38–58.

Smith, B. (2004) Computer-mediated negotiated interaction and lexical acquisition. *Studies in Second Language Acquisition* 26(3), 365–398.

Smith, B. (2005) The relationship between negotiated interaction, learner uptake, and lexical acquisition in task-based computer-mediated communication. *TESOL Quarterly* 39(1), 33–58.

Sommers, N. (1980) Revision strategies of student writers and experienced adult writers. *College Composition and Communication* 31(4), 378–388.

Stahl, G. (2006) *Group cognition: Computer support for building collaborative knowledge.* Michigan: MIT Press.

Stone, C. (1993) What is missing in the metaphor of scaffolding. In E.A. Forman, N. Minick and C.A. Stone (eds) *Contexts for learning: Sociocultural dynamics in children's development* (pp. 169–183). Oxford: Oxford University Press.

Storch, N. (1997) The editing talk of adult ESL learners. *Language Awareness* 6(4), 221–232.

Storch, N. (1998a) A classroom based study: Insights from a collaborative text reconstruction task. *ELT Journal* 52(2), 291–300.

Storch, N. (1998b) Comparing second language learners' attention to form across tasks. *Language Awareness* 7(4), 176–191.

Storch, N. (1999) Are two heads better than one? Pair work and grammatical accuracy. *System* 27(3), 363–374.

Storch, N. (2001a) Comparing ESL learners' attention to grammar on three different collaborative tasks. *RELC Journal* 32(2), 104–124.

Storch, N. (2001b) How collaborative is pair work? ESL tertiary students composing in pairs. *Language Teaching Research* 5(1), 29–53.

Storch, N. (2002) Patterns of interaction in ESL pair work. *Language Learning* 52(1), 119–158.

Storch, N. (2004) Using activity theory to explain differences in patterns of dyadic interactions in an ESL class. *The Canadian Modern Language Review* 60(4), 457–480.

Storch, N. (2005) Collaborative writing: product, process, and students' reflections. *Journal of Second Language Writing* 14(3), 153–173.

Storch, N. (2007) Investigating the merits of pair work on a text editing task in ESL classes. *Language Teaching Research* 11(2), 143–161.

Storch, N. (2008) Metatalk in pair work activity: Level of engagement and implications for language development. *Language Awareness* 17(2), 95–114.

Storch, N. (2009) *The nature of pair interaction. Learners' interaction in an ESL class: its nature and impact on grammatical development.* Saarbrücken, Germany: VDM Verlag.

Storch, N. (2010) Researching grammar. In B. Paltridge and A. Phakiti (eds) *Continuum companion to research methods in applied linguistics* (pp. 205–221). London: Continuum.

Storch, N. and Aldosari, A. (2010) Learners' use of first language (Arabic) in pair work in an EFL class. *Language Teaching Research* 14(4), 355–375.

Storch, N. and Aldosari, A. (2013) Pairing learners in pair work activity. *Language Teaching Research* 17(1), 31–48.

Storch, N. and Wigglesworth, G. (2003) Is there a role for the use of the L1 in an L2 setting. *TESOL Quarterly* 32(4), 760–770.

Storch, N. and Wigglesworth, G. (2007) Writing tasks: Comparing individual and collaborative writing. In M.P. García Mayo (ed.) *Investigating tasks in formal language learning* (pp. 157–177). London: Multilingual Matters.

Storch, N. and Wigglesworth, G. (2010a) Learners' processing, uptake, and retention of corrective feedback on writing. Case studies. *Studies in Second Language Acquisition* 32(2), 303–334.

Storch, N. and Wigglesworth, G. (2010b) Students' engagement with feedback on writing: the role of learner agency/beliefs. In R. Batstone (ed.) *Sociocognitive perspectives on language use and language learning* (pp. 166–185). Oxford, United Kingdom: Oxford University Press.

Strauss, P. and U, A. (2007) Group assessments: dilemmas facing lecturers in multicultural tertiary classrooms. *Higher Education Research and Development* 26(2), 147–161.

Swain, M. (1985) Communicative competence: some roles of comprehensible input and comprehensible output in its development. In S. M. Gass and C. G. Madden (eds) *Input in second language acquisition* (pp. 235–256). Rowley, MA: Newbury House.

Swain, M. (1993) The output hypothesis: Just speaking and writing aren't enough. *The Canadian Modern Language Review* 50(1), 158–164.

Swain, M. (1995) Three functions of output in second language learning. In G. Crook and B. Seidlhofer (eds) *Principles and practices in applied linguistics: Studies in honour of H. Widdowson* (pp. 125–144). Oxford: Oxford University Press.

Swain, M. (1998) Focus on form through conscious reflection. In C. Doughty and J. Williams (eds) *Focus on Form in Classroom Second Language Acquisition* (pp. 64–81). Cambridge: Cambridge University Press.

Swain, M. (2000) The output hypothesis and beyond: Mediating acquisition through collaborative dialogue. In J. Lantolf (ed.) *Sociocultural theory and second language learning* (pp. 97–114). Oxford: Oxford University Press.

Swain, M. (2001) Examining dialogue: another approach to content specification and to validating inferences drawn from test scores. *Language Testing* 18(3), 275–302.

Swain, M. (2006) Languaging, agency and collaboration in advanced second language learning. In H. Byrnes (ed.) *Advanced language learning: The contributions of Halliday and Vygotsky* (pp. 95–108). London, UK: Continuum.

Swain, M. (2010) Talking-it-through: Languaging as a source of learning. In R. Batestone (ed.) *Sociocognitive perspectives on language use and language learning* (pp. 112–130). Oxford: Oxford University Press.

Swain, M., Brooks, L. and Tocalli-Beller, A. (2002) Peer-peer dialogue as a means of second language learning. *Annual Review of Applied Linguistics* 22, 171–185.

Swain, M., Kinnear, P. and Steinman, L. (2011) *Sociocultural theory in second language education. An introduction through narratives*. Bristol, UK: Multilingual Matters.

Swain, M. and Lapkin, S. (1995) Problems in output and the cognitive processes they generate: A step towards second language learning. *Applied Linguistics* 16(3), 371–391.

Swain, M. and Lapkin, S. (1998) Interaction and second language learning: two adolescent French immersion students working together. *The Modern Language Journal* 82(3), 320–337.

Swain, M. and Lapkin, S. (2000) Task-based second language learning: the uses of the first language. *Language Teaching Research* 4(3), 251–274.

Swain, M. and Lapkin, S. (2001) Focus on form through collaborative dialogue: exploring task effects. In M. Bygate, P. Skehan and M. and Swain (eds) *Researching Pedagogic Tasks: Second Language Learning, Teaching and Testing* (pp. 99–118). London: Longman.

Swain, M. and Lapkin, S. (2002) Talking it through: Two French immersion students' response to reformulation. *International Journal of Educational Research* 37(3-4), 285–304.
Swain, M., Lapkin, S., Knouzi, I., Suzuki, W. and Brooks, L. (2009) Languaging: University students learn the grammatical concept of voice in French. *The Modern Language Journal* 93(1), 5–29.
Sykes, J., Oskoz, A. and Thorne, S. (2008) Web 2.0, synthetic immersive environments, and mobile resources for language education. *CALICO Journal* 25(3), 528–546.
Takahashi, T. (1989) The influence of the listener on L2 speech. In S. Gass, C. Madden, D. Preson and L. Selinker (eds) *Variations in second language acquisition. Discourse and pragmatics* (Vol. 1) (pp. 245–279). Clevedon: Multilingual Matters.
Tan, L., Wigglesworth, G. and Storch, N. (2006) Patterns of interaction and mode of communication: Comparing face-to-face and computer mediated communication. Paper presented at the Australian Association of Applied Linguistics, Brisbane, Australia.
Tan L., Wigglesworth G. and Storch N. (2010) Pair interactions and mode of communication: Comparing face-to-face and computer mediated communication. *Australian Review of Applied Linguistics* 33(3), 1–24.
Tarone, E. and Swain, M. (1995) A sociolinguistic perspective on second language use in immersion classrooms. *The Modern Language Journal* 79(1), 24–46.
Thorne, S.L. (2008) Computer-mediated communication. In N. Hornberger and N.V. Duesen-Scholl (eds) *Encyclopedia of language education* (pp. 235–336). New York: Springer/Kluwer.
Thorne, S.L. and Payne, J.S. (2005) Evolutionary trajectories, internet-mediated expression, and language education. *CALICO Journal* 22(3), 371–397.
Thorne, S.L. and Reinhardt, J. (2008) 'Bridging activities', new media literacies, and advanced foreign language proficiency. *CALICO Journal* 25(3), 558–572.
Tobin, L. (1991) Writing between the lines. In J.L. Collins (ed.) *Teaching and learning language collaboratively* (pp. 63–71). Portsmouth, NH: Boynton/Cook-Heinemann.
Tocalli-Beller, A. (2003) Cognitive conflict, disagreement and repetition in collaborative groups: effective and social dimensions from an insider's perspectives. *The Canadian Modern Language Review* 60(2), 143–171.
Trentin, G. (2009) Using a wiki to evaluate individual contribution to a collaborative learning project. *Journal of Computer Assisted Learning* 25, 43–55.
Trimbur, J. (1989) Consensus and difference in collaborative learning. *College English* 51(6), 602–616.
Trinder, R. (2013) Business students' beliefs about language learning in a university context. *English for Specific Purposes* 32(1), 1–11.
van Lier, L. (1996) *Interaction in the language curriculum: awareness, autonomy and authenticity.* London: Longman.
Varonis, E.M. and Gass, S.M. (1985) Non-native/non-native conversations: a model for the negotiation of meaning. *Applied Linguistics* 6(1), 71–90.
Villamil, O.S. and de Guerrero, M.C.M. (1996) Peer revision in the L2 classroom: Social-cognitive activities, mediating strategies, and aspects of social behavior. *Journal of Second Language Writing* 5(1), 51–75.
Vygotsky, L.S. (1978) *Mind in society. The development of higher psychological processes.* Cambridge, Mass: Harvard University Press.
Vygotsky, L.S. (1981) The genesis of higher mental functions. In J.V. Wertsch (ed.) *The concept of activity in Soviet Psychology* (pp. 144–188). Armonk, NY: M.E. Sharpe.

Vygotsky, L.S. (1986) *Thought and language*. Cambridge, Mass: MIT Press.
Wajnryb, R. (1990) *Grammar dictation*. Oxford: Oxford University Press.
Wang, S. and Vásquez, C. (2012) Web 2.0 and second language learning: What does research tell us? *CALICO Journal* 29(3), 412–430.
Warschauer, M. and Grimes, D. (2007) Audience, authorship, and artefact: The emergent semiotics of web 2.0. *Annual Review of Applied Linguistics* 27, 1–23.
Watanabe, Y. and Swain, M. (2007) Effects of proficiency differences and patterns of pair interaction on second language learning: Collaborative dialogue between adult ESL learners. *Language Teaching Research* 11(2), 121–142.
Watanabe, Y. and Swain, M. (2008) Perception of learner proficiency: Its impact on theinteraction between an ESL learner and her higher and lower proficiency partners. *Language Awareness* 17(2), 115–130.
Weissberg, R. (2006) *Connecting speaking and writing*. Ann Arbor: University of Michigan Press.
Wells, G. (1998) Using L1 to master L2: A response to Antón and DiCamilla's sociocognitive functions of L1 collaborative interaction in the L2 classroom. *The Canadian Modern Language Review* 54, 343–353.
Wells, G. (1999) *Dialogic inquiry. Towards a sociocultural practice and theory of education*. Cambridge: Cambridge University Press.
Wenden, A. (1986a) Helping language learners think about learning. *ELT Journal* 40(1), 3–12.
Wenden, A. (1986b) What do second language learners know about their language learning? A second look at retrospective accounts. *Applied Linguistics* 7(2), 186–201.
Wenden, A. (1987) How to be a successful learner: Insights and prescriptions from L2 learners. In A. Wenden and J. Rubins (eds) *Learner strategies in language learning* (pp. 103–117). Englewood Cliffs, N.J: Prentice Hall.
Wenden, A. (1999) An introduction to metacognitive knowledge and beliefs in language learning: beyond the basics. *System* 27(4), 435–441.
Wesche, M. and Skehan, P. (2002) Communicative, task-based, and content-based instruction. In R. Kaplan (ed.) *The Oxford handbook of applied linguistics* (pp. 207–228). New York: Oxford University Press.
Wheeler, S., Yeomans, P. and Wheeler, D. (2008) The good, the bad and the wiki: Evaluating student-generated content for collaborative learning. *British Journal of Educational Technology* 39(6), 987–995.
Wigglesworth, G. and Storch, N. (2009) Pairs versus individual writing: Effects on fluency, complexity and accuracy. *Language Testing* 26(3), 445–466.
Williams, J. (1999) Learner-generated attention to form. *Language Learning* 49(4), 583–625.
Williams, J. (2001) The effectiveness of spontaneous attention to form. *System* 29(3), 325–340.
Williams, J. (2008) The speaking-writing connection in second language and academic literacy development. In D. Belcher and A. Hirvela (eds) *The oral-literate connection* (pp. 10–25). Ann Arbor: University of Michigan Press.
Williams, J. (2012) The potential role(s) of writing in second language development. *Journal of Second Language Writing* 21, 321–333.
Witney, D. and Smallbone, T. (2011) Wiki work: can using wikis enhance student collaboration for group assignment tasks? *Innovations in Education and Teaching International* 48(1), 101–110.

Wood, D., Bruner, J.S. and Ross, G. (1976) The role of tutoring in problem-solving. *Journal of Child Psychology and Psychiatry* 17(2), 89–100.

Yang, M., Badger, R. and Zhen, Y. (2006) A comparative study of peer and teacher feedback in a Chinese EFL writing class. *Journal of Second Language Writing* 15(3), 179–200.

Yarrow, F. and Topping, K.J. (2001) Collaborative writing: The effects of metacognitive prompting and structured peer interaction. *British Journal of Educational Psychology* 71(2), 261–282.

Yu, L. (2001) Communicative language teaching in China: Progress and resistance. *TESOL Quarterly* 35(1), 194–198.

Yule, G. and Macdonald, D. (1990) Resolving referential conflicts in L2 interaction: The effects of proficiency and interactive role. *Language Learning* 40(4), 539–556.

Zeng, G. and Takatsuka, S. (2009) Text-based peer-peer collaborative dialogue in a computer-mediated learning environment in the EFL context. *System* 37(3), 434–446.

Zhang, S. (1995) Reexamining the affective advantage of peer feedback in the ESL writing class. *Journal of Second Language Writing* 4(3), 209–222.

Zorko, V. (2009) Factors affecting the way students collaborate in a wiki for English language learning. *Australasian Journal of Educational Technology* 25(5), 645–665.

Author Index

Abadikhah, S., 42, 46, 55, 80, 173
Adams, R., 12–13, 35–36, 82, 173
Adler, R.P., 160, 175
Aldosari, A., 19–20, 31–32, 34–35, 40, 46, 55, 58–59, 66–69, 90–91, 102–103, 106, 110, 163, 173
Alegría de la Colina, A., 34–35, 46, 54–55, 91, 147, 173
Aljaafreh, A., 84, 173
Alvarado, C.S., 68, 173
Alyousef, H.S., 126, 130–131, 134, 173
Anderson, T., 140–141, 143
Andre, J., 25
Anton, M., 44, 102–103, 173, 176
Aragão, R., 99, 117, 173
Arnold, N., 137, 141, 143–144, 146–147, 154, 167, 173, 177
Asenavage, K., 38, 176
Augar, N., 124–125, 174

Bachman, L.F., 19, 174
Badger, 192
Baker, M., 176
Barcelos, A.M.F., 94, 97, 174, 180
Bassok, M., 175
Basturkmen, H., 177
Bejarno, Y., 19–20, 41, 174
Belanoff, P., vii, 177
Benson, P., 94, 174
Bereiter, C., 22, 174
Bernat, E., 97, 174
Bigelow, M., 9, 179
Biggs, J., 154, 174
Bikowski, D., 138, 143–145, 180
Birdsong, D., 79, 174

Blake, R., 120, 174
Blaye, A., 176
Boggs, J., 180
Borg, S., 95, 174
Boud, D., 124, 174
Bower, M., 126, 130, 134, 174
Bradley, L., 136–137, 142, 149–151, 174
Breen, M., 93, 117, 174
Bremner, S., 25, 174
Brooks, D.B., 100, 174
Brooks, L., 38, 82–83, 88, 174, 190
Brown, A.V., 98, 174
Brown, S., 160, 175
Bruffee, A., vii, 2, 7, 22–23, 42, 175
Bruner, J.S., 192
Butler, Y.G., 18–19, 175
Bygate, M., 20–21, 175

Callaway, R.A., 184
Camps, A., 17, 42, 175
Canale, M., 19, 175
Carless, D., 100–101, 175
Carr, T., 126, 130–135, 148, 175
Carson, J.G., 38, 68, 104, 113, 148, 164, 175, 181
Chang, G., 17, 175
Chao, J.T., 118, 123, 185
Chao, Y-C., 124, 137, 141–143, 175
Cheng, S.T., 185
Chenoweth, N.A., 25, 175
Chi, M.T.H., 16, 66, 175
Chisholm, R.M., 164, 175
Chiu, M., 175
Cohen, R., 174
Cole, M., 126, 134, 175

Colen, K., 25, 175
Coniam, D., 136, 139, 141–148, 153, 159
Connor, U., 38, 176
Coughlan, P., 17, 176
Cox, G., 175
Crookes, G., 11, 19, 182
Cropper, S., 180
Cumming, A., 13, 28, 36–37, 176
Cunningham, W., 123, 182

Daiute, C., 23–24, 176
Dale, H., 7, 23–24, 61, 163, 166, 176
Dalton, B., 23–24, 176
Damon, W., 61, 176
Dansereau, D.F., 185
Davis, R.M., 179, 182
de Guerrero, M.C.M., 15, 84, 103, 176
de la Fuente, M.J., 101
de St Léger, D., 101, 176
Deacon, A., 175
Dewey, J., 23, 176
Dias, P., 25, 176
Dicamilla, F., 44, 102–103, 173, 176
Dillenbourg, P., 3, 176
Dinitto, R., 69, 167, 176
Dipardo, A., 22, 176
Donato, R., 15, 30, 39, 61, 68, 84–85, 100, 105, 174, 176
Dörnyei, Z., 93, 177
Doughty, C., 19–20, 28, 41, 178
Dovey, T., 25, 167, 177
Ducate, L., 125, 137, 141, 143, 147, 166, 173, 177
Duff, P., 17, 176–177
Dunn, A., 56, 177

Eckerth, J., 46, 53, 55, 82–83, 88, 105–106, 177
Ede, L., vii, 2–3, 24–26, 177
Egi, T., 183
Elbow, P., vii, 23, 177
Elgort, I., 125, 127, 130–133, 177
Ellis, R., 11, 19–21, 76, 83, 88, 177–178
Elola, I., 123, 125, 136, 138, 140–143, 146, 148, 153, 160, 162, 177
Emig, J., 22, 177
Engstrom, M., 125, 130, 154, 177
Ewald, J.D., 30, 160, 162–163, 177

Faigley, L., 144, 177
Falodun, J., 186
Felvegi, E., 184
Fernández Dobao, A., 47, 60, 68, 72, 75, 88, 106–107, 162, 177
Fernández-Garcia, M., 120, 177
Ferris, D., 22, 177
Flower, L., 22–23, 178
Fluker, G., 185
Fortune, A., 35, 47, 53–55, 178
Foster, P., 12, 28, 120, 152, 162, 178
Fotos, S., 11, 178
Freedman, A., 22, 176
Freire, P., 23, 178
Fuji, A., 183

García Mayo, M.P., 34–35, 46, 54–55, 91, 147, 173, 178
Garrett, P., 101, 178
Gass, S., viii, 10–13, 36, 53, 178, 182
Glaser, R., 174–175
Godwin-Jones, R., 124, 178
Gollin, S., 25, 178
Gonzales, P., 15, 180
Goo, J., 105
Graham, S., 94, 178
Grant, L., 125, 127, 130–131, 133–134, 136, 144, 178
Green, J.M., 95, 98, 100, 178
Grimes, D., 118, 123
Guasch, O., 175
Guk, H., 101, 178
Gutiérrez, K.D., 19–20, 117, 178–179
Gutiérrez, X., 91, 179
Guzdial, M., 125, 129, 134–135, 167
Gvozdenko, I., 97, 174

Hall, J., 20, 174, 179
Hanaoka, O., 88, 179
Harklau, L., 19, 21, 179
Harley, B., 8, 179
Harris, J., 2, 179, 182
Hayes, J.R., 22, 25, 175, 178–179
Hedgcock, J., 22, 177
Hillebrand, R.P., 72, 179
Hirvela, A., 2, 173, 179
Hood, M., 128, 130–133, 135–136, 153
Horwitz, E.K., 95–96, 165, 179
Hoy, A.W., 159, 161

Huddleston, P., 161, 164
Hughes, J.E., 127, 130, 132–135, 179
Hunter, R., 170, 179
Hyde, M., 98, 179
Hythecker, V.I., 185

Iberri-Shea, G., 180
Ives, D., 68, 95, 97, 99, 101, 103, 105, 107, 109, 111, 113, 115, 117, 179
Iwashita, N., 11, 179
Izumi, S., 9, 20, 179–180
Izumi, Y., 20, 180

Jacobs, G., 105, 180
Jacoby, S., 15, 180
Jewett, D., 125, 130, 154, 177
Johnson, D.W., 24, 124, 180
Johnson, R.T., 24, 124, 180
Jones, P., 124–125, 127, 130–133, 135, 178, 180
Judd, T., 128, 130–131, 133–134, 136, 180

Kalaja, P., 94, 97, 174, 180
Kanagy, R., 186
Kang, S., 101, 180
Karis, W.M., 3, 25, 181
Keck, C.M., 105, 180
Kellogg, D., 101, 178
Kelsey, K., 128, 131–132, 135, 166, 182
Kennedy, G., 180
Kern, R., 95, 119, 180
Kessler, G., 138, 141–148, 167, 180
Kim, Y., 47–48, 55–56, 68–69, 76–78, 80, 104–108, 166, 180
Kinnear, P., 189
Kinsella, K., 115, 165, 181
Knouzi, I., 190
Kormos, J., 93, 177
Kost, C., 136, 138, 141–147, 149–150, 162, 173, 181
Kowal, M., 12, 15, 48, 59, 69, 181
Krashen, S., 8, 181
Kuiken, F., 48, 53, 55, 76, 79–80, 86, 89, 103, 181
Kumaravadivelu, B., 19, 181
Kuteeva, M., 143, 162, 181

Lai, C., 120, 181
Lambiotte, J.G., 185

Lantolf, J.P., 7, 14–16, 84, 173, 176, 181
Lapierre, D., 82, 181
Lapkin, S., 9, 16, 28–29, 34, 36, 52, 56, 80–82, 84, 88–89, 102–105
Larson, C.D., 185
Lavancher, C., 175
Lay, M.M., 3, 25, 181
Lee, L., 118, 120, 123–124, 136, 139, 141–144, 146–147, 159, 179, 181
Leeman, J., 183
Leeser, M., 36, 49, 55–59, 69, 90, 106, 108, 181
Leeuw, N.D., 175
Leki, I., 3, 25–26, 68, 164, 181
Leonard, J.S., 22, 179, 182
Leow, R., 80, 86, 182
Leuf, B., 123, 182
Lewis, M.W., 175
Li, M., 136, 139, 142, 149, 151, 182
Lightbown, P., 105, 182
Lin, H., 128, 131–132, 135, 166, 182
Lincoln-Porter, F., 186
Lindström, B., 174
Linnel, J., 186
Little, D., 95, 182
Littlewood, W., 18, 98, 182
Lo, H-C., 124, 137, 141–143, 175
Lockhart, C., 61, 68, 182
Loewen, S., 76, 82–83, 177, 182
Lomicka, L., 173, 177
Long, M.H., 6–13, 17, 19, 27–28, 32, 35, 59, 66, 76, 93, 120, 130, 133, 154, 156, 175, 178, 182
Lor, W., 94, 174
Louth, R., 24, 183
Lund, A., 14–144, 146, 159
Lunsford, A., vii, 2–3, 24–26, 177

Macdonald, D., 59, 192
Macdonald, J., 161, 167–168, 183
Mackey, A., 11–12, 20, 28, 53, 104–105, 173–174, 178
Mak, B., 136, 139, 141–148, 153, 159
Malmqvist, A., 49, 53, 68, 72, 74, 76, 103, 106, 108
Manchón, R., 2–4, 25, 37, 168, 171
Martínez Arbelaiz, A., 120, 177
Matsuda, P., 22, 183
Matthew, K.I., 124, 128, 130–131, 133

McAllister, C., 183
McAllister, H.A., 183
McCarthey, S.J., 39, 184
McCreary, J., 20, 187
McDonough, K., 1, 48, 55–56, 68–69, 95, 98–100, 104–106, 108, 166, 180
McLoughlin, C., 118, 123–124
McMahon, S., 39, 184
Medway, P., 176
Mercer, S., 97, 184
Meyer, K.A., 119, 184
Millan, M., 175
Mirel, B., 3, 25, 184
Mishra, S., 98–99, 105, 184
Miyazoe, T., 140–141, 143, 184
Moreno, N., 177
Morrison, A., 175
Murphy, J.M., 39, 184
Murphy, L., 183, 187
Myers, C., 118, 184

Nakahama, Y., 11, 21, 184
Narayan, R., 127, 130, 132–135, 179
Nassaji, H., 49, 54–55, 72–73, 76, 78, 80, 84, 89, 184
Navarro, D., 97, 184
Negueruela-Azarola, E., 96, 184
Nelson, G.L., 38–39, 68, 104, 113, 148, 175
Neumann, D., 128, 130–133, 135–136, 153, 184
Ng, P., 61, 68, 182
Niu, R., 33–37, 50, 53, 91, 109, 111, 184
Nobuyoshi, J., 83, 184

O'Donnell, A.M., 72, 74, 159, 161, 185
O'Malley, C., 176
Ohta, A.S., 7, 14–15, 17, 20, 28, 32, 39, 59, 178
Oliver, R., 12, 98–99, 105, 183–185
Ortega, L., 1, 20–21, 118, 120, 168, 180
Oskoz, A., 123, 125, 136, 138, 140–143, 146, 148, 153, 160, 162, 177
Osman-Schlegel, L., 124, 129–133, 135, 148, 185

Pajares, F.M., 94–95, 185
Palmeri, J., 25, 185

Paninos, D., 186
Pare, A., 176
Paribakht, T.S., 77, 185
Parker, K.R., 118, 123, 185
Payne, J.S., 136, 190
Peacock, M, 95–96, 185
Pellettieri, J., 120, 186
Peng, J.E., 97–98, 186
Perl, S., 22, 186
Petelin, R., 25, 175
Petrovsky, A.V., 68, 186
Pfaff, E., 161, 163–164, 186
Phelps, E., 61, 176
Philp, J., 20, 83, 182
Picard, M.Y., 126, 130–131, 134, 173
Pienemann, M., 9–10, 186
Polio, C., viii, 11, 174, 185–186
Porter, P.A., 19, 186
Purpura, J., 76, 186

Qi, 80, 186

Raitman, R., 174
Reichelt, 22–23, 186
Reid, J.M., 98, 186
Reimann, P., 175–176
Reinhardt, J., 171, 190
Ribas, T., 175
Richards, J.C., 19, 175
Rick, J., 125, 129, 134–135, 167, 187
Riley, P., 96, 98–99, 101, 182
Roberts, M., 174
Robinson, P., 10, 183
Roca de Larios, J., 25, 28, 183, 187
Rocklin, T., 185
Roed, J., 120, 187
Rogers, T.S., 19, 187
Roskams, T., 92, 111, 114, 187
Ross, G., 192
Ross-Feldman, L., 13, 35–36, 173, 178
Rreinders, H., 72–73, 76, 79, 187
Rulon, K.A., 20, 187
Rystedt, H., 174

Sampson, J., 174
Samuda, V., 20, 187
Savignon, S.J., 18–19, 21, 187
Scardamalia, M., 22, 174
Schmidt, R., 8–10, 175, 187

Schneider, B., 25, 187
Schrage, M., 2, 187
Scott, V.M., 101, 187
Sheen, R., 101, 105–106, 187
Shehadeh, A., 89–91, 102–103, 111, 113–114, 163, 167, 187
Shekary, M., 82, 120–122, 187
Shortall, T., 99, 101, 178
Singleton, D., 95, 182
Skehan, P., 19–20, 175, 187
Slavin, R.E., 124, 188
Smallbone, T., 129–132, 134, 148, 160, 191
Smith, A., 177
Smith, B., 120, 122, 182, 188
Smørdal, O., 139, 144, 146, 183
Sommers, N., 22, 188
Spilka, R., 3, 25, 184
Stahl, G., 2, 4, 188
Steinman, L., 189
Stone, C., 70, 117, 179
Storch, N., 3, 19–20, 28, 31, 33–36, 40, 46, 50–51, 54–55, 57–59, 61–63, 66–69, 72–76, 80, 85–86, 88, 90–91, 93, 101–103, 105–106, 109–111, 115–116, 147, 151, 160, 163, 176, 188–189
Strauss, P., 3, 25, 189
Sunitham, W., 99, 184
Suzuki, W., 190
Swain, M., viii, 6–13, 15–16, 19–20, 27–29, 34, 36, 38, 48, 51–52, 56, 59, 68–69, 78, 80–85, 88–89, 102–103, 105–106, 110, 117, 156, 174–175, 179, 181–182, 189–190
Sykes, J., 160, 190

Tahririan, M.H., 82, 120–122, 187
Takahashi, T., 11, 190
Takatsuka, S., 82, 120–122, 192
Tan, L., 32, 34, 45, 52, 64–65, 68, 120–121, 150, 190
Tarone, E., 105, 190
Tatsumi, T., 183
Thorne, S., 7, 84, 118, 136, 171, 181
Thornton, K., 97, 154
Thorp, D., 35, 47, 53–55, 178
Tian, J., 49, 54–55, 72–73, 76, 78, 80, 89, 184

Tobin, L., 23, 190
Tocalli-Beller, A., 17, 189–190
Toland, J., 177
Topping, K.J., 90, 192
Tracy-Ventura, N., 180
Trentin, G., 161, 190
Trimbur, J., 24, 190
Trinder, R., 98, 190
Tyler, A., 184

U, A., 3, 25, 189

van Lier, L., 15, 17, 20, 184
Varonis, E.M., 11, 190
Vásquez, C., 136, 141, 191
Vedder, I., 48, 53, 55, 76, 79–80, 86, 89, 103, 181
Villamil, O.S., 15, 84, 103, 176
Vygotsky, L.S., 6–7, 13–15, 23, 84, 156, 190–191

Wa-Mbaleka, S., 180
Wajnryb, R., 3, 53, 191
Walsh, M., 20, 179
Wang, S., 136, 141, 191
Ware, P., 180
Warschauer, M., 118, 123, 180
Warshauer Freedman, S., 22, 176
Watanabe, Y., 52, 68–69, 85, 105, 117, 191
Watters, P.A., 174
Weissberg, R., 42, 191
Wells, G., 14, 17, 175, 191
Wenden, A., 95–96, 179, 191
Wesche, M., 20, 77, 191
Wharton, C.E., 179, 182
Wheeler, D., 124, 130, 133, 191
Wheeler, S., 124, 130, 133, 191
Wigglesworth, J., 28, 31, 34, 36, 40, 51, 55, 72, 74–75, 88, 93, 102, 163, 188, 191
Williams, J., 12–13, 36, 82, 105, 123, 183, 189, 191
Witney, D., 129–132, 134, 148, 160, 191
Witte, S., 144, 177
Woo, K., 174
Wood, D., 14, 192

Yañez-Prieto, C., 181
Yang, M., 39, 192
Yarrow, F., 90, 192
Yeomans, P., 191
Yu, L., 33, 95, 192
Yule, G., 59, 192

Zeng, G., 82, 120–122, 192
Zhang, S., 104, 192
Zhao, Y., 120, 181
Zhen, Y., 192
Zhou, W., 174
Zorko, V., 140–141, 143, 160, 168, 192

Subject Index

affordances, 134
appropriation, 85
assessment, 1, 3–4, 21, 45, 57, 97, 114, 126, 128, 130, 134, 136–138, 140–141, 144, 153–154, 161, 166–168, 170, 177
assistance, 2, 14, 17, 32–33, 37–39, 63, 70, 100, 104, 121, 143, 178
asynchronous, 119, 121, 124, 141, 160
attention, 9–13, 20–21, 27–28, 30, 34, 36–37, 43, 45, 54–58, 61, 82, 91, 119–122, 136, 142, 146–147, 156, 159, 173, 179–180, 182
attitudes, 4, 93–94, 97–100, 111–117, 121, 132, 143–144, 148, 152, 157, 165, 170, 176, 178
audience, 23–24

beliefs, 4, 94–99, 102, 111–113, 115, 117, 157, 164–165, 170, 173–174, 178–180
blogs, 118, 123, 140, 143, 178

chats, 82, 119–123, 138, 140, 146
clarification, 8, 10, 20, 28, 34, 102
cloze, 3, 47, 49–50, 53–55, 72–73, 78, 109, 158
co-author, 2, 24, 38, 43, 88, 91, 135, 166–167, 171, 176
co-construction, 61, 134–135, 157
cognition, 3–4, 174, 176, 179
cognitive conflict, 24, 61
cognitive theories, 6–8, 19
collaboration, viii–ix, 2–3, 22, 68, 71–75, 77–79, 81–82, 90, 117–118, 128, 135–137, 139, 145, 147, 149–150, 152, 154, 157–162, 165–168, 171, 173–174, 176, 178–180, 182

collaborative dialogue, 7, 16–17, 30, 43, 82, 156, 166, 180–181
collaborative pattern, 61, 63, 115, 157, 166
collaborative writing, vii–viii, 1–7, 17–18, 21–28, 31–32, 34–40, 42–45, 53, 55, 57, 60–61, 68–71, 75–76, 82, 84–85, 88–94, 100, 102, 104–106, 111–114, 116–119, 121–123, 125–126, 132, 136–137, 141, 145, 147, 149, 154–182
collective scaffolding, 15, 30, 37, 59, 61, 63–64, 68, 84, 121, 151–152, 160, 176
communicative competence, 18–22, 175
communicative language teaching (CLT), 18–21, 182
composing processes, 22, 25, 154, 169, 177
composition, 3–4, 7, 18, 22–23, 25, 31, 46, 50–51, 54, 56–58, 66, 72–73, 103, 109–110, 115, 125, 129, 147, 154, 174–175, 177–179
comprehensible input, 8–9, 13, 182
computer mediated communication (CMC), 45, 118–120
confirmation, 8, 10, 17, 28, 30–31, 38, 40, 43, 86, 145
consolidation, 30, 33, 83–84, 86–88, 159
cooperation, 3, 121, 148
cooperative writing, 3, 22, 24–25, 61–62, 65, 68, 121, 135, 149–150, 152, 161, 173–174, 180–181
correction, 29, 39, 43, 63, 147
corrective feedback, 39–42, 63, 67, 93, 145, 147–148

data commentary task, 29, 33, 40, 50–51, 55, 61, 72, 74–75, 85, 102, 111, 158
dialogue, 7, 16–17, 30, 41, 43–44, 82, 156, 166, 180–181
dictogloss, 3, 45–49, 51–69, 72–74, 77, 79–80, 82–83, 89, 102–104, 106–108, 110, 121–122, 158–159, 177
discussion board, 127–128, 140, 145
division of labour, 3, 134, 159
dominant/dominant, 61–62, 64, 68, 70, 85, 90
dominant/passive, 62, 66, 68–70, 85, 90, 115, 117, 121, 151
dyads, 8, 11, 47, 57–59, 62, 72, 85, 120

EAP, 114, 138, 146, 181
editing, 2–3, 23, 124, 130, 134–135, 141–142, 144–146, 148, 151, 153
editing task (also editing exercise), vii, 2–3, 34, 44, 46–47, 49–55, 58, 61, 72–73, 78, 82, 85, 103, 109, 115, 139, 158, 188
EFL, viii, 19, 31, 33, 36–37, 40–41, 45–48, 50, 56, 66, 89, 95–99, 103–105, 107–110, 114, 121, 137–142, 144, 146, 148, 151, 153, 168, 173, 178
egocentric speech, 14
elaborate noticing, 79–80
engagement, vii, 3, 16, 18, 20, 35, 54–55, 61, 65, 69–71, 80–81, 85–88, 93, 119, 121–122, 124, 131–136, 142–143, 148, 152–154, 157, 159, 161, 165, 169, 175
error, 29, 31, 73–74, 120, 144
ESL, vii–viii, 12, 23, 29, 31, 33–34, 38, 40, 45, 47, 49–52, 55, 68, 72–75, 78–79, 86, 93, 99, 102, 109, 111, 120, 122, 145, 168, 173, 175–177, 179, 182
essay, 31, 41, 52, 55, 66, 75, 102, 126, 138, 146, 148, 151, 153
exercises, 3–51, 54, 78, 89, 94, 99–100, 102, 109, 160
expert, 14–15, 22, 62, 67–70, 85, 104, 121, 151, 180
expert/novice, 15, 62, 67–70, 85, 121, 151
expert/passive, 68, 85
externalise, 81

face-to-face, 1, 5, 32, 52, 64, 82, 118, 120, 123, 125, 133–135, 141–142, 147, 149, 155–156, 158–162, 164–167, 169, 171
feedback, 10, 12–13, 22–23, 27, 31, 37–43, 61, 63, 65, 67, 82–83, 85, 88, 93, 99–100, 104–105, 111, 120, 137, 145–148, 154, 157, 167–168, 173, 180
First language (L1), vii, 4–5, 7, 10–11, 18, 22–25, 31–32, 35, 42, 47, 61, 72, 74, 90, 94, 100–104, 125–126, 131, 135–136, 144, 153, 157, 162, 166–168, 173, 175
focus on form, 11–13, 19–21, 25, 27–28, 45, 58, 88, 147, 181–182

goals, 1, 69–70, 117, 147–148, 157–158
Google Docs, 1, 118, 123, 138, 146, 168, 171
grammar, vii–viii, 3–4, 19, 34–35, 44–45, 47, 49–50, 53–56, 61, 72–73, 89–90, 94–95, 99–101, 105–106, 109, 111, 114, 116, 145–146, 158–160, 178, 181
grammar tasks, viii, 3, 44, 54–55, 101, 106
group dynamics, 68, 131–132, 148, 164, 166–167
group work, 13, 19, 21, 43, 68, 84, 88, 97–101, 113, 115, 132, 143, 152, 157, 162, 167, 177, 181
grouping, 57–58, 163–164

hypothesis testing, 29, 81

immersion, 8, 29, 34, 48, 51–52, 56, 59, 82, 89, 102, 105, 110, 179
individual (solitary) writing, 22–23, 26, 28–29, 37–38, 43, 70, 72, 171
information gap, viii, 11, 36, 53, 108
inner speech (self-directed speech), 14, 17, 32, 77, 156
input, 2, 8–10, 13, 105, 142, 178–179, 181–182
input hypothesis, 8, 181
interaction, 2, 6–18, 21, 23, 25, 27–28, 30, 32, 36, 40, 45, 56–66, 68–69, 79, 83–86, 88–89, 91, 97, 104–105, 115, 117–120, 124, 142, 148–149, 151–152, 155–156, 160, 162, 164–167, 170, 173–176, 178–182

Subject Index

interaction hypothesis, 6–11, 13, 21, 27–28, 36, 118
interactive, 118, 137, 148, 173, 175, 179
interlanguage, 8, 12, 105–106, 156, 174, 177, 179
internalise, 156

jigsaw, 19, 46, 52–56, 58, 60, 75, 82, 89, 102–103, 107, 121–122, 158

language learning, vii–viii, 1, 3–11, 13, 16–17, 20–21, 25–26, 38, 43, 57, 60, 68, 70–71, 73, 75–91, 93–100, 102, 104–105, 111, 113–114, 117, 119–121, 148, 152, 155–157, 159, 162–166, 168, 170–171, 173–182
language learning beliefs, 4, 94–97, 102, 117, 157, 164, 170
Language Related episodes (LREs), 4, 28–38, 40, 43–44, 54–61, 66, 70, 75–82, 84–88, 90, 105–110, 119–123, 157–158, 163, 178
language-focused tasks, 3, 45–46, 55, 72, 77, 80, 147, 159
languaging, 7, 13, 16–18, 27–28, 30, 43–45, 47, 49, 51, 53, 55–57, 59–61, 63, 65–70, 77, 81, 119, 145, 156, 159–160, 163–164, 174
learning to write, 4, 26, 171, 175–176

meaning-focused tasks, 11, 53–54, 58, 103, 141, 147, 158–160
mediation, 178
metalanguage, 34, 51, 56, 178
microgenetic, 84, 157, 169
missed opportunities, 36
modelling, 45, 47–49, 51–52, 56–57, 104, 108, 159, 166–167, 180
modified output, 12–13, 76, 179
motivation, 2, 73, 98, 130, 134

negative feedback, 10, 13, 37, 40, 43, 120, 173
noticing, 7, 9, 20, 76, 79–81, 88, 173, 179, 181
novice, 14–15, 22–23, 39, 62, 67–70, 85, 90, 121, 151, 176, 180

occasions for language learning, 43, 70, 82
online, 1, 5, 12, 82, 121–122, 124–125, 127, 135, 140, 158, 161, 167, 170, 173–174, 177–181
oral tasks, viii, 11–13, 21, 36, 53, 56, 82, 94, 98, 104, 120
output, 6–13, 16, 76, 93, 122, 160, 173, 178–181

pair work, viii, 5, 13, 15, 19, 57–58, 60, 69, 74, 78, 92, 94–95, 98–101, 104–105, 111, 114–117, 157, 162, 170, 179
pairing, 57–58, 69, 103, 163
patterns of interaction, 63, 68–69, 85, 120, 142, 148–149, 151, 164–165, 167
peer feedback, 22–23, 38, 88, 104–105, 137, 154, 167, 180
positive feedback, 38, 40, 42–43, 63
post-test, 38, 77–85, 89, 91, 100, 122
pre-test, 78–79, 82–83, 85
private speech, 2, 14–18, 30, 42–43, 156
problem solving, 43
proficiency, 4, 10–11, 15, 29, 31–34, 39, 41, 43–45, 55, 57–60, 66–69, 78, 80, 85, 90, 99, 103–106, 112, 114, 117, 121, 136, 141, 146–147, 157–159, 163–164, 173, 176, 179–181
pushed output, 7, 9–10, 16

recast, 10, 29
reformulation, 10, 173
relationships, viii, 59–61, 64, 67, 69–70, 90, 96–98, 101, 105, 115, 117, 122, 135, 148, 157, 163, 169–170, 181
repairs, 8, 32, 35–36, 38, 46, 63, 115, 119, 163
repetition, 20, 41, 176
resistance, 95, 164
resolution (of LREs), 33–35, 55, 57, 59, 78, 80, 85–86, 88, 106–107, 121–122, 135
revision, 2, 18, 22, 24, 32, 141, 147, 151–152, 176–177, 181

scaffolding, 14–15, 17, 30, 37, 39, 43, 59, 61, 63–64, 68, 84–85, 121, 151–152, 160, 176

second language acquisition, 6, 156, 177–179, 181–182
second language learning, vii, 6–7, 25, 38, 95, 105, 156, 173, 175–176, 181–182
second language writing, 175–177, 179
sociocultural theory (SCT), 6–7, 13, 15–16, 84, 156, 181
synchronous, 119, 141, 160, 181

tailor made tests, 76, 81–82, 105
task, 3–4, 6–7, 11, 13–14, 16–21, 25, 28–29, 33–34, 36–37, 40–41, 44–45, 47–48, 50–70, 72–83, 85–86, 91, 94, 101–106, 108–109, 111, 113, 115, 117, 119–122, 126, 128, 132, 134, 136–142, 147–148, 151–152, 154, 156–163, 166–169, 173–180, 182
Task based language teaching (TBLT), 18, 20–21
teams, 24, 126–131, 135, 137–138, 142, 163
technology, 1, 119, 123, 130–132, 135, 143, 159, 168, 171, 173–175, 177–178, 180–181
tests, 38, 45, 76–84, 88–90, 99, 105–106, 121–122, 128, 153, 157, 160
text ownership, vii, 39, 134–135, 162, 170

text reconstruction, 3, 33, 46, 50–51, 54, 61, 72–73, 85–87, 107, 109, 115
tools, 97, 117, 123, 126–128, 130–131, 137–138, 140, 143, 160, 168, 170–171, 177

uptake, 88, 93, 122, 177

verbalisation, 16–17, 35, 156
vocabulary, 4, 15, 60, 63, 67, 77–78, 80, 88, 90, 100, 102–105, 111–112, 114, 145, 156, 177, 180

wikis, 1, 5, 118–119, 123–136, 138, 140–149, 151–155, 157–162, 166, 168, 171, 173–175, 177–182
writing activities, vii–viii, 1, 3–5, 22, 24–25, 27–28, 34, 38, 43, 57, 70–71, 85, 89, 91–92, 94, 111, 116–118, 141, 149, 155–156, 158–159, 164–165, 167, 169, 171
writing instruction, 18, 22–23, 164, 179, 181
writing processes, 113, 172
writing to learn, 4

zone of proximal development (ZPD), 14–15, 173, 176, 178

For Product Safety Concerns and Information please contact our EU Authorised Representative:

Easy Access System Europe

Mustamäe tee 50

10621 Tallinn

Estonia

gpsr.requests@easproject.com